HYACINTH

TRENCH

OSPREY
PUBLISHING
IN ASSOCIATION WITH

IMPERIAL WAR
MUSEUM

TRENCH

A HISTORY OF TRENCH WARFARE
ON THE WESTERN FRONT

STEPHEN BULL

First published in Great Britain in 2010 by Osprey Publishing,
Midland House, West Way, Botley, Oxford, OX2 0PH, UK
44-02 23rd Street, Suite 219, Long Island City, NY 11101, USA

E-mail: info@ospreypublishing.com

Artwork in this volume and the map on p.9 previously published in ELITE 74: *World War I Trench Warfare (1)*, ELITE 84: *World War I Trench Warfare (2)*, ELITE 150: *World War I Gas Warfare Tactics and Equipment* and FORTRESS 24: *Fortifications of the Western Front*.

A CIP catalogue record for this book is available from the British Library

ISBN: 978 1 84603 937 9

Page layout by Myriam Bell Design, France
Index by Michael Parkin
Map on page 9 by The Map Studio
Typeset in Minion Pro and Bodoni
Originated by PDQ Media, Bungay, UK
Printed in China through Bookbuilders

10 11 12 13 14   10 9 8 7 6 5 4 3 2 1

Where possible, all measurements are shown in their imperial form, unless taken from an original source.

Imperial War Museum Collections:
The majority of the photos in this book come from the Imperial War Museum's huge collections which cover all aspects of conflict involving Britain and the Commonwealth since the outbreak of World War I. These rich resources are available online to search, browse and buy at www.iwmcollections.org.uk. In addition to Collections Online, you can visit the Visitor Rooms where you can explore over eight million photographs, thousands of hours of moving images, the largest sound archive of its kind in the world, thousands of diaries and letters written by people in wartime, and a huge reference library. To make an appointment, call (020) 7416 5344, or e-mail collections@iwm.org.uk.

Imperial War Museum www.iwm.org.uk

Front Cover: Men of 'A' Company, 11th Battalion, Cheshire Regiment, occupy a captured German position at Ovillers-la-Boiselle on the Somme, July 1916. (IWM Q3990)
Back Cover: German shock troops practise the attack. (IWM Q47997)
Title Page: Men of the Lancashire Fusiliers carry duckboards over the battlefield near Pilckem, 10 October 1917. (IWM Q6049)
Endpapers: The Mark IV tank of 'H' Battalion, ditched in a German trench west of Ribecourt, Cambrai, 20 November 1917. (IWM Q6432)

Osprey Publishing is supporting the Woodland Trust, the UK's leading woodland conservation charity, by funding the dedication of trees.

www.ospreypublishing.com

CONVERSION TABLE

1 millimetre (mm)	0.0394 in.
1 centimetre (cm)	0.3937 in.
1 metre (m)	1.0936 yards
1 kilometre (km)	0.6214 miles
1 kilogram (kg)	2.2046 lb
1 inch	2.54cm
1 foot	0.3048m
1 yard	0.9144m
1 mile	1.609km

CONTENTS

ACKNOWLEDGEMENTS

As early as my very first glimpse of the Western Front – with my parents, more years ago than I care to remember – I have been working up a significant debt to a band of like-minded professionals, enthusiasts and academics. Over the years they have been unearthing, sometimes quite literally, old, new and at times arcane facts about the Western Front. Their fields of endeavour span armies and regiments, tactics, weapons, engineering, genealogy, geology, archaeology, museology and history – to name but the most obvious. It behoves me to thank as many as possible within the space available.

Perhaps the first candidate for acknowledgement is Dr Paddy Griffith, formerly of the Royal Military Academy Sandhurst, with whom friendly 'tactical' sparring has led to significant results. Simon Jones, formerly of the Royal Engineers and King's Liverpool museums, has frequently helped with questions of gas and mining. Colonel John Downham, Colonel Mike Glover, Jane Davies, Gary Smith and Peter Donnelly have provided access to many specific texts and objects from the collections of the North, South and East Lancashire regiments as well as the Manchesters, Liverpool Scottish, King's Own and Lancashire Fusiliers. Colonel Martin Steiger and Captain John Cornish have been unfailingly supportive in their respective roles with the Duke of Lancaster's Own Yeomanry and 14th and 20th Hussars. On the other side of the Pennines John Spencer of the Duke of Wellington's Museum and Keith Matthews at York Castle have been similarly helpful. Further south I have had fruitful correspondence with Ian Hook of the Essex Regiment Museum and Andy Robertshaw at the Royal Logistic Corps – both former colleagues at the National Army Museum. At the Imperial War Museum, London, Manchester and Duxford, many staff past and present have been of great assistance, most notably David Penn, Fergus Read, Mike Hibberd and Martin Boswell.

I should also like to thank Major Norman Bonney, who was keen to help at an early stage with his extensive experience of grenades and explosives, as was the late Anthony Carter with his remarkable knowledge of bayonets and units. Martin Windrow, Richard Dunning, Gerry Embleton, Julian Sykes, Ray Westlake and Paul Hannon have all given practical assistance at different times – not least with illustrations and contacts. Many of the members of the Western Front Association and Great War Society have similarly been most helpful over the years, and for these the name of Geoff Carefoot must stand in symbolically for the many. Sniping expert Martin Pegler, formerly of the Royal Armouries, is now proprietor of Orchard Farm at Combles on the Somme – one of several bases from whence research has been conducted. Last but not least in this list is David Wollweber, my patient travelling companion along that long, continuous and still controversial battlefield – the Western Front.

Dr Stephen Bull
2010

French troops man a trench in cold weather. Both wear animal fleece, fur side inward, tied with a cord around the body; a brazier is also visible, foreground left. (Author's collection)

INTRODUCTION

The observer who goes up in an aeroplane and looks down on the vast battlefield of Northern France and Flanders sees the country below him marked by minute threadlike cracks, running here and there, into and out of one another; an endless and seemingly confused web. These are the trenches. Tangled though they appear to the unpractised eye, to the expert observer their confusion reveals a plan and system. He reads them as an Oriental scholar reads an Arabic script… Over a part of the front where a lull reigns the eye of the observer aloft might sweep the country for signs of life and movement in vain. The maze of threadlike cracks looks deserted. The prospect seems a desolate solitude of ruined towns, roofless remains of villages, shot torn woods, and fields full of emptiness. Meanwhile on another part of the front the battle rages. There the flash of artillery is incessant. The roar of the guns rises in a hurricane of thunders… Swarms of grey human ants now creep across the ground, and now dash forwards in rushes. The lines of cracks become lines of flashing fire.

Edmund Dane, 1915[1]

In the minds of many it is the bloody Western Front that epitomizes World War I of 1914–18, and the essential character of that archetype is the trench war. Our common vision is that of Tommy, Fritz and the French Poilu 'eye deep in hell' – a chaotic misery of mud, blood and bigoted irrational stupidity, unenlightened by any strategic or tactical reason – and for whom 'the trench' carried an almost demonic overtone as the prime author of their suffering. Yet hindsight and pity are wonderful things. In reality trenches were designed to, and did, save lives.

The digging of trenches was a pre-planned response to the stalling of the attack. Death was far more likely to visit those who showed above the parapet or ventured boldly into No Man's Land. As Crown Prince Wilhelm remarked, 'Trench warfare was the natural outcome of an exhaustion brought on by a failure on both sides to develop a decisive strategy.' Trench warfare was not just planned and systematic but eventually a cruel, even Darwinistic, breeding ground for the innovations that would finally allow the war to become 'mobile' once more.

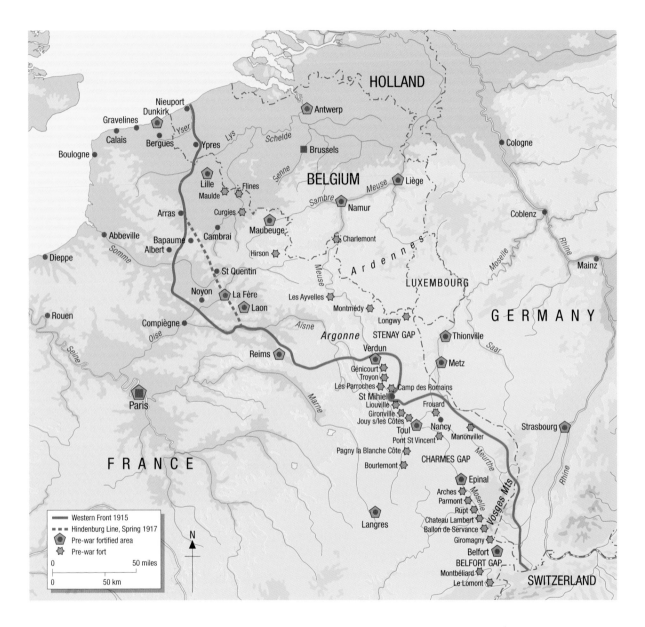

Map of the Western Front.
(© Osprey Publishing)

WESTERN FRONT CHRONOLOGY

1914

1 August	France and Germany declare general mobilization.
3 August	Germany declares war on France.
4 August	German troops enter Belgium; Britain declares war on Germany.
8–16 August	Bombardment and capture of the Liège forts.
19 August	Mülhausen taken by the French.
21 August	Start of battle of the Ardennes.
23 August	Battle of Mons.
26 August	Battle of Le Cateau.
5 September	Fall of Rheims: end of 'battles of the Frontiers'.
6 September	Start of battle of the Marne.
12 September	Start of battle of the Aisne.
25 September	Start of 'Race to the Sea'.
10 October	Surrender of Antwerp to Germans.
19 October	Start of First Battle of Ypres.
21 October	Start of First Battle of Langemarck.
20 December	Start of First Battle of the Champagne.

1915

25 January	First action at Givenchy.
10–13 March	Battle of Neuve Chapelle.
20 March	End of First Battle of the Champagne.
22 April	Start of Second Battle of Ypres; first major gas attack.

9 May	French offensive commences. Battle of Aubers Ridge.
15–25 May	Battle of Festubert.
19 June	First of several actions at Hooge.
25 September	Second Battle of the Champagne and battle of Loos commence.
29 September	French repulsed at Vimy Ridge.
16 November	End of Second Battle of the Champagne.
19 November	General Sir Douglas Haig appointed British Expeditionary Forces commander in France.

1916

21 February	Start of German offensive *Gericht* at Verdun.
25 February	Fort Douamont falls to Germans.
27 February	Start of actions at St Eloi crater.
21 May	*Morte Homme* stormed, Verdun.
24 June	Fleury falls, furthest extent of German advance at Verdun.
1 July	Opening of battle of the Somme.
29 August	Hindenburg replaces Falkenhayn as Chief of the German General Staff.
15 September	Flers Courcelette. First use of tanks.
24 October	French counter-attack commences at Verdun.
1 November	Fort Vaux recaptured by French.
13 November	Battle of the Ancre commences.
18 November	End of battle of the Somme.
16 December	End of French offensive operations at Verdun.

1917

11 January	Re-commencement of operations on the Ancre.
14 March	Beginning of German retreat to the Hindenburg Line.
5 April	Arras offensive begins.
6 April	America declares war on Germany.
9 April	Start of battle at Vimy Ridge.
16 April	Start of French offensive on the Aisne.
15 May	Arras offensive ends.
7–14 June	Battle of Messines.
31 July	Start of Third Battle of Ypres; attack at Pilckem.
20 August	French second offensive starts at Verdun.
20–25 September	Battle of Menin Road Ridge.
12 October	Battle of Passchendaele.

10 November	End of Anglo-Canadian offensives in Flanders.
20 November	Great tank attack at Cambrai.
23–28 November	Capture of Bourlon Wood.
30 November	German counter-attacks commence at Cambrai.

1918

21 March	Operation *Michael* opens German Spring Offensive.
26 March	French battle of the Avre.
9 April	Battle of the Lys commences.
14 April	Marshal Foch appointed Commander Allied Armies in France.
27 May	Start of German offensive in the Champagne.
1 June	Start of US actions at Belleau Wood.
6 June	End of German offensive in the Champagne.
5 July	Beginning of Fourth Battle of the Champagne.
8 August	'Black Day of the German Army' at Amiens.
12–13 September	Battle at St Mihiel. First full-scale US offensive.
17 October	Recapture of Douai.
20 October	Actions commence at Serre and Lys.
11 November	Armistice concluded.

Opposite:
Men of the machine gun section of the 11th Hussars in the trenches at Zillebeke in the winter of 1914–15. Several of the men wear woollen caps, and one maintains one of the weapons. The trench, which lacks revetment, has been cut through tree roots, and at least one tree has been felled to help create improvised overhead cover. From the collection of Major General T. T. Pitman. (IWM Q51194)

CHAPTER ONE

THE ARMIES OF 1914 AND THE PROBLEM OF ATTACK

By 1914 Western Europe had been at peace for more than four decades. Otto von Bismarck's unification of Germany had culminated in the declaration of the German Empire in 1871. There followed a period of equilibrium in which the *Drei Kaiser Bund,* or 'Three Emperors' League', helped hold peace in central Europe; Britain looked outwards to her world empire; and France, though stung by defeat in 1870, lacked power to challenge her new neighbour. Arguably tranquillity began to unravel from 1888 with the accession of Kaiser Wilhelm II, who was famously said to have 'dropped the pilot' when he dismissed Bismarck two years later. Thereafter France moved closer to Russia, whilst German fleet building, plus support of the Boers during the South African War, slowly pushed apart hitherto friendly Anglo-German relations, and a series of conflicts in the Balkans gradually destabilized Austria-Hungary. In theory the assassination of the Archduke Franz Ferdinand of Austria in June 1914 need not have started a war – and certainly not a World War – but in the event it was the spark that lit the fuse that blew Europe apart. Though the immediate *causus belli* lay in south-eastern Europe, and Germany's stated objective was support of Austria, existing alliances and war plans pointed to the West. The Kaiser was said to have been shocked to discover the impracticality of attacking in the East when military plans were based on a preemptive knockout blow to France, firmly framed as the most serious threat. So it was that seven out of eight German armies now swung westwards according to the diktats of a modified 'Schlieffen Plan', the German overall strategic plan for war. In doing so they quickly violated Belgian neutrality, an act that proved the final straw for Britain, which was now facing not only the possible defeat of France, but occupation of the Channel coast by a hostile power.

European armies of 1914 differed in the detail of their weapons, equipment, uniforms and organizations, but a strong common thread ran through their purpose and tactics. Rising populations, increasing wealth, industrialization and conscription in Continental powers had made massive armies possible. Increased tensions and new army laws in France and Germany had made sure that they continued to grow – potentially to

Kaiser Wilhelm II (1859–1941). Seen underneath the portrait is part of the text of a declaration made at his headquarters at Koblenz in August 1914: 'I recognise no parties, but only Germans', an attempt to unify the nation behind the war effort. (Author's collection)

millions in case of war. The universal expectation was that such a war could not be won without movement and attack, and recent historical precedent suggested that the struggle would be both short and decisive. The idea that it would be 'over by Christmas' was by no means as gauche as it now seems. The Austro-Prussian war of 1866 was famously a 'seven weeks' war; France had lasted about six months against Prussia in 1870. The relatively lengthy American Civil War and Boer War were not regarded as reliable indicators of what might happen in Europe. As Captain E. G. Hopkinson of the East Lancashire Regiment put it, 'Few, indeed, thought that the war would last long enough to interfere with the cup final of April, 1915.'[1]

No recent European war had been won by defence. Prussia had defeated its enemies by swift wars of manoeuvre, and Staff colleges still taught the maxims of Napoleon and Clausewitz – in which passivity was tantamount to surrender. With some justification initiative was thought to lie with the offence: for only by advance and attack could one concentrate force against an inferior portion of the enemy and inflict decisive results. For the French in particular attack had assumed an almost mystic quality: a belief persisted that the Franco-Prussian War had been lost partly due to lack of *élan*, and the possibility that the enemy might muster superior numbers seemed to suggest that rapid advance and massed force was the route to military salvation. Whilst there had been numerous technical advances, the most important 'arms of service' were the same in 1914 as they had been a century earlier: infantry, cavalry and artillery.

The artillery was commonly divided into 'field' units which accompanied the fighting troops on the battlefield, and heavier guns, the main purpose of which was to batter fortifications or other fixed positions. The field elements were by far the

One of the 13-pdr guns used by 'L' Battery, Royal Horse Artillery, at Néry, during the retreat from Mons, September 1914. Under machine gun, rifle and artillery fire, the battery fought until its ammunition was exhausted. Three won the Victoria Cross: Captain E. K. Bradbury, who continued to direct the guns despite the loss of a leg, and is now buried in Néry Community Cemetery; Battery Sergeant Major G. T. Dorrell, who took over after all the officers were killed or wounded; and Sergeant D. Nelson, who remained at his post though seriously injured. The gun is now displayed in the Imperial War Museum North, Manchester. (IWM Q68293)

most numerous. On the British 'War Establishment', for example, an infantry division also contained four artillery brigades, three of 18-pdr field guns and one of howitzers, totalling 72 guns. The field piece by which others were judged was the vaunted 1897 model French 75mm. At the time of its introduction this was the 'Quick Firer' *par excellence*. It was equipped with a hydro-pneumatic recoil system, a fast-acting breech mechanism based on a screw, a crew shield and an automatic fuse setter. The ammunition was 'fixed', meaning that rounds came complete in a single unit, with the shell seated in its cartridge case containing the propellant. All the loader had to do was slide the round into the open breech in a single movement. The '75' was mobile by previous standards, had a maximum range of about 4 miles, and for short periods could average more than a dozen rounds a minute. Firing air-bursting shrapnel it was in its element breaking up concentrations of attacking troops. The individual gun section comprised six gunners, six drivers and a corporal, with limber and ammunition wagon, commanded by a sergeant. Over 1,000 four-gun batteries of 75s existed at the outbreak of war, and more than 17,000 pieces were manufactured by 1918. Tactically the field artillery was usually deployed in close support, often firing at relatively close, directly observed targets. The French *batterie de tir* did not usually begin shrapnel fire until within 4,400 yards.

By common consent the Germans were best equipped with heavy artillery. By 1913 the 'Foot' artillery disposed 24 regiments, organized into 48 battalions, each of four batteries of heavy guns, or two of 21cm *Mörser*. Approximately half of the howitzers were 15cm types, the latest model of which was capable of throwing shells over 9,000 yards. At the super heavy end of the spectrum were a relatively small number of massive fortress-busting mortars. The biggest of all was the 42cm, whose shell stood taller than its crew. A smaller 30.5cm Austrian model was also on the inventory, and it was these weapons, together with the 21cm, which were destined for the smashing of the Belgian forts that threatened to impede the speed of the German advance. Firing the bigger guns was no light matter, as US Corporal Amos Wilder explained:

> With the shells came also bags of powder and fuses. When a gun was fired one member of the crew adjusted the barrel for the required direction and trajectory; another rammed home the shell after screwing on its fuse; another added the powder charge (a bag not actually of powder but of thin yellow strips); a fourth closed the breech block; then all seven of the gun crew put their fingers in their ears as the last, at the officer's command, pulled the lanyard.[2]

The range of such weapons was remarkable. The German 15cm howitzer could fire anything from 3–6 miles depending on the model and type of shell; the mighty 42cm mortar could lob approximately 8 miles. Some of the naval guns eventually deployed on land would comfortably double even this distance.

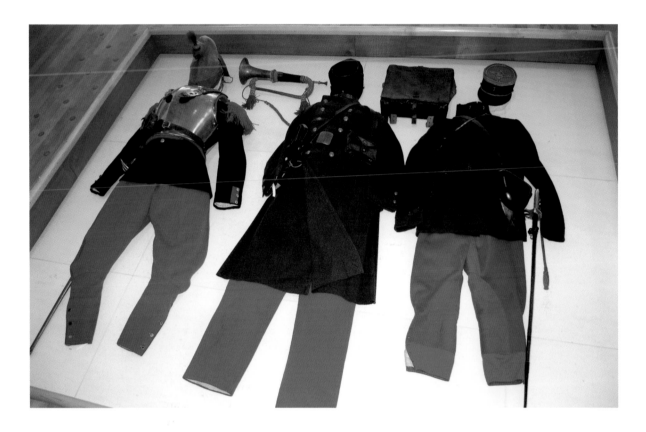

In many early engagements of the war the artillery would fight at comparatively close ranges, often firing over 'open sights' against targets observed from the gun line. Once fronts became fixed this would change quite rapidly with the use of 'forward observers' who positioned their observation posts amongst, or even slightly forward of, the main infantry positions. Map or 'predicted' fire similarly became more important as the war progressed. Artillery would take a significant toll in the 'battles of the Frontiers', but if anything its position as killer-in-chief would become more obvious later. Overall artillery was easily the most deadly weapon of World War I, far outstripping even that reviled newcomer, the machine gun. According to a sample of 212,659 wound cases examined at British casualty clearing stations, over 58 per cent of wounds were caused by shells and trench mortar bombs; 39 per cent by bullets from rifles and machine guns combined; 2 per cent by grenades, and less than one-third of a per cent by bayonets. Tables considered by the Munitions Design Committee in 1916 showed shell and mortar wounds outnumbering all others by more than two to one. Figures cited by Winteringham and Blashford-Snell suggest that in the period 1914–15 about 50 per cent of German casualties were caused by artillery, rising to a staggering 85 per cent from 1916 to 1918. Aggregating these statistics brings us to the conclusion that two-thirds of all deaths and wounds on the Western Front having been caused by artillery is very close to the mark.

French uniforms of 1914, in the Historial de la Grande Guerre, Péronne. Left to right: cuirassier, with distinctive breastplate; infantry, with greatcoat and pack; and officer. The famous red trousers would disappear in 1915 with the adoption of an 'horizon blue' uniform. (Author's collection)

The impact of shells, which tended to get bigger, more frequent and more impressive in their performance as the war progressed was quite literally stunning. Captain McKinnell of the Liverpool Scottish described the largest varieties as passing 'like an express train' even if aimed at a distant target. As C. E. Carrington of the Royal Warwickshires related, old soldiers learned to recognize a shell by its sound: some whistled, others shrieked. The smallest projectiles leaving field guns in the distance might sound like 'champagne corks'. The wounds and deaths caused by shells involved the most shocking sort of disfigurement and dismemberment. As Frederic Manning of the King's Shropshire Light Infantry observed, though all the dead were equally dead, 'it is infinitely more horrible and revolting to see a man shattered and eviscerated, than to see him shot'.[3] Gustav Ebelshauser, 17th Bavarian Infantry, was witness to just one tragedy amongst thousands:

> Aldrich had been struck by a large steel splinter that had made a clean cut through flesh and bones slightly beneath the belt, slicing his body in almost two equal halves. A strip of cloth at the back of his uniform prevented the two pieces from falling apart. Instead it had caused them to open, fully exposing to view their ghastly contents. The splinter hit with such force that Aldrich's head had been forced between his legs. But his face looked as though it were still alive...[4]

Many memoirs include incidents in which bodies are so shredded to odd fragments that they have to be scraped up into sandbags for burial. Seaforth Highlander Norman Collins was appalled to see how much of a man's intestines could be blown out, whilst the victim yet remained alive. There were also bizarre wounds, such as that of the

German officer seen by Australian E. P. F. Lynch, who was relatively healthy bar a neat slicing off of his top lip.

Some had the narrowest of escapes. Artillery officer N. F. Tytler remembered taking cover as a round hit nearby:

> As soon as the shell had burst I looked out just in time to see a red lump rising out of a red pool… I pulled him into one of the trench dugouts and started a party to clean him up and then report damages. Extraordinary as it appeared, he was perfectly untouched… The shell must have burst on the back of one of the horses, as there was no crater in the ground.[5]

Blasts could quite literally throw men around, though it did not always kill them. As Unteroffizier Hundt remembered:

> The shells came over in great salvoes, exploding with ear-splitting detonations. Then bits were flying in all directions: clods of earth, stones, pieces of wood and showers of loose earth which came down everywhere like rain … there was an almighty explosion right next to me, which seemed to get me right in the stomach and innards. I was seized by its irresistible violence and flung into the air. When I came round I had been thrown 3 metres into a hole and covered with a light layer of earth. I jumped to my feet and saw a huge shell crater right next to me. A man of my section, who had been shot through both legs, was being carried off. Despite the most energetic efforts, no trace was found of three of my men…[6]

A carte de visite style hand-coloured studio portrait of a Prussian guardsman, Potsdam, c.1913. The Haarbusch, or falling plume, was a parade item not usually worn in other orders of dress, its holder then being replaced with the spike. (Author's collection)

Perhaps surprisingly the most remarkable statistic about shells was that a majority of those fired actually killed nobody. From March to November 1918 alone British forces on the Western Front expended more than a million shells each week, and sometimes two or even three. This was more than half a dozen for every single German under arms, even allowing for a generous margin of 'duds'. Conversely, unlucky strikes on bunched or vulnerable targets could prove catastrophic. Mortar crewman Stuart Chapman reported a hit on a crowded *estaminet* in Arras that killed 28; on another occasion he was witness to a German 15cm shell that hit a house and killed not just 12 soldiers, but seven civilians, and a further four troops were wounded. Most could recall some such disaster.

Yet the significance of the artillery was not in any one round, but the marshalling of bombardments to multiply effect and even deny whole areas to an enemy. During one bombardment at Delville Wood in 1916 it was calculated that 400 German shells per minute were raining down on the South African positions. Private Charles Dunn returned to the wood after such a pounding:

> Dead men were lying all about. At some parts one was obliged to step over the dead bodies of Germans, Britishers [sic], South Africans and Highlanders. And some awful sights there were. Some men with half bodies, heads off, some were in a really awful state. All the time that I spent in Delville Wood in one large shell hole a dead Jock was sitting upright, he had evidently died from loss of blood. On his left lay half a man – he was a Jock too. All that could be seen of him was his kilt and two legs.[7]

Little wonder that bombardment became one of the greatest trials of the soldier; fear and exhaustion, combined with brain-shaking concussion, would lead ultimately to the as yet little understood condition of 'shell shock'. This ailment was not named until February 1915 when the term was coined by Dr C. S. Myers writing in the *Lancet*. Yet, interestingly, few could actually agree what shell shock was. Sufferers seldom felt their real problem was understood while the authorities believed that 'shell shock' was a cover for cowardice and malingering. Both sides could point to specific instances to support their views. The treatment, if any, varied radically depending on circumstance and the experience of the medical staff involved. Some victims of nervous breakdown were treated simply as disciplinary cases, others as lunatics, and at the most extreme end of the spectrum were given a primitive form of electric shock therapy, which, it was observed, was useful at least in the sense that it sometimes exposed those who had been shamming their neurosis. Some were handled much more sympathetically and rested behind the line. Perhaps the biggest surprise was that there were not more shell shock casualties: in 1915 for example there were just over 20,000 cases of 'nervous disorders' of all types requiring medical intervention. This total amounted to less than 4 per cent of all British hospital cases, and covered things that were not actually 'shell shock'.

Not until the institution of a War Office Committee of Enquiry in 1922 was the issue systematically examined. Then there was broad agreement that the phrase 'shell shock' was not really useful, Dr W. H. Rivers being just one of many medical practitioners who pointed out that stress was the main factor in most cases, 'shock' being merely the last straw. Some were physical victims of concussion to brain and spine; many more simply collapsed under the strain of combat; some presented complex mixtures of the physical and emotional. Major General H. S. Jeudwine, former commander of 55th Division, iterated the opinion that shell shock had been used as a portmanteau term to cover everything from the 'badly frightened' to those suffering serious derangement of nerves or health. Its incidence happened to have been greatest in the middle of the war when the armies were static under fire. Historian John Fortescue offered the surprisingly modern conclusion that stress was cumulative and everybody had his limit where combat was concerned, as 'even the bravest man cannot endure to be under fire for more than a certain number of consecutive days'.[8]

The cavalry were no longer the decisive fighting force they had been in the Napoleonic era. Nevertheless they retained a significant, though reduced, niche in the order of battle. Horsemen could move faster than infantry, at least for short periods, and could screen army movements as well as probe enemy positions. They could also act as 'mounted infantry' and defend outposts, act as a spoiling or surprise force, or could exploit gaps or enemy retreats. Likewise they could seize important positions until the main body came up to secure them. The old distinctions between 'heavy' and 'light' cavalry, and 'dragoons' had become increasingly blurred: indeed German cavalry were now issued with lances whatever their theoretical designation. In the French mounted arm all had lances except the heavy Cuirassiers. Perhaps surprisingly the cavalry also retained swords as well as a carbine or rifle. Even after the first clash of arms British instructions issued as part of *Notes From the Front* stated that cavalry patrols should 'invariably carry their swords – not their rifles – in their hands for immediate use'. The official default action on meeting enemy cavalry, even if superior in numbers, was to 'charge at once at the gallop'.

Men of the 16th Queen's Lancers on the retreat from Mons, September 1914. The 16th were part of 3rd Cavalry Brigade, and engaged as early as 22 August when they gave chase to an enemy patrol, and then overran a party of Jäger. During the retreat they attempted to screen the crossing of the Crozeat canal, but were driven out of Jussy on 29 August. On 12 September they succeeded in ambushing the 13th Landwehr Infantry Regiment, killing or capturing almost a complete company. (IWM Q56309)

The basic mounted unit was the regiment, divided into squadrons. In 1914 cavalry were sometimes deployed in complete brigades, but were also attached in smaller units to infantry divisions. In the German order of battle a cavalry regiment formed part of

Vorwärts – 'Forwards' – a German patriotic postcard of 1914 showing an infantry standard bearer on the advance. Too often dug-in troops brought such popular heroics to a premature halt. (Author's collection)

each division; in the British, a squadron. The French cavalry were widely acknowledged as amongst the best, animated with 'patriotic spirit' and having good march discipline and well-informed officers. A British report of 1912 stated that French horse could manage a steady 8 miles per hour, and that in a patrol action it was possible for small groups of half a dozen to cover anything up to 45 miles in a morning. Perhaps less sensibly they displayed 'contempt' for rifle fire, and were not inclined to admit that they required infantry support.

Infantry were by far the most numerous of the fighting troops, and also took the vast majority of the punishment. Not only did German drill manuals warn the foot soldier this was so, but British statistics proved it. According to that great digest *The Military Effort of the British Empire*, no less than 86 per cent of all casualties fell on the infantry. Captain Henry Dundas of the Scots Guards did not survive the war, and so was without benefit of hindsight when he wrote:

> The infantry in the line, who bear the brunt of the whole thing, get nothing done for them, get paid a pittance compared to anyone else, and then get butchered in droves when the fine weather comes. No one would object to being *condamnés à la mort* as the French pithily describe the infantry, if there was a little fattening up attached to it.[9]

Pour la France
VERSEZ VOTRE OR

L'Or Combat Pour La Victoire

LES MONNAIES D'OR SONT ÉCHANGEES A LA BANQUE DE FRANCE

A French poster by Jules Abel Faivre – 'Give your gold for France: gold fights for victory'. The German infantryman is confronted by an angry French cockerel and crushed by the weight of money. (Author's collection)

The infantry were universally armed with bolt action rifles. In the four decades leading up to 1914 the 'infantryman's friend' had changed almost out of recognition. The rifle was no longer a single-shot large-bored beast, but a relatively slender, relatively high velocity, precision tool with a magazine. These improvements had been made possible by the perfected, powerful, smokeless powder, brass cartridge – now usually with a pointed jacketed bullet – which was easy to handle, and worked reliably though the loading mechanism. The penetration of such a bullet is astounding to anyone who has not seen it first hand. At 200 yards a .303 round will cut through a house brick. According to British training anything under 600 yards was close range, and most rifles were sighted up to about 2,000 yards. In 1915 Corporal W. F. Lowe of the 10th Durhams reported an incident in a crowded trench in which one man – being wounded in the act of reloading – suffered an accidental discharge. His bullet went straight through his neighbour's head and ricocheted through the arm and thigh of a second man, before landing in the stomach of a third.[10] What happened when a man was hit varied considerably and depended greatly on where he was struck and at what range. Canadian Herbert McBride explained some of the possibilities:

> At short ranges, due to the high velocity, it does have an explosive effect and … when it strikes, it sounds like an explosion. Bullets may be cracking viciously all around you, when all of a sudden, you hear a 'whop' and the man alongside goes down. If it is daylight and you are looking that way, you may see a little tuft of cloth sticking out from his clothes. Wherever the bullet comes out, it carries a little of the clothing – but it is unmistakable… And the effect of the bullet, at short range, also suggests the idea of an explosion, especially if a large bone is struck.[11]

Modern experimental techniques show that where any significant body mass is hit by a fast-moving projectile a temporary cavity is formed, and often the bullet begins to tumble – massive tissue damage being the result. French soldier Marc Bloch saw a comrade's skull quite literally shattered by a bullet that left half the face hanging, 'like a shutter whose hinges no longer held'.[12] Rifleman John Asprey of the 1st Royal Irish Rifles was killed by a ricochet that 'turned at right angles' – and hit him in the left temple. Usually entry wounds were deceptively small and neat: as Private R. G. Bultitude of the Artist's Rifles put it, 'bullets drill a fairly clean hole'.[13] Exit wounds, on the other hand, were often ugly and gaping. When Siegfried Sassoon took a sniper's bullet and slumped against the side of a sap his initial impression was that a bomb had hit him from behind. Stomach wounds were nasty, and often fatal – slowly. Lieutenant D. W. J. Cuddeford of the 12th Highland Light Infantry saw one such at Arras in 1917:

> He was only a boy, obviously not more than about 17 years of age, but he had always refused to be sent back to the Base Depot along with the other 'under ages'. The bullet struck him in the belly, and as is usual with one of these abdominal wounds he rolled about clawing the ground, screaming and making a terrible fuss. Certainly, to have one's guts stirred up by a red hot bullet must be a dreadful thing, and that a bullet is really hot after its flight through the air is well known to anyone who tries to pick up a newly spent one. However, they got the boy back into the trench, opened his clothes and put a bandage around his middle over the wound, but of course we could see from the first it was hopeless.[14]

Conversely there were some men, hit in non-vital areas, who had lucky escapes when a round passed clean through without inflicting serious injury. McBride similarly described a long-range, and probably low-velocity, impact where a bullet slipped into a soldier's leg and the man remained unaware for sometime that his minor injury had been caused by a bullet.

Bayonets were taken seriously by military authorities, and drill with 'cold steel' featured prominently in training. Generally it was assumed that the longer the bayonet, the better 'reach' its user would have in a fight. The bayonet charge was the final phase of the attack, intended, as British instructions put it, to give 'moral and physical advantages' over a stationary line. Though useful in the dark, or for the intimidation of an unwilling prisoner, few bayonet wounds were actually inflicted. Nevertheless soldiers found other applications for them and strict injunctions had to be issued against using them as pokers or toasting forks. Jean Norton Cru, French veteran of Verdun, was particularly scathing. He had never seen a bayonet used, stained with blood, nor stuck in a corpse. True bayonets were 'fixed' at the start of an attack, 'but that was not a reason for calling it a bayonet charge, any more than a charge in puttees'.[15]

In the infantry the principal tactical units were the battalion, of about 1,000 men, and the company, four of which made up the battalion under German, British and French organizations. The infantry attack was similar in the doctrine of all the combatant nations. Battalions would advance on the enemy, starting off in columns of various types for ease of movement, fall into skirmish lines for maximum deployment of their weapons, then engage. Having gained the upper hand with fire they would charge forward, taking the fight to the enemy, perhaps with the addition of reserves thrown in at a vital moment. There were, however, differences in the detail. In the British synthesis, as outlined in

Designed specifically with fortress destruction in mind, the 42cm mortar was the ace in the pack of German heavy artillery in 1914. Though designated 'mortars' in German terminology, these pieces were effectively super heavy howitzers – throwing monster 2,000lb shells more than 8 miles. Along with Skoda 30.5cm and 21cm ordnance this class of mortar was deployed against the forts of Liège, Namur, Antwerp and Maubeurge. Though many guns have been popularly dubbed 'Big Bertha' this was the original – being nicknamed after Bertha Krupp (1886–1957) of the Essen armaments dynasty. (IWM Q65817)

MASH VALLEY

The infamous 'Mash Valley' from the 'Ovillers' trench map, sheet 57D S.E. 4, 1:10,000, with German trenches, in red, corrected to 27 April, and British trenches, in blue, corrected to 11 June 1916. The red dots are identified as German 'earthworks'. On the morning of 1 July, Ovillers, at the top of the area shown, was the main objective of the 8th Division assault – but some of the attackers had 700 yards of open ground to cross, overlooked and under fire from more than one direction. The 2nd Middlesex actually entered the German line but suffered 540 casualties, including their commanding officer, who was wounded, and had only one officer and 28 men remaining at the end of the day. The 8th King's Own Yorkshire Light Infantry were similarly hard hit, and the 8th York and Lancasters lost 597. The 8th Division suffered a total of 5,121 casualties.

Ovillers was eventually taken during intensive fighting from 15–17 July, the last 128 German defenders being officers and men of 15th Reserve Infantry Regiment and Garde Fusiliers, who were finally winkled out by bombers of 11th Lancashire Fusiliers. Three German machine guns, still operative, were also captured. The Ovillers British military cemetery, designed by Sir Herbert Baker, is just one of several in the area. It commemorates 3,440 Commonwealth servicemen, and also contains 120 French burials. One of the graves here is that of Captain J. C. Lauder, 1st/8th Argyll and Sutherland Highlanders, son of Sir Harry Lauder, killed in December 1916. The remains of La Boiselle, located at the bottom of the plan on the spur between Mash and Sausage valleys south of what was once the main road to Albert, were attacked by Tyneside Scottish and Irish battalions of 34th Division at the cost of 6,380 killed, wounded and missing – the highest number lost by any division on 1 July.

Men of 'A' Company, 11th Battalion, Cheshire Regiment, occupy a captured German position at Ovillers-la-Boiselle on the Somme, July 1916. Note that the trench has been 'turned', and is now being defended from its parados, or rear lip. One man keeps sentry, using an improvised fire step, whilst his comrades rest. Picture taken by Lieutenant J. W. Brooke. (IWM Q3990)

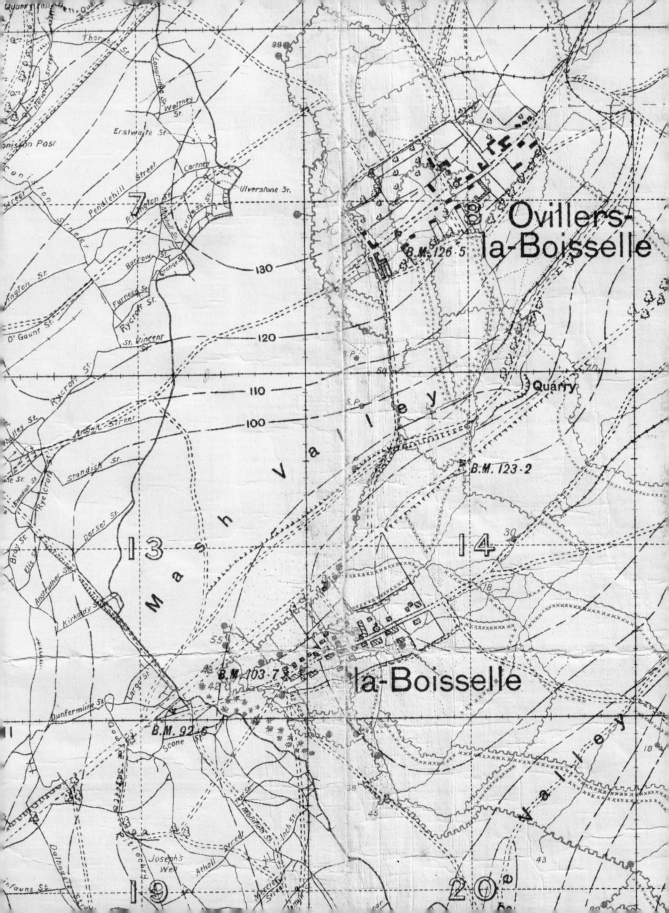

the 1914 *Manual of Infantry Training*, the troops were divided into firing line, supports and 'local reserves'. Ideally a portion of the force held the enemy by fire, and the crucial blow was struck by the general reserve. The attack would begin as a 'determined and steady advance', though the routes forward would be planned with an eye to concealment and opportunity for 'covering fire'. The attackers were not to halt until 'compelled to do so', and fire was to be used with the object of making 'advance to close quarters possible'. When checked by 'heavy and accurate fire' the infantry would resort to advances by rushes, using either the whole line, or parts, as the manual explains:

> The fact that superiority of fire has been obtained will usually be first observed from the firing line; it will be known by the weakening of the enemy's fire, and perhaps by the movement of individuals or groups of men from the enemy's position towards the rear. The impulse for the assault must therefore often come from the firing line, and it is the duty of any commander in the firing line, who sees that the moment for the assault has arrived, to carry it out, and for all other commanders to co-operate.

In the German system, as laid down in the *Infantry Drill Regulations* 1906, the attack was described as consisting of 'firing on the enemy until close range is reached, if this is necessary. Victory is made complete by charging with fixed bayonet.' Following deployment into skirmish lines the infantry would move as close as possible before opening fire, and though open ground was best avoided or crossed swiftly by 'well extended forces', in extremis it could be used for the attack. The desire to press forward was to 'animate all units of the attacking force'. Despite this bullish approach, organized 'mutual fire support', breaking into smaller units to take difficult targets, and rushes were all part of the plan. Rushes were commonly of platoon size units, as smaller bodies tended to break up fire effect, and larger ones made mutual fire support difficult. 'Regularity' in the advance of units was positively to be avoided, though interfering with the fire of neighbouring units was strictly forbidden. Before the outbreak of war the British General Staff was in no way complacent about the comparative merits of the Continental infantry. Whilst it was thought that British troops had the edge in 'musketry' and 'minor tactics', a report of 1912 suggested that the French infantry were superior in marching. British observers noted some units covering 30 miles in a day. The 'spirit, discipline, endurance and marching powers' of the Prussians and Saxons in the German Army was acknowledged as 'in every sense admirable'.

The machine gun was something of a Cinderella on the battlefields of 1914, for though it had existed in its modern form for three decades there was still disagreement about its best tactical use. Performance in colonial wars was not thought to be a particularly good guide as to what might happen when 'civilized' enemies, who also had machine guns, were encountered. The models in use at the outbreak of war were neither available in very large numbers nor of particularly mobile designs. Most nations, including Britain and Germany, fielded water-cooled

French gunners with the 8mm Hotchkiss machine gun. The air-cooled Hotchkiss was a reliable weapon, usually fed from strips of 24 or 30 cartridges. Despite the lack of a water jacket the equipment was still heavy – with the gun and the mount weighing about 53lb each. (Author's collection)

Maxim designs; the French air-cooled guns were mainly of the Hotchkiss type. Water-cooled weapons were better for long periods of sustained fire but required a supply of water and a can. Sometimes this was easier said than done, and many crews had to resort to what Georg Bucher would delicately call the 'human water spring' – with the result that a hot gun stank. Moreover boiling liquid gave rise to steam which could sometimes reveal the position of an otherwise well-placed gun. Air-cooled guns did not suffer these inconveniences, but were less useful in prolonged actions. All machine guns were heavy – though the air-cooled models were generally a little lighter – and the British and French guns were mounted on tripods, the German MG 08 on an elaborate 'sledge mount'. The Germans had kept their machine guns in separate units until comparatively recently, but then, like the British, had allotted them, two per battalion, to the infantry, though *Jäger* battalions had a complete company of six guns. British regulations described the machine gun as a weapon 'of opportunity'. In the event they were somewhat cumbersome in the attack, but would prove devastating in defence.

One thing that contemporaries did agree on was that, whilst they occupied a relatively small space, machine guns were remarkably powerful – equalling from 30–50 riflemen depending on the authority quoted. Moreover, as an Austrian report translated by the British General Staff in 1911 observed, the effect of machine weapons was not just physical:

When we think of the heavy loss which can be caused by machine guns over a restricted area in a very short period of time we see that the influence which they exert on the enemy must be very great. Nor must we forget that the bullets which fail actually to hit have also great moral effect if they get close to the enemy. They force him down under cover, disturb his aim, and thus enable our own infantry to fire more effectively.

In the British Army at the outbreak of war the old .303 Maxim was already slated for replacement by the Vickers model of 1912, an essentially similar, but somewhat improved gun. George Coppard remembered the Vickers as the most successful, being highly efficient, reliable and compact:

The tripod was the heaviest component, weighing about 50 pounds; the gun itself weighed 28 pounds without water. In good tune the rate of fire was well over 600 rounds per minute, and when the gun was firmly fixed on the tripod there was little or no movement to upset its accuracy. Being water cooled, it could fire continuously for long periods. Heat engendered by rapid fire soon boiled the water and caused a powerful emission of steam, which was condensed by passing it through a pliable tube into a canvas bucket of water.[16]

So much for the technology and tactics – which might have worked were it not for a number of strategic and technical matters that confounded all expectations of a swift and emphatic encounter. One important factor that made the occurrence of trench warfare more likely on the Western Front was the relatively fine balance of the opposing forces. Germany was strong, but needed to retain a defence in the East against Russia: her seven armies involved in the initial onslaught in the West therefore totalled approximately 1.5 million men, with the greatest concentrations at the northern end of the front. Against this France could initially dispose just under 1.2 million, but with the enemy advance into Belgium other forces also came into play. The Belgians numbered approximately 120,000, and, though poorly equipped in some respects, on the defensive they benefited from existing fortifications, notably those at Liège and Namur. These forts of the Meuse were not new, having been completed in 1891; nevertheless they were extensive, involving 21 individual forts, concrete shelters and an investment of 72 million Belgian Francs. Their presence impeded enemy use of the Belgian railway system. The arrival of the British Expeditionary Force (BEF) from 12–17 August added another 100,000 men. Though traversing Belgium gave more space in which to deploy, and offered the tempting prospect of avoiding the main concentration of French forces, it also increased the distance the German armies had to travel. The spearhead of the German offensive, First and Second Armies, would strike Belgians, British and French in turn – and would cross hostile territory, while the British and French were welcomed as friends.

With time any initial German numerical advantage evaporated as the Entente powers gained strength faster than their enemy in the West – and more effort was required to hold in the East. In his memoirs von Falkenhayn went so far as to claim that as early as mid October 1914 the German Army was significantly outnumbered on the Western Front, having just 1.7 million troops to the 2.3 million commanded by France and its allies. This is something of an exaggeration; nevertheless Germany could never bring as many reinforcements to the Western Front as her opponents, at least until Russia finally capitulated. We may therefore see that although it proved possible to create local advantages on specific sectors the total numbers deployed on either side at the start of war were similar. When we consider that modern commentators expect that successful attacks will require perhaps three times the force of a prepared defence, the difficulty of achieving any decisive opening campaign becomes apparent.

Sheer numbers also created inertia. The dramatic European campaigns of earlier centuries had been mounted by much smaller armies, formed from smaller populations, with less effective communications technology. In simple terms this had meant that previous armies fighting in the 'cockpit of Europe' had more space and time in which to manoeuvre. There were simply not enough troops to maintain continuous lines across the Continent, and no observation aircraft or telephones to provide early warning. Forces could, and did, slip around each other, and sometimes remained undetected at relatively short distances. In 1914 the Germans quickly ran out of physical space, though doubtless the inescapable mathematical calculation of men and frontages had been one of the factors influencing the decision to enter neutral Belgium in the first place. On the right the German First Army, under Kluck, has been calculated as packed to a density of 18,000 men per mile of its front, whilst even Sixth Army, which was spread over 70 miles on the least crowded sector, had 3,100 men for each mile. As events would prove, simply cramming more men into less space did not make matters easier. Railways did speed troop movement behind the lines, and created what has been famously dubbed an opening 'war of timetables', but once the railhead was reached mobility slowed to walking pace. The attack being joined, railways and roads favoured the defender who could now usually move forces more quickly than the attacker. The 'miracle of the Marne' was at least in part due to the ability of Joffre to reorder his forces to the left-hand end of his line under Maunoury, meeting strength with strength.

The technical improvement of weapons also played their part in the stalemate. In the opinion of Marshal Foch, commenting on 1914:

> Generally speaking, it seemed proved that the new means of action furnished by automatic weapons and long range guns enabled the defence to hold up any attempt at breaking through long enough for a counter-attack to be launched with saving effect. The 'pockets' which resulted from partial attacks which were successful and seemingly even decisive, could not be maintained, in spite of very costly losses, long enough to ensure a definite rupture of the adversary's line.[17]

More men with more effective arms certainly made closing with the opposition or breakthrough more difficult. In 1814 the musket-armed infantryman would have been lucky to achieve three aimed shots to an effective range of 100 yards; by 1914 the magazine rifle made ten or more rounds per yard to 500 yards perfectly practicable. Artillery, with a rate of fire of perhaps one solid round shot per minute to 1,000 yards, had advanced to a state where shrapnel shells were being thrown ten times per minute to much greater ranges. Machine guns, which had not existed at all in 1814, were effective surprise or defensive weapons, creating 'beaten zones' out to ranges of hundreds of yards. Such walls of fire certainly made a significant contribution to the creation of the 'empty battlefield': units remaining in plain sight of the enemy for very long were likely to be crippled as an attacking force.

Opposite:
A French soldier using a Bellard-type 'hyposcope' rifle through a loophole. The firer uses a dummy 'set down' stock, and takes aim by periscope, viewing through the rifle sights. The purpose of the device was to ensure that return fire could not strike home, the hyposcope operator being protected below the loop or parapet. Many different models were patented by inventors internationally during the course of the war: others included those of Horton and Liebmann; Duerr; Pochielli and Pavesi; Gérard; Boult; Sangster; and Evans.
(IWM Q69982)

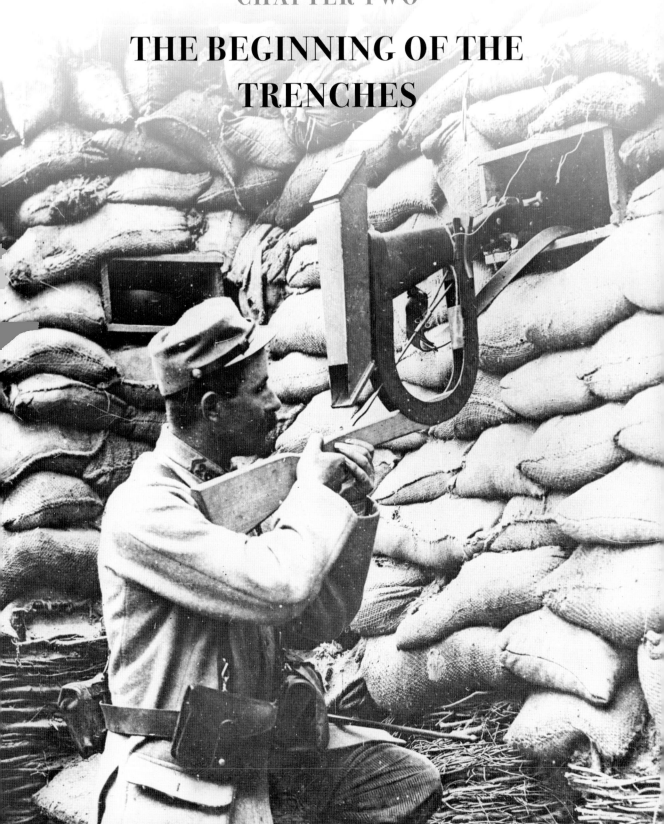

CHAPTER TWO

THE BEGINNING OF THE TRENCHES

Many histories of World War I on the Western Front draw a clear distinction between the 'open' warfare of the 'battle of the Frontiers' and the 'trench' warfare that supposedly characterized fighting after the battle of the Marne. In fact this difference would only become clear with hindsight because temporary use of trenches and fieldworks started in many sectors not long after the outbreak of hostilities. Even at the time of the Marne large parts of the front had already achieved a somewhat uneasy 'stability'. By 9 September 1914, for example, much of the French front from Switzerland to the Argonne had become fixed. The subsequent 'race to the sea' as the armies attempted to manoeuvre around each other's northern flank, led not to breakthrough, but effectively cemented the remainder of the Western Front. As Edmund Dane observed, not 'a spade stroke' of the effort required to create the trench lines was wasted.[1] Digging served to protect the troops in relatively inactive sectors, freeing up units for the attempts to outmanoeuvre or break through that were made.

The British *Official History* dates 'the beginning of trench warfare' on the Aisne, perhaps over-precisely, to 14 September 1914, a day on which alternate attack and counter-attack ended with no decisive result. Two days later Field Marshal Sir John French issued orders that the line now held should be 'strongly entrenched'. The *Official History* described the first British trenches as 'rarely continuous', being more usually:

> a succession of narrow pits capable of holding a few men. Generally they were of the narrow type, 18 inches to 2 feet wide, with tiny traverses, 3 to 6 feet wide. These days were afterwards spoken of in jest as the 'Augustan Period' (August 1914) of field fortification. The narrow trenches, though giving good cover, were easily knocked-in by high explosive shell, and proved the graves of some of the defenders, for men were occasionally buried alive in them.

Nevertheless nobody in overall command consciously chose general 'trench warfare' as the preferred strategy, and Sir John French's orders also stated that he intended to 'assume a general offensive at the first opportunity'. Often trench warfare began simply as the pre-programmed response of units halted by enemy resistance in vulnerable positions. As German Chief of Staff Erich von Falkenhayn later explained:

> GHQ was fully conscious of the disadvantages involved by the transition to trench war. It was chosen purely and simply as the lesser evil … the transition to trench war was not effected by the independent decision of the Chief of the General Staff, but under the stern pressure of necessity.[2]

Almost from the outset the Entente powers suffered from some disadvantages in the siting of their trench lines. For the French, giving up national ground voluntarily in order to place defences in ideal positions was an anathema. For the British, whose Expeditionary Force moved to the Ypres sector in October 1914, there were other problems. Little of Belgium remained unoccupied, and to yield its last significant town when the freedom of that country had been one of the main objectives of war was unthinkable. The result was the dogged defence of what soon became ruins, within a precarious salient, ringed on the Eastern flank by low hills occupied by the enemy. British strategy on the Western Front would now involve not only attempting to assist both France and Russia at their various times of need, but holding suitable Channel ports, and attempting to push the Germans back from their stranglehold on Ypres. In much of Flanders both sides struggled with low lying ground and a water table close to the surface. Excavations soon filled with water and required continuous pumping, or else 'box' trenches or 'breastworks' had to be built up on the surface, becoming magnets for artillery fire. Such constructions were described by Lieutenant F. P. Roe of the Glosters as, 'not actually trenches at all' but 'sandbag fortifications all above ground'.[3] According to the history of the South Wales Borderers parts of the Festubert sector were at times so waterlogged that they actually became a series of islands which the troops had to struggle to reconnect before a line could be established.

Though 'trench warfare' often became a chaos enacted amongst shallow ditches, shell holes and morasses of featureless mud, creating 'fieldworks' was a default position in the teaching of every army, and one of the main purposes of digging in

The Boyau de Mort, *or 'Trench of Death', Dixmude, Belgium. Defended by Belgians and French marines, the town of Dixmude was heavily bombarded and fell on 10 November 1914 and was not reclaimed until 1918. Though extensively repaired by the Belgian Army in 1974, and replete with cement sandbags, the* Boyau de Mort *is an original, and the fire trench with its 'supervision' trench behind can clearly be discerned. Further work to the site was still ongoing in 2008. (Author's collection)*

was to economize on lives. Moreover the distinctive characteristics of what would, by happenstance, become the trenches of 1914, had been laid down several years before the outbreak of war. The only thing that was unexpected was that these works, rather than being temporary features of part of the front, quickly occupied the entire distance from the English Channel to Switzerland.

The document that determined the layout and appearance of the first German trenches was *Feld-Pionierdienst Aller Waffen*, or 'Field Pioneer Work for all Arms', a general instruction first published in 1911. One of the main objectives foreseen by this manual was the holding of ground with 'relatively little effort'. The trenches themselves were to have free and open fields of fire, with the *Schützengraben* or 'fire trenches' near to the crest of a rise, and the *Verbindungsgraben*, 'connecting' or 'communication', trenches providing access from the rear. Though a depth of 70 inches was the model, exact dimensions and detail of design would depend on the level of the water table, with piled up excavated earth to the front to compensate for shallow trenches. Fire steps were notionally 16 inches wide, and doubled for seating. Walkways were to be a minimum of 24 inches wide. Natural cover such as folds in the ground or foliage would disguise positions. Ideally the fire trenches were to have *Schulterwehren* (shoulders or traverses) at 8–11 yards intervals, as protection against enfilading fire and explosion.

In the fully developed German trench system the communication trenches led to a *Deckungsgraben*, or 'cover trench' in the rear, and there were spurs leading to dugouts and posts. These included a *Verbandraum* or 'dressing station', a *Fernsprechstelle* or 'telephone position', and latrines. Trenches were not portrayed as a negative development but as fire positions and jumping off points for future aggressive action. Key points from the official manual were also reproduced in semi-official and private digests during 1914 and 1915. Notable amongst these were Rabenau's edition of *Dienstunterricht des Deutschen Pioniers,* or 'Service Instructions of the German Pioneers', and Heinrich Fitschen's lively little pocket book *Der Spatenkrieg*, or 'The Spade War', both published in Berlin in 1915.

The British appreciation, as outlined in the *Manual of Field Engineering* (1911, reprinted 1914), was similar. Field fortifications were desirable under certain circumstances but were always to be regarded as a 'means to an end'. Trenches were to be used to protect troops and allow them to use their weapons to the 'greatest effect'. They were also intended to 'reduce losses' in one theatre or part of a field of battle, specifically to allow men and resources to be released for more useful application elsewhere. Usually infantry would entrench only when further progress became impossible, though artillery would take advantage of fieldworks 'whenever possible'. In strengthening a locality it was important that the defenders should consider the tactical requirements; economy of men; deception of the enemy; screening; free movement within the position; the hampering of the enemy; and fields of fire. Most significant in terms of bringing fire was the 'last 300 or 400' yards of the approach, which might well benefit from the clearance of cover.

The dimensions of British field fortifications varied with opportunity, tactical employment and the conditions, but standard instructions took into account the important basic parameters of the physique of the average soldier and the ballistic resistance of the materials used in their construction. Hence the standard gap between the fire step and elbow rest of a trench was 4 feet 6 inches, and the usual thickness of an earth parapet 3 feet 6 inches. Unrammed earth was to be 40 inches thick to stop a rifle bullet; turf or peat 80 inches; chalk 15 inches. Fire steps were to have a maximum width of 18 inches, and the best trenches were wide enough to admit the passage of a stretcher without interfering with the garrison firing out. Most trenches would be constructed by the infantry, with planning and assistance from the Royal Engineer field companies as available. Tools were carried by the troops, and in 'first line' transport. The most important of these were the pick and 'Shovel GS', and the 'entrenching implement' which formed part of the standard 1908 equipment. Standard infantry battalion allocation was 226 shovels; 151 picks; 936 'implements'; 25 axes (hand and 'felling'); 63 bill and reaping hooks; 32 saws; eight crow bars, and 24 pairs of wire cutters. Cavalry were not as well equipped, and on occasion resorted to bayonets and anything else that came to hand.

The *Official History* states that during the early fighting on the Aisne, 'except in one sector of the II Corps area', the trenches 'stood vertical without revetment'.

Left:
Illustration showing the overhead cover for two men in the firing line, from E. J. Solano Field Entrenchments: Spadework for Riflemen, *1914. (Author's collection)*

Right:
Diagrams showing trench details from the Manual of Field Engineering, *1911.(Author's collection)*

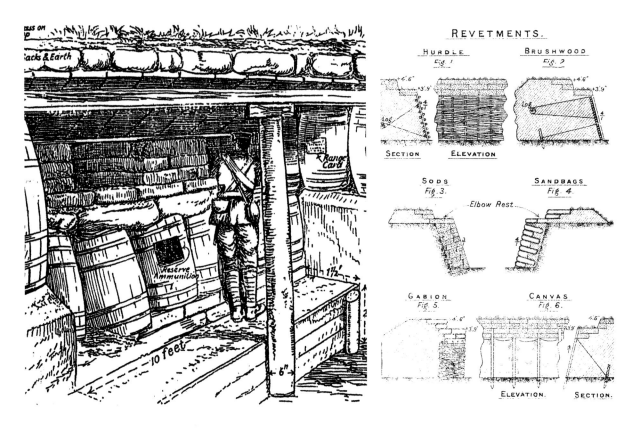

Moreover sandbags were not the only form of revetment shown in the *Manual of Field Engineering*, and initially bags were in very limited supply. There was soon widespread use of gabions (cages filled with soil), sods, sacks and timber for reinforcement, and in many places these methods would persist. Early photographs of the Nieuport coastal sector show wood, barrels and other detritus in the defences. Perhaps the most extraordinary revetments were observed by Captain Billie Nevill of the East Surreys near Fricourt in 1915. These included 'bedsteads, sideboards, table legs, cart wheels, bricks, fenders and any old thing you can think of'.[4] In many places, as in parts of Ploegsteert Wood, a mixed construction would remain the norm – with a shallow trench revetted with corrugated iron or other materials, and a parapet of sandbags. Near Bois Quarante, Ypres, Territorials of the South Lancashire Regiment were confronted by stubborn tree roots and poor drainage, as well as lack of sandbags. Here trenches were left unsupported, and in such sectors maintenance was particularly problematic. Guy Chapman of the Royal Fusiliers recorded that early in the war, at the time of the most dire shortage of sandbags, some women in England had re-supplied his battalion. These bags were not issue rough tan hessian, but 'beautifully stitched' in a range of colours.[5] Though some 'barbarians' actually used them for the intended purpose, Chapman stowed his boots and wash kit in them. Private Edward Roe described the 1st East Lancashire trenches of October 1914 as:

more or less irregular ditches following twists and angles without any apparent meaning, through turnip fields, across roads, through badly pulverised villages and farm houses; in some places they run through cemeteries. One would imagine that

Drawings from Dienstunterricht des Deutschen Pioniers, *1915, showing forward saps and methods of wiring. (Author's collection)*

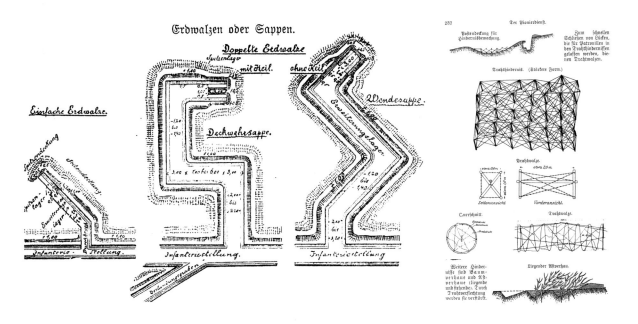

the trench line was the result of accident; they were not like the elaborate affairs we used to dig on the Curragh…[6]

French instructions made but limited reference to the sandbag, focusing upon earth, gabions, planks and logs. Even late in the war the manual of the platoon leader continued to feature an entirely subterranean 'Russian Sap' which was unsupported except by virtue of its arched profile. French trench work was considered slovenly by many British observers, including Robert Graves of the Royal Welch Fusiliers, whose description of their works on the Somme was 'tumble-down' and 'too shallow in many places, and without sufficient traverses'. Burying the dead in the bottom of the trench was not unknown. The French attitude may have been more casual, but there were also good reasons why their efforts were less elegant than those of their Allies. The French front was longer, much of it was first established at an early stage, and industrial capacity to produce elaborate construction materials was more stretched. Shallow fieldworks were not purely a phenomenon of Gallic workmanship either: natural erosion and damage tended to fill up any unnatural voids in the landscape, and muddy, water-filled trenches presented particular problems. Too often the solution to wet feet was laying another layer of duckboards where the first had disappeared into the mire. Recent archaeology has discovered places where three duckboards have been placed one upon another, and when in use this must have made the trench increasingly shallow over time.

Likewise, though German trench construction had a reputation for thoroughness, there were considerable local variations. Indeed, mixed media was the norm, rather than the exception. Quite late in the war photographs of the Bayernwald, near Wytschaete, showed extensive use of posts and wattle. This sort of construction was flimsy compared to sandbags, but some British observers noted that under bombardment hurdles made from wattle were more inclined to flex when more robust materials failed catastrophically. In many other German trenches the use of planking persisted. At Violanes German soldiers burrowed into the extensive brick stacks for cover, and in some rocky areas trenches acquired revetment of stone. Such works had considerable permanence and resistance to the elements but, if they suffered direct hits, could turn into showers of lethal fragments. Temporary works, dug as jumping off points, or saps to forward positions could be very sketchy. Even if they were well built, bombardments degraded trenches and interfered with repairs.

Cover of the privately produced German manual Der Spatenkrieg *– 'The Spade War' – by Heinrich Fitschen, Berlin, 1915. Like unofficial British manuals this drew heavily upon official sources, in this case the* Feld-Pionierdienst Aller Waffen *of 1911. For Fitschen the spade was the prime 'defensive weapon in modern war' for the construction of trenches and shrapnel-proof dugouts. In short, Schweiß statt Blut – 'sweat saves blood'. Yet Fitschen also saw the spade as a preserver of health, in cleaning up the latrines and 'dead animals', and useful in the attack. (Author's collection)*

Wire, seen in dense deep masses almost everywhere by the middle of the war, was also in limited use in 1914 and supplemented with broken glass, planks studded with nails and caltrops. These last were an invention of Roman times, and were made up of four small sharp metal prongs, one point of which presented upward whatever way the device fell to the ground. A minor inconvenience in daylight out of the zone of fire, at night they were major impediments to columns of horses.

In preparing trenches concealment was vital. Skylines were best avoided, but when they had to be used earth and turf were piled up behind to ensure that the defenders were not silhouetted against the sky. Provided fields of fire were good, parapets could be low or even omitted. According to standard tables it took a man three minutes to excavate a cubic foot of earth, and six hours to dig a proper fire trench sufficient to accommodate a single rifleman. Sandbags could be filled one every three minutes, but making a brushwood gabion took several hours. Given the time required to construct a proper trench system incorporating standing cover, many of the first excavations were begun as simple scrapes in the ground for prone riflemen, and only subsequently improved – perhaps through an intermediate stage of 'kneeling cover'.

The British soldier was taught that a hole a foot deep and 6 feet long was adequate in an emergency, and such 'lying down' cover should be started from the rear of the position to first create a 'hollow for the disengaged arm'. According to E. J. Solano in *Field Entrenchments: Spadework for Riflemen*, effective protection by this method took about 35–45 minutes to complete. Covering the head and shoulders certainly had some 'moral value', but on the downside the mound of earth created could itself provide an aiming mark if carelessly executed. In French, German, and, later, American manuals illustrations were included showing how soldiers could work in pairs to dig in. The shallow French scrape was officially described as a 'skirmisher's shelter trench', during the digging of which the riflemen were encouraged to place their packs to the fore for a modicum of concealment, firing as they could whilst throwing up a 'light parapet'. In the summer of 1914 Marc Bloch of the 272ème infantry observed the enemy doing the same thing opposite, burrowing to create a 'yellowish ramp' over which just their hands were exposed from time to time as they cast out the earth.[7] Leipzig student Walter Limmer described his own position as 'a sort of grave like hole which I dug myself in the firing line'.[8] In the American method, elaborated in Major J. A. Moss's *Manual of Military Training*, 1917, the prone soldier was taught to scrape a shallow 18-inch wide trench 'back to his knees', then roll into it and dig a deeper foot-wide extension. This was then occupied whilst the whole scrape was enlarged to full size. Again two men could work together, alternately providing covering fire. Small scrapes were a handy first line of defence against the rifle, but users remained vulnerable to shrapnel from above.

The general threat posed by artillery was quickly recognized. As the British document *Notes From the Front*, Part 1, explained:

Owing to the accuracy of the enemy's artillery fire, it is desirable that ground which is to be held defensively or to assist further advance should be entrenched. Trenches should be commenced at once with the light entrenching tool and improved later as opportunity occurs. They should be kept deep and narrow and show as little above the ground as possible, and all trenches should be traversed at intervals of five to ten rifles. When siting trenches it should be borne in mind that the enemy is adept in bringing enfilade artillery fire from flank positions. At any point, such as a salient, at which trenches are particularly liable to this form of fire, great care should be taken as to their siting and they should be especially heavily traversed. Where head cover cannot be provided, cover from shell fire for the troops when not actually using their rifles can readily be obtained by making recesses in the trenches on the side nearest to the enemy… If immunity from shrapnel fire can be obtained up to the moment of having to resist the infantry attack, no more can be hoped for.

Primitive 'recesses' under the front lips of trenches had been seen in the Boer War, and were described in the 1911 *Manual of Field Engineering* as small square cut chambers between 2 and 4 feet 6 inches in width, ideally roofed over with brushwood, boards or corrugated iron, 9–12 inches of earth, and preferably integrating a layer of shingle. In building them it had to be borne in mind that they should not weaken the parapet; not curtail the number of rifles that could be brought to bear; and should be easy to evacuate, the preference being for large numbers of simple shelters rather than a few elaborate ones. In practice many such shelters were unsophisticated rabbit burrows – often known by the term 'funk holes' – from which limbs and equipment often protruded untidily into the trench. Some of Sidney Rogerson's

Men of 2nd Royal Scots Fusiliers manning a trench at La Boutillerie, winter 1914–15. The soldiers use loopholes rather than exposing themselves to fire by shooting over the top of cover. (IWM Q49104)

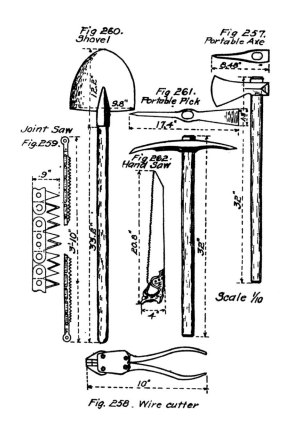

Fig 260.
Shovel

Fig 257.
Portable Axe

Fig 261.
Portable Pick

Joint Saw
Fig. 259.

Fig 262.
Hand Saw

Scale ⅒

Fig. 258 . Wire cutter

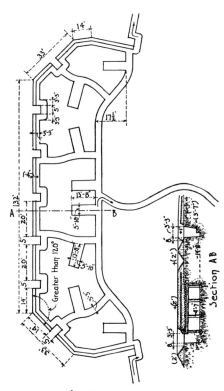

Fig. 54.– Trench For a Section.

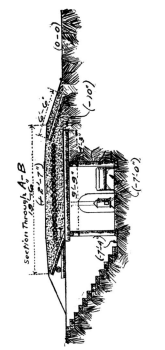

Fig. 79.– Cover for Commanding Officer.

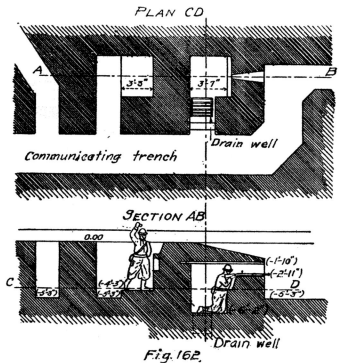

PLAN CD

Communicating trench

Drain well

Section AB

Drain well

Fig. 162.

brother officers dug out funk holes lengthwise alongside the fire trench, and could be seen lying there like 'crusader effigies'.[9] Others secured 'greater privacy' by means of a ground sheet hung like a curtain. All nationalities had burrows off trenches, the Germans giving them the rather more heroic nickname of *Siegfried* dugouts. Sometimes any dugout was better than nothing, but those that were too flimsy could easily become death-traps. As one anonymous diarist of the 12th East Surreys recorded, 'there were two nights when I preferred to sleep outside of my dugout, because the shelling made it rock so much, and as I was in at the far end, I had no wish to be suffocated or buried if a shell should knock it down'.[10]

Naturally headquarters were accommodated in dugouts as soon as possible. Lieutenant John Reith described an early battalion headquarters of 1st Cameronians as 'half dugout and half hut', into which he was received with 'great cordiality':

> What an astonishing place it was; how odd for a regular Colonel to be so circumscribed – this hole in the ground, the mud on his clothes. It was, however, a comfortable hole. It was lit by two oil lamps; there were two tables, a bookshelf and ledges all round cut out of the clay for seats and bunks. There was moreover a coal fire burning in an excavated clay fireplace. They were only eighty yards from the Germans. Eighty yards – three and a half cricket pitches. I wondered what the Germans were doing and why they stopped there, and whether they would continue to stop there anyhow till my visit was over.[11]

From the start machine guns were often placed within, or near, the trench system. As *Field Engineering* explained they were best situated 'with a view to bringing a powerful enfilade or oblique fire on the attackers after they have reached effective infantry range, to flanking supporting works, and to sweeping any gaps that have been left in the line of obstacles'. If the actual MG posts were in a trench:

> a platform of earth at the requisite depth can be left as the trench is being dug, or it can be built up subsequently. The crest of such an emplacement may take the form of an arc of a circle, the length of which will depend on the extent of the ground it is desired to sweep with fire.

Head cover for such a position was desirable, but was to be made to appear similar to any provided elsewhere, and a 'splinter proof' shelter for the detachment was to be made nearby.

For many an 'other rank', the first encounter with the communication trench would be one of life's little mysteries. As Private Edward Loxdale of the Civil Service Rifles put it in 1915 – somewhat tongue in cheek – the communication trench was:

> a species of rabbit burrow, with entrances, carefully concealed, a long way behind the firing line. On first entering them one is irresistibly reminded of the burrow in

Opposite:
Illustrations from French Notes on Field Fortifications, *showing tools (Fig 257–262), a trench for a section of troops (Fig 54), cover for a commanding officer (Fig 79), and methods for defending a communication trench (Fig 162).*
(Author's collection)

Wonderland, down which little Alice followed the rabbit, and chased after him ever so long with his tail almost out of sight in front. We stumbled along the burrows in 'Censorland' for, as it seems, an interminable period, tripping over ourselves in the dark and the mud, and no matter how desperately we strive to catch up, the pack of the man in front is always just on the point of disappearing round the corner.[12]

Trenches soon acquired names, very often painted on boards. This was homely, but also highly practical, since one trench could look very much like another. Sometimes such appellations made little apparent sense, but often they had a regimental or geographic significance. Under the most orderly schemes sectors were identifiable by the fact that all the trench names began with the same letter or followed a theme – such as types of weather condition or the names of towns or famous streets back home. Nevertheless there were some real curiosities, as for example 'Nonsense', 'Bluenose', 'Baby' and 'Doris'. Perhaps the French claimed the oddest trench name with one in the enemy line they christened 'Tranchée des Homosexuels'.

Diagrams from Notes From the Front, *Part 1, 1914. Plate VIII shows German rifle trenches while Plate IX illustrates German support and communication trenches. (Author's collection)*

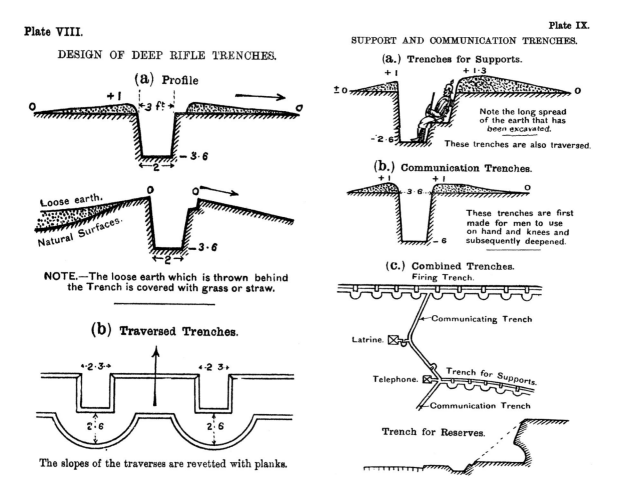

In some ways the beginning of trench warfare was more miserable than what was to follow. As Edmund Dane remarked in 1915:

It is sometimes forgotten that in trench warfare the worst test comes first. The worst time is that in which, in fire trenches hastily thrown up, men are called upon to hold a front at all costs. The trenches are rude and undrained. Dugouts have yet to be

French troops manning a fire trench, 1915. There is a wooden fire step, and the riflemen aim through loops in the parapet rather than over it. The floor of the trench has both a walkway and a separate drainage channel. The cylindrical objects, foreground, are food containers. (Author's collection)

THIEPVAL

Thiepval and Thiepval Wood from sheet 57D S.E.1 & 2, 1:10,000, showing the German trenches, in red, corrected to 15 August 1916. The furthest extent of the British trenches is shown only by the blue line – and many, including 'Elgin Avenue', 'Whitchurch Street' and 'George Street', overlaid old French systems within the wood. On 1 July the 36th Ulster Division assembled ten of its battalions in the wood and attacked the network of trenches and strong points to the north and west of Thiepval known as the 'Schwaben Redoubt'. Though hemmed in by the marshy ground of the Ancre, the Ulstermen were able – by dint of the ferocity of their charge, and the closeness of their final jumping off points – to make dramatic early progress. The 32nd Division, committed to attack the fortified remnants of the village, were repulsed by machine guns untouched by the barrage. Though the Ulstermen actually reached right through to the German second line they were unsupported and subjected to bombardment and counter-attacks – which ultimately forced them back, and cost the division 5,104 casualties by the end of the day. However, fighting in and around Thiepval continued for months with the 'battle of Thiepval Ridge', which involved Canadian troops as well as the British 49th and 18th divisions, finishing only at the end of September.

Now dominated by the massive Lutyens-designed 'memorial to the missing', which was formally unveiled in 1932 on the site of the old chateau, and the much smaller Ulster Tower, the Thiepval sector remains one of the most interesting on the Western Front. Cemeteries in the vicinity include Connaught Road close to the wood, and Mill Road where subsidence caused by the dugouts and tunnels of the Schwaben Redoubt led to the headstones having to be laid flat. Extensive archaeological work has been done both in Thiepval Wood and, in 2003–04, on the site of the new visitor centre. In the area of the visitor centre the trace of a trench was uncovered and the remains of four German soldiers were recovered, along with personal effects, including a harmonica, comb and clasp knife. Other artefacts found include parts of gas masks, more than 1,000 grenades of several different types, and a range of artillery munitions up to and including 9.2inch shells.

Above: British trench in Thiepval Wood after re-excavation. From these trenches the Ulster battalions went 'over the top' on 1 July 1916. Duckboards and the sandbag parapet have been replaced. In an age of photography, reference works and eyewitness accounts, World War I archaeologists have a wealth of archival material and documentary evidence that can only be envied by those researching most other periods. (Author's collection)

Top right: Men of the Border Regiment in 'funk' holes at Thiepval Wood, 1916. The sergeant, left, wears the padded 'winter' cap. The man lying on the top is using a groundsheet as bedding and has laid out his 1908 Pattern webbing with small pack, entrenching tool and water bottle by his feet. (IWM Q872)

Bottom right: A 4.5inch howitzer emplacement at Thiepval, September 1916. (IWM Q1537)

S. 3062.

REFERENCE.

Enemy {
Any trench apparently organised for fire.
Other trenches. Important ones are shown
by thick line. Old or disused by dotted
line.
}

British front line trench.

Entanglement or other obstacle.

Ground cut up by Artillery fire.

Enemy's tracks.

Buried pipe line or cable.

Trench railway.

Supply dumps........△ Observation posts.

Dug-outs........■ Earthworks.

Mine craters.....⊕ Mine craters fortified.

Hedge, fence or ditch. (Unknown which).

Ditch with permanent water.

Conspicuous points. (Position of point is
centre of circle. Dot shows that point is
trigonometrically fixed.)

Church   Any trig   Mill
            point

	Fenced	Unfenced
1st Class		
2nd Class		
3rd Class		
Footpaths, Cart tracks.		

Roads

Railways {
Double
Single
Light or Tramway
}

NB.—The fact that an obstacle is not represented on the map does not necessarily mean that there
is none there. It is often impossible to distinguish obstacles or to identify their character. It
may be assumed that there are obstacles in front of all fire trenches (shown by thick line).

All heights in metres.

constructed. Communication trenches have not yet been cut. To reach or leave the fire trenches at all is a race in which a man takes his life in his hands. In the darkness he has to dash from one bit of cover to the next, to crawl behind ruined walls, or across planks laid over streams and gulleys. Reliefs have not yet been organised. In place of hours his spells in these trenches may extend to weeks. The 'front' is gradually working and shaking itself into a system as fast as the struggle with a bitter enemy will let it. As fast as possible it is elaborating itself into a system of entrenched positions. One by one the features of the underground world shape themselves. The streets of dugouts are being built, and 'finished off' at night, with all the derelict doors and boards available. The communication trenches are in the course of being cut. Meanwhile the front trench is a freezing puddle; the trench pumps and braziers are luxuries yet to be.[13]

In the first phases of trench warfare many types of supplies and equipment were in short supply. The Indian Corps, which appeared in the line late in 1914, did so clothed for the plains of the subcontinent in uniforms of light khaki drill. Pullovers, balaclavas and blankets were added wherever possible – but for a while the Lahore Division had to make do with eiderdowns and whatever civilian kit could be had. Greatcoats were generally banned to the British forces in the front line trenches and it was a while before goatskins and padded 'winter caps' could be provided. Badges were lost or given away to civilians, and were difficult to replace. The Canadians made the alarming discovery that their Ross rifles, highly accurate on the range, now quickly clogged. The French found that their famous red trousers were hardly suited to conditions of economy, mud and need for concealment – but had to do with various substitutes before a new uniform of blue grey was issued. The Belgians, reduced to a rump of their former nation, quickly became dependent on their Allies for almost everything. On the German side of the line huge demands on the clothing and equipment systems could only be satisfied by cutting details. Corduroy trousers; spiked helmets of pressed rabbit felt; simplified 'ersatz' (substitute) bayonets; and soon canvas replacements for leather items made their appearance.

THE EVOLUTION OF 'DEEP' DEFENCE, 1915–16

As testified by many accounts and photographs, the trenches of 1914 and early 1915 were often densely manned, forming only a relatively shallow crust to the battlefront. Frequently they were regarded as protection for entire units *in situ*. Such arrangements maximized firepower, but conversely exposed the garrison to considerable risk if an unlucky shell pitched into a bay, or a machine gun could be pushed forward to flank a length of the defences. They were also highly problematic in terms of the stresses imposed upon individual battalions. As more, and heavier, guns were deployed, dangers increased.

A German General Staff report of April 1915 titled *Experiences Gained in the Winter Battle in Champagne* explained:

The main characteristic of the French attacks was an irresistible artillery preparation, defying all description, directed against the portion of the line which they intended to break, on a front sometimes 2–3 kilometres wide, sometimes considerably less. This preparation consists of deliberate preliminary ranging, followed by fire from massed artillery, like the roar of thunder, in bursts of fire sometimes lasting for hours without interruption, methodically distributed from both field and heavy guns, which destroys our obstacles and parapets, demolishes our shelters and buries them in the debris, destroys our telephone communications, kills some of the men holding our positions and puts the remainder to flight. The morale of everybody behind the front line was affected by the noise, the clouds of smoke and dust rising like a gigantic wall above the battle line and the shower of splinters raining in every direction. It was scarcely possible for commanders, owing to the moral effects of this bombardment, to grasp the situation clearly or to give their orders calmly.

Remarkably, the French infantry did not make use of 'successive lines of attack', but, though densely deployed, issued from 'trenches, sap heads and depressions in the ground'. Fresh troops replaced the attackers after one or two assaults. The German trenches, which were often on commanding forward slopes, were frequently located by enemy observers and pounded until 'not a vestige of shelter' remained. Attempts to repair such works were harassed or frustrated by rifle grenades, mortars and rifle fire.

The German trenches at Festubert suffered almost as much under British attack in May and June 1915. As the chronicler of 1st/4th Battalion, Loyal North Lancashire Regiment, recorded:

Illustrations from From E. Dane, Trench Warfare, *1915, showing the development of a fire trench. (Author's collection)*

The German trenches after two days' bombardment were in a bad state. In many places they had been completely destroyed, and when we took them we found them piled deep with German dead. The dugouts, which had been made in the parados, seemed whole but were full of dead and wounded, probably the work of the bombers [grenadiers]. The communication trench was also partially destroyed, and littered with German dead. The whole series of trenches were full of German equipment in great confusion. Like our trenches they were built of sandbags, but their communication trench was very deep and well traversed, and was probably intended to serve as a fire trench… There was an abandoned German machine gun in the fire trench in a stretcher carriage, which could not be moved. There was a good amount of German equipment outside the trench about the point 'Z'. This place was the wildest

FIG. 2.   FIRE COVER OF OLDER TYPE—SECOND STAGE.

FIG. 3.   OLDER TYPE OF FIRE TRENCH COMPLETED.

spot, a mass of shell holes and fragments of works. The German barbed wire was very strong, of abnormal thickness in closeness and strength of spikes and in the wire itself. The ditch in front of the sap was heavily wired under water.

That trench systems should be developed to meet the risks was widely recognized, and during the Champagne battles the Germans increased the depth of their position to about 2 miles. The new works were not regular, but represented a scheme that convinced its defenders that it would be possible to hold even in the event of a 'local breach'. The general conclusion that a single line of trenches was inadequate was quickly absorbed and became official German policy:

> we have learned by experiment and experience that what was required was not one, or even several, fixed lines of defences, but rather a fortified zone which permitted a certain liberty of action, so that the best use could be made of all the advantages offered by the configuration of the ground.[14]

New German plans started by identifying the 'key tactical point' upon which a trench could be designated as 'the main line of defence'. This would be as far as possible out of enemy observation, avoiding accurate incoming artillery fire being accounted more significant than the field of fire of the defence. In front of the main line were dug further fire trenches, listening posts, mortar pits and machine gun posts linked to the main line by communication trenches. Behind the main line were to be further trenches, presenting a sort of *cul-de-sac* into which the enemy ventured at his peril. Fire through trench parapets using loopholes and steel shields was best but would be supplemented by fire over the parapet. Dummy trenches and batteries served to confuse the enemy and dissipate his fire. Flanking positions, particularly for machine guns, were critical, and obstacle zones were to be of several lines, preferably with low wire securely anchored to iron posts. Individual *Gruppe*, or sections of men, were to be supplied with their own dugout, preferably with two entrances, and covered by 3 yards of earth. Dugouts further back accommodated supporting troops. One point that would have crucial import for the future was that German tacticians also noticed that enfilading positions could often control an area of ground without frontal defences, and even in the absence of obstacles.

The new blueprint was gradually applied to the German front through 1915, and the High Command soon ordered the construction of a 'second line' behind the first. The parts of the line facing the French were first priority, with the British sector doubled soon afterwards in answer to the build up of troops. So was constructed what the German public learned to call *Gottesmauer* – 'God's Wall'. Though Allied development was slower, and attack took priority in 1915, the differences in approach were not as great as is sometimes supposed. Indeed a copy of German instructions was soon in enemy hands and later widely circulated.

The corollary of good cover was the truly 'empty battlefield' on which not only was one seldom seen, but one seldom saw the enemy. As war reporter John Masefield put it:

In the fire trench they saw little more than the parapet. If work was being done in No Man's Land, they still saw little save by these lights that floated and fell from the enemy and from ourselves. They could see only an array of stakes tangled with wire, and something distant and dark which might be similar stakes, or bushes, or men, in front of what could only be the enemy line. When the night passed, and those working outside the trench had to take shelter, they could see nothing, even at a loophole or periscope, but a greenish strip of ground, pitted with shell holes and fenced with wire, running up to the enemy line. There was little else for them to see, looking to the front, for miles and miles…[15]

A good summary of the model appearance of the fully developed British trench system from the middle of the war onward was provided in the instructional booklet *Notes For Infantry Officers on Trench Warfare*. The initial line consisted of three trenches, the main fire trench behind an obstacle zone, support and reserve. The fire trench itself might either be continuous, or consist of a series of short 'T' or 'L' shapes projecting

An 'abatis' defending a Flanders canal line. Such obstacles featured in the manuals of all the combatants, and were widely used early in the war wherever materials were available. The British Manual of Field Engineering described the abatis as 'formed of limbs of trees firmly picketed down with the branches pointed and turned towards the enemy … strands of wire interlaced between the branches add still further to their efficiency'. A less tidy 'tree entanglement' could be made by lopping off trees as they stood, felling them in the same direction. (Author's collection)

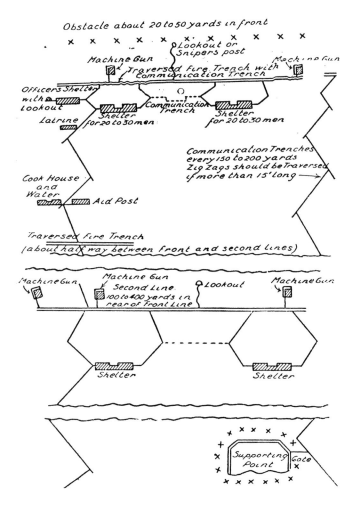

Obstacle about 20 to 50 yards in front

Lookout or
Snipers post

Machine Gun   Machine Gun
Traversed Fire Trench with
Communication Trench

Officers Shelter
with
Lookout
Communication
Latrine   Trench
Shelter   Shelter
for 20 to 30 men   for 20 to 30 men

Communication Trenches
every 150 to 200 yards
Zig Zags should be Traversed
if more than 15' long

Cook House
and
Water
Aid Post

Traversed fire Trench
(about half way between front and second lines)

Machine Gun   Machine Gun
Second Line.   Lookout
100 to 400 yards in
rear of front Line   Machine Gun

Shelter   Shelter

Supporting
Point   Gate

A diagrammatic sketch of the organization of a defensive line from Notes From the Front, *Part 3, 1915. (Author's collection)*

forward from a 'supervision trench'. Trenches might be entirely below ground; above ground as breastworks; or a mixture of both – with just a parapet built up. The layout was to be irregular, and in no instance was the trench to be perfectly straight. Trenches held for any length of time were to be revetted and floored. Fire steps were to be of contained earth or stout, well-supported planks: sandbags were not thought suitable for fire steps. Traverses were massive, ideally 9–12 feet in thickness, and provided every 18–30 feet. To the front of the trench under the parapet were exits in the direction of the enemy, for use by patrols, or to enter forward saps. The tops of the parapets themselves were to be irregular, to provide concealment for riflemen or observers. A few loopholes for fire through the parapet were provided with a metal plate and a shutter – where it was possible a man might be silhouetted in the aperture a cloth was arranged behind his position. Another useful defensive addition was the provision of a bombing trench, or 'bombing pits', behind, but within throwing range of, the fire trench. *Notes* suggested that certain features of the trench should be matched to the strength of the garrison. Loopholes, for example, were normally needed one per section; listening posts one per platoon.

Obstacle zones were best placed about 20 yards forward of a trench, and made at least 10 yards deep. Wire was generally kept about 2 feet 6 inches high, though plans existed for both 'high' and 'low' wire entanglements which were used in varying circumstances. In any case there had to be provision for the wire to be observed and accessible to defensive fire. Ideally the wire was not under the direct observation of the enemy, and by placing it in a fold in the ground, or a trench, its presence could be kept a surprise. Sunken wire was also less liable to damage.

Ideally communication trenches were numerous, between the support line and fire trench in particular, and machine guns positioned to give flanking fire either from within the system, or from 'small inconspicuous emplacements' behind. As in the earlier German scheme reserve trenches allowed for a swift local counter-attack, or for a tactical withdrawal, and were ideally 70–100 yards back from the front line. The support line was 400–600 yards further back again. In the rear of the main trench system there might be 'keeps' or 'strong points' with all round defence. These were to be carefully concealed, and break up any attacks that penetrated the main system. The defenders of the keeps were to 'hold out to the last'. Other strong points might be included within trench systems at important locations. Very deep dugouts in the foremost areas were not encouraged, being difficult to exit quickly and prone to filling with gas, and undermining the lip of a trench was now actively discouraged. Splinter-proof positions were deemed useful, ideally in the 'supervision' trenches. Further back more substantial dugouts were provided, and here various sandwich constructions were recommended – including a 'burster layer' near the surface to detonate incoming shells before they reached the interior. Before the Somme became an active sector it was home to some of the most commodious accommodation. Captain Nevill had a good look around the dugouts of the 8th East Surreys:

> In one of them is a lovely case of stuffed birds, a beautiful four poster bed, some nice chairs, a good big table, towel horse, ivory wash stand etc. and endless bric-a-brac. They are all furnished magnificently from the cottages here and are jolly cosy. The beds are a great treat. Company HQ is a wonderful place… We're hidden away, quite snugly in a little dip, we've got our signal section dug in next door, a room for our servants and messengers and a store place.[16]

He joked that if he stayed here very long he would be sending home for a badminton set.

In low-lying areas in winter it was otherwise. Lieutenant N. F. Percival of the Duke of Lancaster's Own Yeomanry had his first experience of both trenches and dugouts near Bois Grenier in December 1915:

> At dusk we marched to our billets – a farm on the outskirts of Bois Grenier – it was a beastly wet evening and cold. We stayed four days in these billets but we were not allowed to show ourselves much in the daytime, in case the Hun should discover our billet; as it was practically the only undestroyed building in these parts; so time passed slowly. Beckett was an excellent fellow and took me up to the trenches one morning to see the sector we were to hold. The trenches here were breastworks and to get along one has to walk in the open field behind, which appears very unsafe at first. I was much amused to see an officer building a dugout with a rifle by his side, with which he sniped at the Hun lines by way of recreation, he was also sniped at himself.[17]

A few days later Percival found himself at the Bridoux Salient – a place of 'evil repute'. Here he was accommodated in a large dugout:

> but practically surrounded by water and thoroughly uncomfortable, the Hun being about 50 yards away, and one met droves of rats. The dugout was big and roomy but about 2 feet deep in water. Our servants baled out water all night.[18]

Opposite:
Artwork illustrating the British
trench system, 1914–15.
Details shown include:
A) Use of pegs inside the spoil
of the parapet to hold revetting
in place.
B) Multicoloured sandbags
of the improvised type made up
by civilians at home.
C) Vickers machine gun sited to
fire en enfilade, taking attackers
obliquely.
D) Layered logs and earth
capable of resisting light shell
fire and shrapnel.
E) Litter around the parapet –
which sometimes concealed
snipers' embrasures.
F) Loophole firing through
the parapet.
G) Reliefs advancing along
a communication trench.
H) Detail of sniper's loophole,
lined with timber.
(© Peter Dennis, Osprey
Publishing)

The wherewithal to maintain the trench system was usually gathered at a 'brigade workshop', at a location as close to the trenches as possible consistent with reasonable safety. This was administered by the staff captain of the brigade and an NCO, and manned by 12–20 men drawn from the battalions, chosen specifically for their skills as artificers or carpenters. As explained by *Notes*:

> Its functions are to make up the material obtained from the Royal Engineers into shapes and sizes suitable for carrying up to the trenches, to construct any simple device required for use in the trenches, and to carry out the distribution of the material. The brigade workshop makes up, for instance, barbed wire 'knife rests', box loopholes, rifle rests, floor gratings, grenade boxes, signboards for communication trenches etc.

As Edmund Dane observed no trench system was 'complete all at once' – rather they tended to grow in size and complexity in an almost organic manner. One company might add braziers in a quiet period; new communication trenches might be excavated in answer to a higher plan. Later, dugouts might be added or enlarged, or posts modified to suit the latest weapons and equipment. As one side or the other pushed forwards, saps, tunnels and mines grew, and reserve lines became fronts – perhaps 'turned' so that a modified trench now faced in the opposite direction. Improving or repairing a trench system often involved unpleasant surprises, from mangled bits of uniform or bodies, to rifles that went off as soon as they were prised up by an entrenching tool. Worst of all, as in Rudyard Kipling's evocative description of the tribulations of the 2nd Irish Guards, were the faces that 'stuck out of the mixed offal, and were hideously brought to light'. In the sunken road at Guillemont Leutnant Ernst Jünger set his men to digging funk holes only to discover that the dead had been buried around them in layers, where one company after another had crowded in and been killed by barrages. The road itself and the ground to the rear was full of Germans; the ground to the front was strewn with British. Everywhere 'arms, legs and heads were sticking up, torn limbs and bodies were lying in front of our funk holes partly covered in ground sheets to avoid the dreadful sight'.[19]

Some observers, like Lieutenant W. Congreve of 3rd Rifle Brigade, were aware as early as 1914 that what was being created as soldiers fought was the archaeology of the future – with bodies and trench detritus being formed in 'strata'. Sometimes, as in the case of Thiepval Wood, where British troops replaced the French, a complete new system overlaid a pre-existing one – with evidence of sequencing surviving in the archaeology. Edmund Blunden of the Royal Sussex saw this process in action:

> The French had modelled Auchonvillers comprehensively as a large redoubt, complete with a searchlight, but now it all seemed out of use and in need of an antiquary. There were many dugouts under houses and in the gardens, but of a flimsy, rotted and stagnant kind; the Somme battle had evidently swamped all old defence schemes, and destroyed

the continuity of 'taking over'. Forward, the trenches were numerous and reliable, although they, too, had got out of hand, thanks to the confusion consequent on July 1. It was remarkable that they remained as serviceable as they were, and Colonel Harrison soon re-elected me Field Works Officer.[20]

One time in a million the overlaying of old with new was a lifesaver.

Private Lomas of the 1st South Wales Borderers had a very narrow escape when his dugout entrance collapsed under shelling, killing several men: Private Lomas and two others, finding themselves virtually buried, started groping about, and Lomas in doing so pushed aside a waterproof sheet and found himself in a narrow passage. Calling his companions to follow him he crawled along it until he finally emerged in No Man's Land, though on the far side of our wire. The second man had also reached the open when a fall of earth caught the third near the end of the sap. Being unable to release him Lomas had to leave him for dead, but made his way back to our lines to report, whereupon Private Ravenhill, Colonel Collier's runner, went out and eventually extricated the poor fellow after he had been half buried for 12 hours.[21]

German troops with a portable French flame thrower captured in the Argonne. Modern flame weapons made their debut in 1915 as a method of trench clearance.

Lomas, who received a Distinguished Conduct Medal, had inadvertently stumbled upon a forgotten French sap. Even where battlefield areas were deliberately conserved after the war it may be the case that what we see is artefactual evidence from more than one period. Such is certainly the case at Beaumont Hamel, where the Newfoundland Park area focuses on the action of 1 July 1916, but on ground fought over both before and after that date.

Opposite:
A sentry of 10th Gordon Highlanders, 15th Scottish Division, at the junction of Gourlay Trench and Gordon Alley, Martinpuich, Somme. Though neatly named the trenches are unrevetted: the final portion of the wrecked village was not captured until 15 September. In some places where trenches were very narrow or crowded, one-way systems were operated. (IWM Q4180)

CHAPTER THREE

'TRENCHTOWN'

By 1915 the trench struggle was recognized as a special type of war requiring new regulations to govern the day-to-day activity of the units that manned these ossified and heavily protected battle lines. This was what Edmund Dane would memorably dub 'Trenchtown in the Making'. In the British instance many battalions, brigades or divisions modified instructions issued by the General Staff to suit local circumstances, or produced their own 'Trench Standing Orders'. Many of these directions contained common elements such as notes on how to enter and exit the trench system; a basic daily routine; a list of stores to be accounted for; a list of paperwork to be kept complete; instructions on sanitation, cleaning and dress; rules on sentries and salvage; and anti-gas preparations. These basics of trench life are often picked up fragmentarily in soldiers' memoirs, but have rarely been examined systematically – as perhaps they should, since they can provide a surprisingly complete picture of the soldier's life in the trenches. Some orders, such as those of the 2nd South Lancashires from November 1916, laid out a full daily timetable:

Part of the French town of Armentières seen from the air. Closest to the camera can be seen the distinctive crenulated outline of a fire trench: zigzagging communication trenches follow hedge and tree lines back towards the ruined suburb. (Author's collection)

(Time unspecified)	'Stand To'
8am	Breakfast
8.30–9am	Washing and cleaning of dugouts
9–12.30am	Work
12.30–2pm	Dinner
2pm–4.30pm	Work
4.30–5pm	Tea
5pm	'Stand To'

Men who had been on night duties were excused morning activities.

The first action of a unit about to commence trench duty was a 'preliminary visit', usually performed by company commanders accompanied by company sergeant majors (CSM). The purpose of this reconnaissance was to examine the trenches, make a tactical appreciation, note the locations and numbers of listening and other posts, and to allow the CSM to make lists of stores present, or required, during daylight hours. Materials were then signed for, either counted or as 'unchecked'. Hot on the heels of the preliminary visit came the battalion specialists, machine gunners, signallers and snipers – also during daylight. This enabled vital points to be manned and firepower and communications put in place before the very vulnerable moment when the bulk of the troops were set in motion. Finally the main body moved in under cover of darkness. As was explained by the *Trench Standing Orders: 124th Infantry Brigade*:

> The strictest march discipline will be maintained by all parties proceeding to, or from the trenches. An officer will march in the rear of each company to ensure that it is properly closed up. Reliefs will be carried out as quietly as possible. No smoking or lights will be allowed after reaching a point to be decided on by Battalion Commanders. Guides at a rate of one per platoon, machine gun, or bombing post will invariably be arranged for by Brigade Headquarters when Battalions are being relieved, a similar number of guides will be detailed by them to meet relieving units.

Ideally the relieving unit would move into the walkways behind the fire steps, each platoon smoothly relieving a similar number of men – so ensuring that fire positions

An impressive heap of battlefield relics at Péronne. Items visible include German body armour; British, French and German steel helmets; barbed wire; canteens, mess tins and cutlery; ammunition; and petrol containers. The main drawback of a collection like this is that unconnected to their archaeology the individual pieces say little; moreover, red-brown 'live' rust suggests that most have a finite lifespan. (Author's collection)

Men of the Lancashire Fusiliers carry duckboards over the morass of the battlefield near Pilckem, 10 October 1917. (IWM Q6049)

remained manned, and no post was inadvertently left unguarded. Such was the theory; but in darkness, and especially under fire, things could easily go awry. Near Lesboeufs, on the Somme, Sidney Rogerson participated in a relief that took seven hours. On the previous day his battalion of the West Yorkshires had departed punctually, before dawn, each company guided by a member of the Devonshires. The route crossed a valley of shell-ploughed ground on the way to Dewdrop Trench, a former German reserve line, whereabouts the ground was 'carpeted with the dead, the khaki outnumbering the field grey by three to one'. Desultory shelling accounted for two men. Two companies occupied this first position, but the remainder had to wait for the following dusk to struggle through mud like 'caramel', into which the feet stuck fast with every step, looking for forward trenches which had been created by joining shell holes. None of the niceties had been performed in advance. At last:

> There followed much jostling, scrambling and cursing; men floundering in the mud, officers and NCOs wrestling with the farce of handing over receipts for stores and ammunition they not could see, much less count; until at last the Devons were clear and we had taken over the sector.[1]

What individual soldiers actually carried with them into the trenches varied, but after a while it became usual for the large pack which formed part of the 1908 web equipment to be left behind with any extraneous bulky items. Later in the war many units published a standard list of what was to be carried into the line. That produced by 42nd Division in February 1918 comprised 'full marching order without the pack', but with full water bottle, ammunition, iron rations and two spare pairs of socks; rifle with cover and 'four by two' flannelette for cleaning; periscope (if the soldier possessed one); towel, soap and shaving kit; and grenades 'as ordered'. The steel helmet was worn, but the soft service dress cap was left in the rear with the pack.

One of the first duties of the company commander was to ensure that he was in contact with the units to either side, then re-check the locations of supporting troops, ammunition and machine guns. A telephone report was then made to the battalion commander that the relief was complete. Platoon commanders were normally expected to remain with their men, even if this entailed not having a designated dugout.

Within 24 hours of arrival the company commander was expected to make a more detailed return to his battalion commander. Typically this included: garrison return; notes on the condition of the trench, and its drainage, fields of fire and loopholes; the state of the wire; ammunition and grenade stocks; anti-gas materials and warnings. Additional reports might be required on visibility conditions; enemy shelling – type, amount and direction; any observed results of outgoing fire; casualties; and expenditure of stores. A typical list of stores returned by a company of the South Lancashire Regiment in August 1916 read as follows:

TRENCH STORES		FORWARD DUMP	
Bombs, Mills, Boxes [of]	25	Bombs, Mills, Boxes	60
Vermorel Sprayers [anti-gas spraying tool]	2	Rifle Grenades, Boxes	3
Tins of Hypo [anti-gas solution]	4	SAA	3
Gas Gongs	3	Rockets, Red, Flares	48
Rockets [for signalling]	100	Rockets, Green, Flares	1
Shovels	150	Barbed Wire, Rolls	10
Mauls	4	Wire, Trench, Coils	5
Axes	5	Stakes, Iron, Screw	30
Bill Hooks	3	Ladders, Scaling	5
Loophole Plates	5	Rations, Iron, 2 Boxes	40
Barbed Wire Rolls	40	Sticks, Rocket	6
Trench Coils [wire]	10	Handsaws	2 [2]
Stakes, Iron, Screw [to secure wire]	25		
Stakes	6		
Tins, Petrol	17		
Boxes, SAA [Small Arms Ammunition]	10		
Rations, Iron, 2 Boxes	40		

DETAIL OF THE HINDENBURG LINE AT BASKET WOOD

From the Honnecourt sheet, 57B S.W. 3, 1:10,000, showing the German trenches, in red, corrected to 8 November 1917. Planned in the autumn of 1916 the Hindenburg Line was an arc of new defences behind the existing German front. 'Hindenburg Line' was an Allied expression, the general German term being *Siegfried Stellung*. There were also different names for different sectors, and for the second and third lines backing the outer crust. The most important elements included the *Wotan Stellung* from near Lille to St Quentin; the *Siegfried Stellung* proper, from Arras to St Quentin; the *Alberich Stellung*; the *Brunhilde Stellung*; and the *Kriemhilde Stellung*, which extended at far as Verdun in the south. Codenamed Operation *Alberich* the retreat to the Hindenburg Line in the spring of 1917 straightened the front and spared the use of perhaps ten divisions, easing manpower problems, whilst the Allied armies were forced to advance over a wasteland – part created by previous battles, part by a ruthless 'scorched earth' policy. It is less often noted that the move also enabled the Germans to build their new defences in the best possible locations. Construction lasted about four months, and the workers included not only Germans but also local labour and Russian prisoners. Basic design elements included an anti-tank ditch, multiple obstacle zones and trenches, and concrete works.

This detail of the main line at Basket Wood, seen here, was located behind the additional cover of the St Quentin canal, and includes the formidable strong points of the village and quarry of la Terrière. The outposts were further forward on the canal line, and machine gun and observation posts, some linked to the main line by saps, may be seen west of the village. The major obstacle zone is massive, having four belts of wire in front of the first fire trench. Communication trenches connect with a second line of fire trenches, which are themselves covered by two more belts of wire. Screens and further MG and observation posts cover the back of the main line, before the second or *Catelet* line is reached. The various small red rectangles represent dugouts, listening posts and concrete works; red dots other earthworks. Behind the *Catelet* line, not seen here, was the *Beaurevoir* line – another double trench zone defended by two or more obstacle zones.

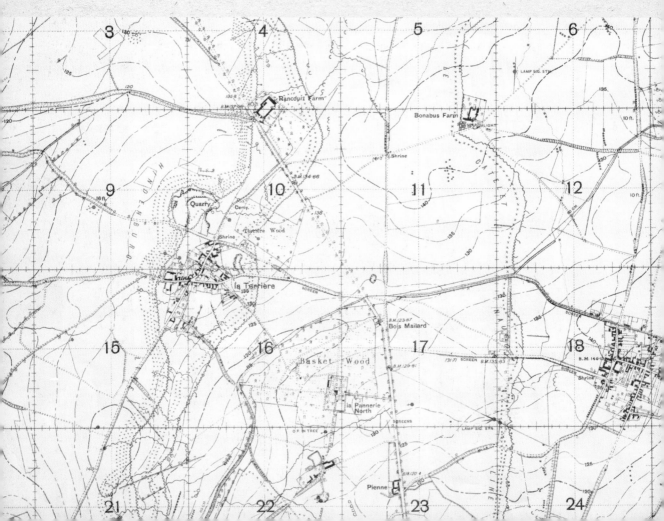

Above: A German front line Granatenwerfer post, showing two model 1916 weapons, and operation by means of a lanyard allowing the firer to remain under cover away from the launchers. The Granatenwerfer spigot mortars are mounted on a raised platform with sandbags weighting their bases. The small bunker provides storage for projectiles, or emergency cover during surprise bombardment. The fin stabilized fragmentation round weighed just under 2kg, and had a range of up to 500 metres. Allied nicknames for the weapon and its bomb included the 'Priest' and the 'Pigeon'. (Author's collection)

Left: Front line German observation and gas alarm post c.1917. The trench features a sturdy fire step, and revetment of wood and wattle, though the overhead cover is at best splinter and rain proof. One man watches using a concealed periscope with a rifleman on guard. Foreground right is the gas alarm bell, and grenades hung by their belt hooks for convenient close defence. (Author's collection)

Often company commanders held a 'Company Meeting' in the evening at which some of the Platoon commanders and NCOs were called together. Here they were given work schedules, briefings and sometimes a chance to 'discuss' other matters. The fact that only selected personnel were present meant that enough were left at their posts in case of attack, and at the same time gave the company commander freedom to air selected issues with specific subordinates. One of the company commander's most important companions in his work was the soft-backed Army Book 152, or *Correspondence Book*, in which was usually recorded not only stores handovers, but copies of reports on raids, casualties, working parties, work reports – and often enough condolence letters to next of kin. Just one of many *Correspondence Books* that survive is that of Captain Prior M. C., of 'C' Company, 8th Battalion, the South Lancashire Regiment, which contains vivid evidence of fighting in the Leipzig Salient area of the Somme during August and September 1916. In it we see that on 28 August five men were killed and 11 wounded. On 29 August the enemy shelled all morning with howitzers and 'whiz bangs', so by 3.10am, in the small hours of the next day, Prior could 'not say definitely how many men are left in 'C' Company, but there are approximately 60'. One of the Lewis guns was put out of action on 1 September, but nevertheless supplies were holding out well as there were still 17,000 rounds of ammunition and 120 boxes of grenades in the company position. Though company commanders were responsible for detailed paperwork for individual trench sectors, much more went on at battalion headquarters – home of the adjutant as well as the battalion commander. The work of the adjutant, assisted by clerks, might include not only collating returns but also recording communications between battalion and brigade, distribution of orders, disciplinary matters and noting incoming stores. The adjutant was also responsible for keeping the 'War Diary', a daily record of the doings of the battalion that was kept in duplicate, and ultimately retained by both the regiment and the War Office.

Posting sentries, making sure that they were alert and changed frequently, was an important precaution. Standing orders of 75th Brigade for December 1916 were that sentries should stand guard for a maximum of two hours, a time period that was to be reduced in bad weather and at night. Each sentry post was to be provided with a periscope and wooden range card, and each machine gun was to be attended by two alert men at all times. *Notes on Trench Routine and Discipline*, 1916, suggested, 'Sentries should always have one hours rest before posting. Bear in mind any physical weakness of a man before putting on sentry, e.g. bad hearing, natural tendency to sleepiness, disability, nerves etc.' Sentries were also prevented from wearing anything over their ears. Despite wintry weather 2nd South Lancashires' standing orders of 1916 were very specific:

> Balaclava helmets are on no account to be worn by sentries in the trenches. They may be worn by men in the support and front lines, but only in such a way as the ears are not covered up and hearing interfered with. The steel helmet must always be worn.

In the 19th Manchesters word was slow to get round and two comrades of Albert Andrews got 'names taken' by the commanding officer for wearing the flaps of their caps down when on sentry.[3] Sadly both were killed by a shell when reporting to battalion HQ regarding this offence.

Some old hands would place their rifle, bayonet attached, under their chins – effectively preventing any 'nodding' during a quiet shift. If anything the sentry's job was more important at night when the enemy might be expected to launch raids, and listening was even more vital than looking. Often a sentry covered more than one trench bay during the day, but after dark it was usual to put a man in each. For maximum vigilance some standing orders demanded that the trench should be 'practically silent' at night, perhaps with periods of total silence whilst special efforts were made to listen for enemy miners. Sentries usually kept their weapons charged, with a round ready in the chamber, but the safety catch applied. Though the prime purpose of the sentry was early warning of raid or attack, his secondary task was to report the unusual, such as lights at night, increased or deceased activity, and changes to enemy works or wire. According to Corporal Robert Rider, 14th Royal Warwickshires even went so far as to have a battery-powered bell push system installed for sentries in the most dangerous position. The alarm was raised by pushing a button which sounded a bell in the company commander's dugout.

In the British Army the ultimate penalty for falling asleep on sentry duty was death; but, though widely publicized, this was a sanction carried out extremely rarely. More often officers and NCOs on hourly rounds would kick sleepy soldiers into wakefulness, and remind them of the possible results. In Delville Wood a particularly sympathetic South African junior officer was remembered by his men as saying loudly into the ear of any apparently dozy soldier, 'are you awake?' As the only possible answer was 'yes', this meant that the man was alerted, and startled, without need for formal action. Sergeant Hall of 26th Battalion Royal Fusiliers was rather less genteel, but his sexual expletives fulfilled much the same function – despite the danger of attracting enemy attention. The young E. C. Vaughan, working 'by the book', put a sleeping sentry on a charge – but a more experienced colleague pointed out the possible consequences, so the man received a thorough bawling out instead. The records of 1st Irish Rifles also reveal that even when cases of 'sleeping at post' did reach Courts Martial, lesser punishments were usually inflicted. No fewer than nine men of the battalion were convicted, of whom two were briefly condemned to death – but not one was actually executed. The penalties finally handed down ranged from a very stiff ten years' penal servitude, down to as little as a suspended one-year sentence.[4]

Christopher Stone, a junior officer with the 22nd Royal Fusiliers, described a typical routine night round of his sector of the Cambrin trenches in December 1915:

FIFTH AVENUE

RESERVE LINE

CHEERO TRENCH

Visé Paris 763

F. Mackain

Sketches
of Tommy's life
Up the line — Nº 10

Sometimes you get so far in the rear, marching in, you are as good as lost
when you come to a spot where different trenches branch off.

Most of the trenches have foot boards laid down in them which keeps them fairly clean but greasy. I go up the communication trench first of all… Macdougall is said to be out in front by himself examining the wire. I go on to the fire trenches and then turn right handed. It's all zigzag of course: a bay and then a traverse, a bay and a traverse, endlessly from the North Sea to the Swiss frontier without a break! In about every third bay there are two sentries standing on the fire step and looking over the parapet. At the corners of the bays there are often glowing braziers and men sleeping round them or half asleep: and you pass the entrance to dugouts and hear men murmuring inside, and the hot charcoal fumes come out. On and on: sometimes I clamber up beside the sentries and look out. There's little to see, rough ground, the barbed wire entanglement about 15 yards away, the vague line of the German trenches. If a flare goes up it lights the whole place for about 30 seconds and is generally followed by a good deal of rifle fire. You see the flash at the muzzle of the rifle. If you hear a machine gun you duck your head. The bullets patter along the parapet when they do what they call traversing: backwards and forwards they patter… In my wanderings I come to a sap and go along it – very deep mud here that nearly pulls off my boots – 100 yards out towards the Germans, and at the end find three or four bombers on guard in case the Bosche tries to come across.[5]

True words spoken in jest: a cartoon postcard showing Tommy standing in water, heavily laden, and lost on his way up to his company in the trenches. The name boards are not as unrealistic as they look – without a potentially suicidal look 'over the top' the trench system could appear very much like a directionless maze. Troops therefore followed names, or looked out for distinctive features such as a wrecked piece of heavy equipment or even an unburied body. (Author's collection)

Early in the war whole units had been forced into the front line fire trenches, sometimes shoulder to shoulder in an effort to bring maximum weaponry to bear: but in the face of artillery massed troops soon suffered heavy casualties – even within the protection of the trench. The shambles seen by Claude Prieur, an officer of the French Fusiliers Marins at Dixmuide, in November 1914, was by no means exceptional:

> The trench began to choke with wounded and the dead. The men of the 11th Company, and Belgian machine gunners who had taken refuge. The scene caused the morale of our men to plummet: they were driven to distraction. All attempts to prevent them running were as nothing – they were completely done out. Others lay on the floor of the trench without shooting, and they were taken prisoner.[6]

After such early mistakes with overcrowded trenches British instructions acknowledged that, in daytime, 'front line trenches should be held as lightly as compatible with safety'. Brigade and battalion commanders were therefore encouraged to regulate garrison strength to match the tactical situation, and to take advantage of whatever supports and communication trenches were nearby. The basic minimum was to add some snipers to

A sentry of 55th (West Lancashire) Division uses a mirror periscope in the front line trenches at Blaireville, 16 April 1916. In this simplest of devices there is only one mirror, so that the soldier places the mirror on the rear lip of the trench and actually observes with his back to the enemy. The original steel shrapnel helmet seen here was patented by J. L. Brodie as early as August 1915, with an updated model produced from early 1916. It was well nigh universal in the British trenches by mid 1916. (IWM Q534)

the sentries, and position a few bombers covering any disused communication trenches, or places where the enemy line ran uncomfortably close. As a rough yardstick *Notes For Infantry Officers on Trench Warfare* recommended that at night at least one man in four, and by day at least one man in ten, should be 'on lookout in each trench'. This could be regulated quite easily by regarding six men under an NCO as a basic group for a section of trench, and two men would be on watch at night, and one during the day. The number of groups required would be varied to match such circumstances as the proximity of the enemy trenches and nature of the ground.

The 2nd South Lancashires' orders from 1916 stated specifically that one officer per company and one NCO per platoon would be 'on duty' at all times. Both the duty officer and the NCOs would patrol their areas frequently. In addition to normal duties of those in charge of sections, NCOs in charge of trench sectors were expected to be knowledgeable regarding the geography and dangers of the trench system, and to be able to pass on relevant information to the men. Specific points they needed to be acquainted with included ranges to defined objects, and tactical features such as enemy trenches; the positions and names of neighbouring garrisons and listening posts; the presence of friendly parties and patrols; routes to important locations such as headquarters, and danger spots. Naturally NCOs also had a role in relaying standing orders. Commonly men in the front line trench were given discretion to fire as and when an opportunity presented itself, but if large or important targets were seen these were to be reported up the chain of command and machine guns or supporting weapons alerted. Sleeping in the fire trenches at all was generally discouraged if there were support trenches nearby.

However a trench was garrisoned, the assumption that it was to be held tenaciously remained common currency until late in the war. The 1917 *Trench Standing Orders* of 63rd Royal Naval Division stated explicitly that 'the main front line of trenches must be held to the last, whatever happens'. Whilst lines were thinned out it was the duty of the immediate supports to reinforce the front 'without waiting for orders', or to 'counter-attack at once without hesitation'. Commanders new to the line were to make plans for such counter-attacks, making particularly sure that key positions were accounted for. Launching counter-attacks quickly was vital since if an enemy was allowed to establish himself, attempting to retrieve the situation was likely to be 'very difficult and costly'.

Before dawn, at the time of greatest danger, came 'Stand To', when the garrison stood ready to arms, a moment also usually chosen for the inspection of men and weapons. A dirty rifle was accounted a particular sin, and to avoid clogged mechanisms and continuous cleaning many men took to covering the action with an old sock. Later they were issued canvas breech covers. Ammunition might likewise be inspected with a view to avoiding malfunctions. According to *Notes on Trench Routine* each platoon was to have one or two boxes of ammunition to hand in addition to what they carried, and each trench bay was to have a further emergency

Next spread:
A trench scene showing German soldiers posed with a captured Maxim gun. Other details include the use of a loophole plate, and right, a trench periscope. The shaft of the periscope has been shrouded in fabric to blend more effectively with the sandbag parapet. The troops carry slung gas mask tins. (Author's collection)

box, with its wooden lid 'eased' ready in a recess. In the trenches the usual instruction was for equipment, including ammunition pouches, to be worn at all times. Though seen in many photographs the untidy festooning of men or trench with cotton ammunition bandoliers was officially discouraged. There were also frequent prescriptions against the wearing of greatcoats in the front line trench, and early in the war Henry Williamson, with the London Rifle Brigade, recorded that his own became so sodden and heavy that he hacked off a length in desperation.[7] Henry Ogle much preferred the leather jerkins and cape-style groundsheets that appeared later in the war.[8] In some units Stand To was at a set hour, or a given period before daylight; however, particularly canny commanders did not publish a set clock time, since this would enable an alert enemy to lay his plans accordingly. Often there was also a dusk Stand To, and the whole procedure, including inspections, might last more than an hour. When trouble threatened Stand To could be extended almost indefinitely. When 55th Division was in imminent danger of German raids or attack in May 1918 elements were kept on Stand To all night, several nights running.

Rum might be issued after Stand To. The letters 'SRD' on the ceramic rum jars were the subject of much irreverent speculation, but actually stood for 'Supply Reserve Depot', which was where the containers came from. Though some were teetotal, many troops appreciated the morale-raising quality of a communal tot of fairly rough alcohol after the strict observances of Stand To. From the point of view of officialdom the key factor was to ensure limited quantity but reliable and equal distribution. Quite naturally many men wanted more, and a rum jar was prized loot. To prevent this, many units placed guards on their supply and followed the rule that rum should be issued and drunk in the presence of an officer. True alcoholics were reasonably rare in disciplined units, most being weeded out before they actually reached the trenches. Perhaps paradoxically, alcoholism was more possible amongst officers who carried the stress of responsibility as well as the common dangers and discomforts of the front line – and were able to afford to have spirits sent out to the front, or provided through the officers' mess.

After morning Stand To it was usually time for the company commander's morning rounds, just one of many being described by the chronicler of the 1st/4th Loyal North Lancashires in late 1916:

> After breakfast comes cleaning and inspecting rifles, while the Company Commander, who has already had a look round and detailed the day's work to the Company Sergeant Major, completes and sends down by runner to the Battalion Headquarters his Trench State and account of ammunition expended; then adjusting his Tube helmet and box respirator and tightening his belt carrying his revolver and glasses (it is a standing order that everyone must wear his equipment all the time in the front line), he sets out to inspect his lines, finding, if he knows his job, a cheery word for all and sundry, and receiving often better than he gives, taking stock of everything, including slackers,

and generally tuning up for the day, well knowing that if he misses anything, the Commanding Officer, or, worse still, the Brigadier, will spot and strafe him! Each sentry post has its standing orders pinned up on a board, with a duty roster showing each man's work through 24 hours, and ensuring that each gets eight hours in which

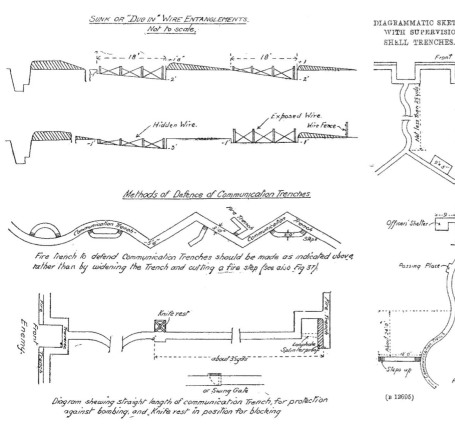

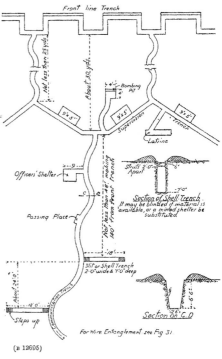

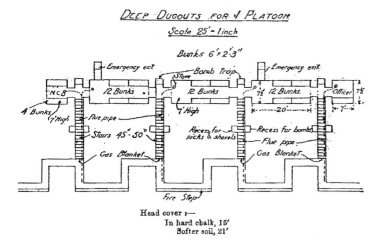

Illustrations from Notes on Trench Warfare for Infantry Officers, Revised Diagrams, *December 1916, showing sunken wire entanglements, a diagrammatic sketch of portion of a front line, methods of defence of communication trenches and deep dugouts for one platoon. (Author's collection)*

he may try to sleep, and a sheet for intelligence, which is collected by the intelligence officer every morning when he visits the sniping post. 'Dinners up' is the signal for a general break and a repetition of the breakfast scene, but the food is stew or roast meat and potatoes or rissoles. At 1.30pm casualty returns and special incidents have to be at Battalion Headquarters, and at 3.30 a report on the direction of the wind.[9]

Many units offered more extensive advice to their officers than that given in official manuals. Late in the war Major General Solly Flood produced a 31-point memorandum for 42nd East Lancashire Division entitled *Questions a Commander Should Ask Himself at Frequent Intervals in the Trenches*. In this officers were reminded that they were 'here for two purposes – to do as much damage as possible to the enemy and to hold [their] part of the line in all circumstances'. To achieve these ends it was the unit commander's duty: to ensure that he knew as much as possible about his territory; maintain contact with the adjoining formations; do everything in his power for the comfort and safety of his men; attempt to leave the trenches and dugouts in better condition than he found them; and check for all signs of 'slackness and slovenliness'. Interestingly, 42nd Division also advised its officers on the niceties of man management, such as setting an example in punctuality, turn out and cheerfulness, and in taking part in games and skill at arms competitions. Whilst cultivating an aggressive attitude towards the enemy and enforcing strict discipline, officers were also enjoined to 'be human'; for example, getting to know men's circumstances and offering whatever assistance might be possible with 'troubles at home'.

Keeping the trench, and its garrison, clean and in good order was something that took time, even in quiet sectors. Men were encouraged to wash and shave, tasks completed away from the fire trench, and in 124th Brigade the general order was that men should be as clean and smart as 'circumstances would allow'. Bathing was out of the question until the troops were away from the line: then hastily converted breweries and other premises were pressed into service as rough and ready bath houses and de-lousing areas. Officer Christopher Stone soon discovered that 'wearing the same pants and breeches for six days and nights without taking them off' gave him, 'tremendous sympathy with the working classes'.[10] Latrines were kept in good order by designated orderlies with disinfectant. The best system was one of buckets 'evacuated nightly', but there were also pit, and various cut and cover systems in use. *Notes on Trench Routine* carried a strict injunction on indiscriminate urinating. Nevertheless 'unofficial' arrangements existed in many areas, of which relieving oneself in an empty tin and throwing it out of the trench as far as possible was one of the least objectionable. On the other side of the line sanitary arrangements were the subject of much Teutonic merriment where the wooden *Donnerbalken,* or 'Thunder beam', over a pit, was the main item of sanitary ware. Interestingly many pictures of German soldiers in the latrines exist, whilst British sensibilities make this subject something of a rarity. George Coppard of the Machine Gun Corps – no stranger to hardship or death – professed

himself shocked by such exhibitions.[11] Latrines were ideally positioned as far away as possible from fighting and living spaces, whilst maintaining 'convenience'.

Rats, which would ultimately become massive beasts of legend, were not equally prevalent everywhere. It was the worst trenches that attracted the most rats – because they found plenty to eat in the form of corpses and discarded food. Perhaps the most unpleasant and memorable image was the sight of these creatures gnawing on the faces of the dead: but they had other tricks, running over the living in their sleep, or making acrobatic endeavours to get at rations which wary soldiers had hung up within dugouts. Some units had regular rat hunts, clubbing or even shooting the vermin. Photos of the aftermath of particularly successful drives survive, showing the creatures laid out in rows or hung like the game bag of some noble shoot in the Black Forest or Scotland. For Lieutenant N. F. Percival of the Duke of Lancaster's Own Yeomanry in the Bois Grenier sector rat hunting was a set fixture of the day, for, 'after breakfast every morning we used to hunt rats which swarmed everywhere'.[12]

The first line against trench litter was usually sandbags 'hung up for the collection of rubbish'. Securing bags by means of spent cartridges or bayonets driven into the trench wall was officially discouraged but often seen. Ideally the refuse was divided into used cartridge cases and chargers for recycling, and other waste. 'Sanitary men' were detailed to collect and remove the non-recyclable material, carrying it, if

Preserved trench system at Sanctuary Wood. Originally named 'Sanctuary Wood' in 1914 because it lay in a quiet sector, by 1915 this had become a key part of the Ypres battlefield. Much of the trench system here has been re-dug since 1918, and despite new industrial strength revetting, soil movement demonstrates the difficulties of keeping trenches open to public access. The site also has a fascinating, if eclectic, museum. (Author's collection)

German soldiers in festive mood: ominously the notice attached to the candlelit Christmas tree tells us that this scene is in front of Verdun in the winter of 1915. The billet is probably a shed, but has been made more homely with photographs and shelving. Many yuletide traditions were held in common by British and Germans, due at least in part to the connections of the royal families in the 19th century. (Author's collection)

possible, 50 yards away from habitation and burying it in marked pits layered with earth and lime. In a perfect world wounded men were sent rearwards with their arms and equipment, but ammunition was left behind. Field glasses, tools and the effects of the dead were sent to battalion headquarters. Enemy rifles and parts of rifles were regarded as salvage, and unusual enemy shell fuses or similar items were supposed to be handed back down the line, like museum exhibits, with labels showing their provenance. Complete dud shells and rifle grenades were exceptions to the rule, being regarded as too dangerous to be moved. Correct procedure was to report them: but in active sectors most were ignored, and in quiet places souvenir-hunting accidents were not uncommon.

Interestingly, certain captured items were regarded as legitimate spoils of war: *Extracts from Routine Orders* of 1917 catalogued these as German helmets, caps, badges, numerals and buttons. These could be, and often were, sent home. Henry Williamson's final haul included three German helmets, a cap, two bayonets, a 'sack of clothing' and, rather less legitimately and much to the consternation of his nearest and dearest, two boxes of hand grenades.[13] Sidney Rogerson of the West Yorkshires

had the uneasy feeling that 'souvenir hunting' was really a euphemistic looting of the enemy dead. One of his colleagues foraged on a purely commercial basis, selling his artefacts to men of the Army Service Corps who were rarely far forward enough to encounter the Germans. Another, more altruistic soldier went through the pockets of a 'huge German' who lay sprawled by a communication trench to find a piccolo, which he promptly gave away.[14] What many 'Souvenir Kings' prized most was the Iron Cross – small and easy to carry, yet commanding 'a very good market'.

Apart from collecting rubbish the ubiquitous sandbag could be used for almost anything. Henry Ogle with 7th Royal Warwickshires was a great fan of the 'blessed sandbag':

> I scrounged them whenever there was a chance. We carried rations in them, slung fore and aft over the shoulder; we used them … on our legs; folded they saved hips and ribs from the extremes of cold or hardness or from temporary damp. I used one as a pillow inside my steel helmet in the line or on my boots out of it. I always carried a spare.[15]

In fact Ogle omitted a few possibilities. With a slit the bag formed impromptu head camouflage; sliced open down one side, a hood for use when carrying dirty supplies or bags of earth; carried into action it was the raw material of protection; cut completely open the material could be used to camouflage periscopes, or made into helmet covers.

'Trench foot' was a vexatious complaint – but one that struck very differently at various times and places. In wet conditions, particularly in winter early in the war, it was a veritable epidemic that led to serious debilitation and even deaths. In the summer, in dry sectors, it was rare and far less serious. Medically speaking trench foot and frostbite were similar – both being related to loss of circulation – though trench foot was caused by standing in mud or water, rather than freezing. Both struck hard in the winter of 1914 to 1915 and caught the army ill prepared. A pamphlet entitled *Prevention of Frost Bite or Chilled Feet* was produced, but by then much of the damage had been done, and over 26,000 men required treatment for one or other condition. Shortly afterwards the subject was revisited in *Notes From the Front*, Part 3, which noted that cold and wet were the prime culprits and that tight puttees and poor circulation were contributory factors. Yet means of prevention, such as warm dry feet, fresh socks and decent duckboards above water level were often easier to identify than to achieve. Greasing the feet was also recognized as helpful, though naturally unpopular.

Private Edward Roe of the East Lancashires viewed the foot smearing procedure with incredulity. The grease was a 'tinned transparent substance' resembling lard:

> We are standing in water up to our knees. We are supposed to take our puttees, boots and socks off, smear our feet with this substance (it is solid and cold as an iceberg), put our wet socks, boots and puttees on again and stand up in water to our knees. Well we won't do it.[16]

Next spread:
Australians in a trench shelter, Fleurbaix, June 1916. In this example the shelter has been prefabricated as a wooden frame and the sandbagging built up around it. Boards keep the occupants clear of the ground. This arrangement was ideal for 'box' or 'breastwork' trenches, fabricated on top of, rather than dug into, the ground. More usually shelters were dug into the side of the trench. (IWM Q668)

Roe might not have done, but many did. One unit that took trench foot extremely seriously was 2nd Battalion Royal Welch Fusiliers. In the winter of 1914 its cooks saved all grease from cooking, and 'after stand to each morning the men rubbed each other's feet vigorously with it'.[17] A man from each company was also detailed to the battalion laundry, and a pair of clean socks for every man was brought up with the rations. Socks were also sent from home in huge numbers, so eventually men were throwing them away after a single wearing. The happy result of this obsession was that only one man of the battalion had trench foot that winter, even though wet trenches were frequently occupied. Gumboots and thigh-length 'trench waders' gradually became more common, and undoubtedly helped – but were not suitable for duty involving swift movement. Also, as *Notes For Infantry Officers* pointed out, they were clammy and best kept on only for limited periods. Nevertheless the general incidence of trench foot and frostbite was reduced with time, so that though the BEF grew to many times its original size the numbers treated for these complaints were marginally reduced in latter years. Captain F. C. Hitchcock of the Leinsters records that having frostbitten feet was eventually regarded as 'disciplinary' – this added insult to injury but may have encouraged additional care.

In the trenches drinking water was usually stored in rum jars and barrels, and, where possible, brought up in battalion water carts at night. Biscuit tins and camp kettles were also used as impromptu water carriers. Bottled soft drinks were rare, but not unknown, unlike amongst the enemy where bottled mineral water was fairly common. Strict prohibitions were issued against using potentially contaminated streams, wells and shell holes – but in extremis, men isolated during major battles could, and did, drink anything. Whatever the source water was safest boiled, and much of Tommy's liquid did in fact come from tea, often carried cold in the water bottle. Chloride of lime was the main alternative to boiling, but usually left the liquid unpalatable, if not undrinkable. Sensible officers kept a rough check on the amount of water to hand and stopped washing and shaving if levels ran low, or allowed potentially contaminated 'surface water' to be used for washing only. 'Water parties' were sometimes needed to fill bottles or collect tins, but were best kept nocturnal and as small as possible to avoid attracting enemy fire.

Tinned 'iron rations' for one day, two if possible, were supposed to be carried up to the line with each relief. These were not, however, to be consumed as a matter of course, being intended only to be opened on the orders of an officer when normal supplies were interrupted. Wherever possible cookery was not done in the foremost trenches, but as a company level activity in support areas. Naturally showing smoke during daylight was strictly forbidden. Nevertheless in many places braziers were improvised out of buckets, and small quantities of food and water were heated over candles. Later some troops acquired somewhat more efficient pocket cookers, or primus stoves. Larger commercial solid fuel stoves were occasionally lugged into dugouts with chimneys. Using any of these devices in enclosed spaces carried risks of fire and suffocation, and

there were accidents. The recommended way to bring food forward was during the night immediately before it was required, but fumbling with an odd assortment of comestibles in mud and darkness was inviting spoilt food and missed deliveries. The answer given by 124th divisional orders was that the quartermasters should make up each company's rations and pack them systematically in sandbags. Each bag was to have the company marked 'on a piece of tin', a second tag under the first denoting the platoon. The marks, being impressed, could be read by touch. Water and other drinks were often brought up in old petrol cans or large iron 'dixies', and memoirs abound with accounts of tainted tea. Nevertheless later in the war there were insulated cylindrical backpacks with screw closures allowing the carrying party free use of both hands whilst delivering tea, stew or other non-solid supplies.

Some staples appeared over and over again: hard biscuits, bread, and tins of stew or pork and beans – the latter being mainly beans and a suggestion of pork. Private Dolden, a cook with the London Scottish, recalled that plum and apple jam was issued so frequently that a single appearance of apricot was warmly welcomed.[18] 'Bully beef' became the stuff of legend, being fried, stewed or simply sliced: but if badly stored, and served warm, might literally be poured from its 12oz tin. For starving Germans late in the war it was regarded as a delicacy – the French were mystified by British 'bully' and derided all tinned meat rations as 'singe' or monkey. Officially each British soldier was given 4,300 calories a day in mid 1916, a laudable target when achieved. Yet nutritional knowledge was not advanced and fresh ingredients were often lacking, particularly in the front line. Moreover the intervention of the enemy, the weather and a good shaking in a sandbag could turn even good food into an unpalatable mush. Sometimes nothing turned up; sometimes the amounts were so small that neighbouring sections would agree to take rations alternately rather than have tiny amounts more frequently. Acting Lance Corporal Eric Hiscock of the Royal Fusiliers remembered the final division of his section rations as an 'art form', with a loaf of bread, stale cheese and other items having to be split into eight precisely equal portions. Albert Andrews of the 19th Manchesters fared rather better – remembering a typical day's trench rations as bacon and tea for breakfast, a 'dinner' of stew, a tea with bread and jam and a cup of tea at midnight.[19] The young Ernest Parker of the Durham Light Infantry mused that teenagers were 'always hungry' – and like many of his compatriots spent any spare pay in the local *estaminets* whenever they were accessible.[20]

During times of particular stress to the supply system, or gluts after the delivery of parcels from home, nourishment turned distinctly bizarre. Lieutenant Roe of the Glosters improvised porridge from hot water, hard biscuits and jam. With the Royal Warwickshires E. C. Vaughan recalled a breakfast of 'tinned herrings and sherry', and supervising a work party near Courcelles he once enjoyed the rare treat of sandwiches and a bottle of English beer. Edmund Dane noted a rifleman who 'imported a box of kippers' to the front line at Givenchy, whilst Henry Williamson continually pestered his mother for cakes.[21] In 1916 the officers of 18th King's Royal Rifle Corps were not unique in enjoying a full Christmas dinner, but embellishments including curried prawns, caviar and 1906 Veuve Cliquot Champagne probably marked them out as the best diners of the festive season. Early in the war the Germans also enjoyed bountiful *Liebesgaben* (presents) from home, with sausages, cigars and spirits particularly popular gifts. At Christmas 1914 Martin Müller had almost too many seasonal goodies to carry, including sausages, gingerbread, marzipan, jam, cake and a bottle of concentrated tea and rum.[22] Yet plenty was all too brief, and towards the end of the war Ernst Jünger would leave vivid descriptions of surviving on paltry *ersatz* (substitute) rations, and the delight occasioned by the rare appearance of dumplings or beans. German dried vegetables acquired the well-earned nickname *Stacheldracht* – barbed wire.

There were some sectors where men felt that they were in the waiting room of death. Places such as 'Shell Trap Farm' and 'Hellfire Corner' got their names for a reason. One particularly nasty area just south of Passchendaele was occupied by the 3/5th Lancashire Fusiliers in mid November 1917. Officially the great Flanders offensive had ended the very day they had arrived but nobody had told the Germans, or the heavens, that the battle was over. At the end of October the unit had had a 'trench strength' of 21 officers and 499 other ranks – but attrition and sickness soon took their toll. Three weeks later 20 men were dead, 39 wounded, seven missing and 70 sick. Of the officers lieutenants Forshaw and Lovell were dead; Lieutenant Simpson wounded.

A German soldier fights from a shallow ditch that might once have been a trench, next to the body of a Frenchman. The German wears the new Stahlhelm; the Adrian helmet of the battered corpse lies nearby. Photograph taken by a German official photographer near Fort Vaux during the battle of Verdun, 1916. (G. Theodore Collection. IWM Q23760)

Three more were sick. Of all ranks a total of 142, or just over 27 per cent, were *hors de combat* even though there had been no attack by either side. As the regimental journal remarked, here 'the weather and general conditions of life in the trenches was more expensive than the enemy'.

Though active sectors and keen, aggressive commanding officers effectively exhausted both the time and the energy of the private soldier, most areas had some experience of boredom. Some happy places, where the enemy was quiescent, were filled with boredom. In the winter of 1915 the 5th South Wales Borderers battled the elements at Festubert and Neuve Chapelle, but lost not a single man throughout November and December. This their history ascribed to their 'having learned to work very silently and to be careful not to leave things about to attract the Germans' attention'. The 10th Lincolns struck particularly lucky near Armentières, in good weather, during February 1916. Here Major Walter Vignoles found the trenches 'really quite comfortable' and 'in good condition', with the enemy doing no more than containing the British occasionally with small arms fire. Despite the presence of snipers Vignoles' company was unscathed. In such circumstances amusements were at a premium. Many played cards. 'Crown and Anchor' was also a popular gambling pastime, using a fabric playing surface the soldier could pack away in his pocket at a moment's notice – a particularly useful characteristic given that technically it was banned. Nevertheless many officers winked at its existence, provided that the game was peaceful and not played in plain sight of authority.

Diaries were also frowned upon, though quite a few were kept. Writing letters and filling field postcards was actively encouraged and was a significant morale raiser, though officers censored the outgoing post. Despite this, and specific prohibitions against mentioning units and places, many men managed to convey a surprising amount of information by means of hints, or outright encoding. One method of indicating location was to write that you were 'back at the same place' as you were when some memorable event had happened at home. Another was to scatter the letters of a vital word at set intervals throughout the message. Though the Army Postal Service was part of the Royal Engineers who brought the mail most of the way, the last and usually most difficult part of the journey was in the hands of a unit postman – commonly a corporal or lance corporal. Christopher Stone described him as a 'poor devil' who 'trudges about 10 miles a day with a bag over his shoulder through incredible sludge and mush'.[23] From 28 August 1914 sending letters home was free: relatives posting to the front paid 1d. Usually, and unless an offensive intervened, delivery took about ten days.

Reading was popular with some, particularly where a unit was static for a while. Perhaps surprisingly, quite a few officers managed to get fairly current newspapers and periodicals delivered directly to the front. These might come by subscription from the publisher, or through an intermediary at home. Many soldiers were given abbreviated 'Soldier's Testaments' or other religious works by societies or well wishers, and other books made it to the trenches in packs, or were found amongst ruined buildings. Divisions and chaplains might have their own libraries, though fewer of those volumes were actually taken to the front line. Trench newspapers were also published by soldiers, for soldiers. These varied in quality and execution, and might actually be prepared in the trenches, or in camps behind the line. Many papers were the product of specific divisions; others were less tidy in their parentage. In the British case trench newspapers generally had a high quotient of humour, leavened with a little news, and brainteasers or drawings.

The majority bore splendidly evocative titles such as *The Gasper, The Dump*, or *The Open Exhaust,* but most famous of all was undoubtedly the *Wipers Times*. This was a 24th Division production, edited by Captain F. J. Roberts of the Sherwood Foresters, who was fortunate to discover a disused Ypres printing works with 'parts of the building remaining', and the type spread over the surrounding countryside. With the machinery quickly reassembled by a sergeant who had formerly been a printer, production of the journal commenced with 'issue one' on 12 February 1916. Later, when the division moved to the Somme the title changed to *Somme Times*, and, later still, to *BEF Times*. In 1918 the March edition was lost to the German offensive, and printing was not resumed until November 1918. *Blighty* was an interesting periodical, for though it bore many of the characteristics of the 'trench' productions, was supplied to the war zone, and contained 'pictures and humour from our men at the front', it was actually printed in London and numbered Field Marshal Haig and Lord Jellicoe amongst its patrons. Unlike a good deal of the 'advertising' in *Wipers Times* which was satirical, *Blighty* carried paid sponsorship from major businesses such as insurance companies, Players cigarettes, BSA and Austin cars.

The French also had a vibrant trench publication market – though distinctively different in tone. Where the British tended to be almost uniformly irreverent, surreal and indefatigably humorous, some of the French material was by turns more jingoistic, philosophical and downbeat. In August 1916, for example, *Le Poilu* explicitly stated that its purpose was to draw together the ties of friendship of the regiment that had given it life. In 1917 *Le Crapouillot* became distinctly more cynical and less funny, in tune perhaps with the atmosphere of seriousness and mutiny in the French Army at the time. Realistic or dramatic accounts of actions, deaths and obituaries were all rather more common than in the British papers. Criticism of the home front was also overt, and boiled over into some very direct opinions, as in a piece in *L'Echo des Tranchées* in May 1917:

> There are civilians who cannot approach a man on leave without asking him, 'Why aren't you advancing?' Why can we not make use of this ardour of civilians greedy for offensives? We could take them into the front line trenches and urge them to advance. We bet that anyone returning from such an expedition would no longer enquire why one does not advance.

Though private cameras were banned, photography in various forms did have its place in the trenches. Quite a few officers ignored the prohibition and carried with them a 'pocket Kodak', or similar small camera of the type that was coming into use beside the old tripod-mounted wood and brass contraptions of the professional. Most regimental collections contain at least some of the pictures by officer photographers alongside those taken by official bodies, or those passed for release through the press. Moreover commercial photographic studios in and near military camps did a roaring trade throughout the war, and as long as materials were available. Literally millions of portraits of individuals or groups were produced. Most were made as multiple prints and given to friends and relatives, whilst soldiers took pictures of their families with them to the trenches. The most salubrious dugouts usually contained one or more pictures, including perhaps a pin-up of a pretty girl, a cartoon or, less commonly, a more patriotic piece. Eventually the war, and the trenches themselves, became the subject of moving pictures such as the remarkable film *Battle of the Somme*, which was widely shown in British cinemas. It is estimated that more than a third of the entire population of the British Isles saw this production within months of its release.

Artistic endeavour was not entirely absent from the trenches either, and indeed a whole genre of applied decoration and crafts has acquired the general description of 'trench art' – what the Germans called *Soldatenkunst*. In fact quite a bit of 'trench' art was made behind the lines, as cottage industry, or as commercial exploitation of war surplus. Some trench art even originated as a by-product of workers' free time in UK factories. Nevertheless many pieces were made by the soldiers themselves, sometimes in the front line. Though drawings and watercolours are not unknown, most trench art was three-dimensional and often had some sort of practical element. Common items included letter openers fabricated from discarded brass or shell splinters, vases, ashtrays and boxes from shell cases, walking sticks, rings and crucifixes. Also seen are cigarette and matchbox holders; lamps; miniature tanks; and decorated bayonets and water bottles. In certain sectors soldiers carved their regimental badges into pieces of chalk, or created larger designs as permanent features of the trench. In the very front line music was usually out of the question, except for that most exceptional Christmas of 1914. Nevertheless second line trenches and dugouts could sometimes boast a musical instrument and the odd rendition of a popular ballad. There are even stories of enterprising souls who managed to get a piano underground. Gramophones were certainly seen in HQ dugouts and billets. The officers of 22nd Royal Fusiliers received a 'Decca' and half a dozen records in January 1917, though the junior officers would later complain that the choice of music was monopolized by the colonel.

Smoking was so common that non-smokers were marked out as unusual, and cigarettes and tobacco came up with the rations as well as being sent from home. The amount issued appears to have varied, with some getting 2oz a week early in the war, others up to 30 cigarettes later. Pipes had been more popular than cigarettes in the

Victorian era, and various wood or briar models now predominated: Henry Ogle of the Warwickshires puffed away on 'Digger Mixture' in a corn cob until his mouth 'felt like pickled leather'. A few, like Corporal Fleet of the East Lancashires, still favoured the old-fashioned clay pipe. Cigarettes appear to have become more popular during the war, at least in part because they were small, quick and convenient – easier to hide from NCOs and the enemy, and less of a disaster if they had to be thrown away. On the other side of the line the traditional long German pipe was sometimes seen, and indeed this was recognized as the mark of a man who had served out his conscription time and passed into the reserves; cigars were also popular until they were exhausted. Germans also received tobacco rations, and when available these were supposed to be two cigars and two cigarettes, or an ounce of pipe tobacco per day. Smoking was widely seen as a comforting tonic for the nerves, and, unlike drink, left the soldier in fighting shape. Unless matches were struck in view of the enemy, or a soldier smoked at the wrong time, it was accepted as completely normal. At Christmas 1914 Princess Mary's fund sent a special brass presentation box to every British soldier, the majority of which contained smoking materials along with a card. Though very welcome the massive deliveries clogged the already well-used delivery systems. When Private Edward Roe ran out of tobacco he resorted to an unsatisfactory mixture of substitutes including tea leaves.[24]

How 'comfortable', or how 'diabolical', a trench system became was dependent on many factors, not least location, weather and enemy action. As early as May 1915 the adjutant of a Loyal North Lancashire battalion was intrigued to discover the 'elaborate way' the enemy had dug himself in. In one captured Festubert trench was discovered a dugout room, 'about 15 feet square, with doors and a window, lined throughout with wooden planking covered in cloth, and furnished with leather covered chairs and a table'. In another was found a 'quantity of feminine underclothing', the purpose of which caused considerable speculation. At the same time the ground recently occupied by the Lancashire battalion was described as 'strewn' with bodies, and defended only by waterlogged trenches 2 feet deep.[25]

The 'working party' became a feature of life as soon as the trenches were dug, though fortunately it was realized that drawing men from reserve areas rather than the front line trenches, except when the front line trench was needing attention, was the most effective utilization of manpower. For technical tasks they often acted under orders of the Royal Engineers. Working parties repaired support and communication trenches, cleared drainage, prepared supplies, helped to erect huts – and a dozen other things – but often they were 'carrying parties' by another name. As such they encountered all the trials of the trench relief, but often under even heavier burdens. As the history of the 1/4th Loyal North Lancashires explained, in bad weather the communication trenches turned into quagmires:

> very dirty, being in no place less than boot deep and in many places thigh deep in pestilent liquid mud. The boards placed at the bottom of the trench were quite covered over, and, being extremely slippery, were mainly useful in leading the way to the deeper, wetter, part of the trenches! Working parties at night and in heavy rain had very great difficulty in making progress.[26]

Near Festubert at 9pm on the pitch dark night of 10 June 1915 a Loyals working party under the splendidly named Captain Crump picked up spades, hurdles and sandbags and headed for the front line trench. Though the distance was less than a mile not all of them arrived, and the time taken was about three hours.

Though there were some long periods in the front line early in the war, and the Germans in particular were forced into semi-permanent occupation, most troops had surprisingly short periods of actual 'trench warfare'. At Verdun in 1916 the French *Noria* system of rotating troops may well have saved the battle, for by May, 40 divisions had been passed through 'the mill on the Meuse'. The idea that trench duty was finite, and that the majority rather than a minority would emerge after a given time, was a considerable boost to morale. In the British instance a division at the front was usually placed with its brigades in line, side by side. At least half the strength was held back from the foremost line, so that each brigade had a battalion each in 'support' and 'reserve', respectively. Therefore only six battalions of the division were actually facing the enemy in the trenches, and of these only half would be in the fire trenches, posts or immediate supports. At any given moment many men were

Fig. 138. Mobile shields. French. One-man type, 1917

Personal armour protection of the trench war. The mobile shields mainly proved impractical, but body armour saw some use right up to the end of the war. (Author's collection)

Fig. 139. Mobile shield, or one-man tank. English model, 1917

Fig. 74   Fig. 74A   Fig. 74B

Fig. 74. Dayfield body shield, simple model

BEAUMONT-HAMEL

From the Beaumont sheet, 57D S.E.1 & 2, 1:10,000, showing German trenches in red, corrected to 15 August 1916. The British line is marked in blue outline only, and the hamlet of Auchonvillers (known to Tommies as 'Ocean Villas') is just behind the British line, off plan, to the west. Parts of squares '10' and '16' are now occupied by the 'Newfoundland Memorial Park' with its famous Caribou statue and preserved trenches. 'Y' Ravine, which sheltered deep German dugouts, is clearly marked in the south-eastern quadrant of square '11'. On 1 July 1916 British 29th Division attacked this sector with a 'first objective' of advancing right through Beaumont-Hamel. The onslaught was prefaced with the explosion of the double mine at Hawthorn Redoubt – which damaged a portion of the enemy line, but also alerted the defenders to the imminence of the attack. Two brigades had gone in before the Newfoundlanders, who now ignored the narrow but safer communication trenches, which were already clogged with casualties, and went over the top ahead of 1st Essex. They met concentrated fire unsupported – whilst bunching to avoid uncut wire.

Much of interest remains in this area. In addition to the visitor centre and trenches of the memorial park there are several memorials, including those to 51st Highland Division and 29th Division, and a variety of cemeteries including the tiny circular 'Hunter's Cemetery' – which is probably this shape because it began as a large shell hole. Recent archaeology has served to emphasize the fact that this area was a battlefield long before, and long after, the tragic Newfoundland attack. Excavation in pasture adjoining the park tentatively identified part of the 'Carlisle Street' communication trench, but also discovered trenches of what appeared to be an earlier French design and unearthed masses of small arms ammunition. A large proportion of this was French and bore dates of manufacture as early as 1901, but not later than 1915 – which fitted neatly with the period before this sector was handed over to the British. Other artefacts included French, British and New Zealand uniform buttons as well as water bottles, medical items, tin cans and other 'domestic' objects. Remarkably Beaumont-Hamel was not taken until 13 November 1916, when the Highlanders of 51st Division cleared its dugouts and cellars, capturing the staffs of 1st and 3rd battalions of German 62nd Infantry Regiment.

Above: Trench in the Beaumont-Hamel Newfoundland Memorial Park, Somme. Once somewhat disorganized, the Newfoundland site has undergone considerable work in recent years – with, for example, duckboards being added to the trenches, and a new 'Canadian style' visitor centre. Most of the barbed wire pickets, still present in the 1970s, and all the trench debris have now gone. Though essentially commemorating 1 July and the 800 Newfoundlanders missing on land and at sea, the park encompasses many memorials and graves to other units, and at the rear the famous 'Y' Ravine. (Author's collection)

Left: Excavated trench leading to a cellar used as a bunker at Auchonvillers, Somme. The building, now used as a tea room and guest house, was rebuilt after the war. The 'Ocean Villas' project, run over many seasons, revealed that part of the trench near to the building had been floored with brick, and also the sequence in which it had fallen into disuse and been back filled. (Author's collection)

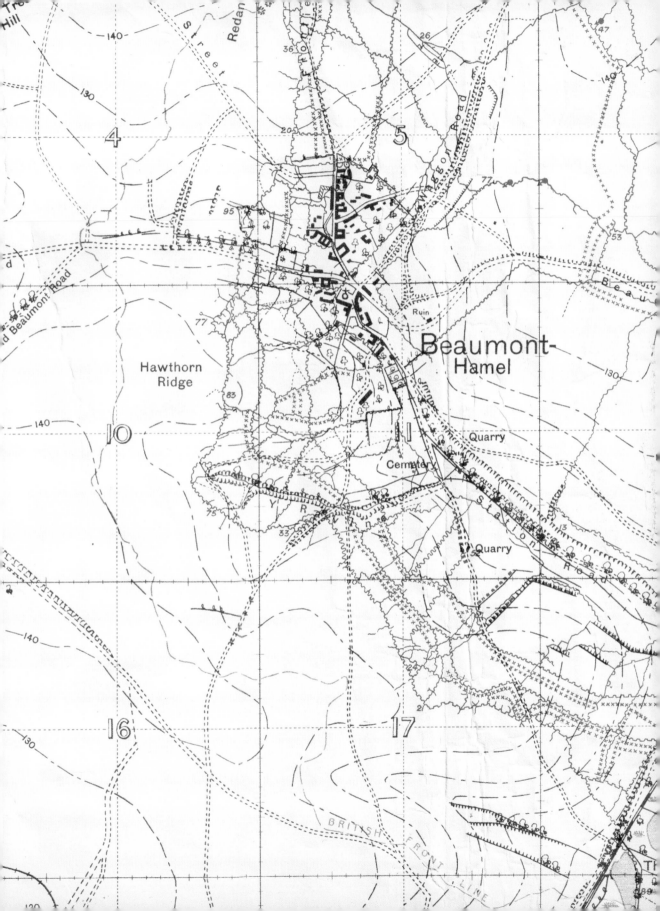

deployed on tasks behind the line, and Royal Artillery personnel were not usually at the sharp end – unless as forward observers. The Army Service Corps, veterinarians and many other support troops had no real place in the trenches. According to one calculation, therefore, a typical division with perhaps 10,000 infantry usually had no more than 1,000 men in possible 'contact' with the enemy, though it needs to be borne in mind that most of the others could be, and sometimes were, subject to often unpredictable shelling.

Quite how long a unit stayed in the trenches varied according to how active the area was, whether attacks were in progress, and the total number of troops available. One of the longest front line sojourns was that of 13th York and Lancasters, who spent an incredible 51 consecutive days in the front line during the Somme, though from a few days to a week or so in the front line trench was a far more typical average. During big attacks, and particularly when heavy casualties were suffered, it was usual for battalions to be taken out of the front line very quickly indeed – sometimes being extracted within 24 hours. According to the history of the 2nd East Lancashires, describing the latter part of 1916, a 'normal' trench tour of duty was 16 days, which might be extended to as many as 24. The battalion was rotated by companies with two in the front line trench and one each in support and reserve. The total time in the front line trench therefore varied from eight to twelve days.

At various times British divisions also enjoyed the comparative luxury of deployments to quiet sectors, or even away from the front. In this respect the British were better situated than their adversaries, who often spent months on the same spot – though with sub-units still rotating between the actual front and local reserve. To mention but a few examples at random, German 1st Reserve Division were in and around Arras for roughly two years up to August 1916, and were then redeployed to the Somme; 16th Bavarian Landwehr were in the Vosges for roughly two years in 1916–17; 25th Hessian Division spent a year on the Somme from late 1914 to late 1915; and the 26th Wurttemberg had similarly been on the Somme for about a year prior to almost total destruction in 1916. As the Crown Prince explained, 'we did not enjoy the invaluable advantages of our enemies, who were able to make good the wear and tear of nerve strength by frequent reliefs and periods of rest'.[27]

Opposite:
Smoking his pipe 2nd Lieutenant L. J. Barley, 1st Cameronians, watches as a rifle grenade is prepared for firing from a trench at Grande Flamengrie Farm, Bois Grenier sector, February 1915. The wooden firing stand is simply constructed, but allows steady shots at a consistent angle. The grenade is a 'No 3' Hale type which had a range of about 160 yards and usually burst into about 175 fragments. Best results were achieved with several rifle bombers firing a salvo, or, failing this, a series of rapid shots to saturate an area. (IWM Q51587)

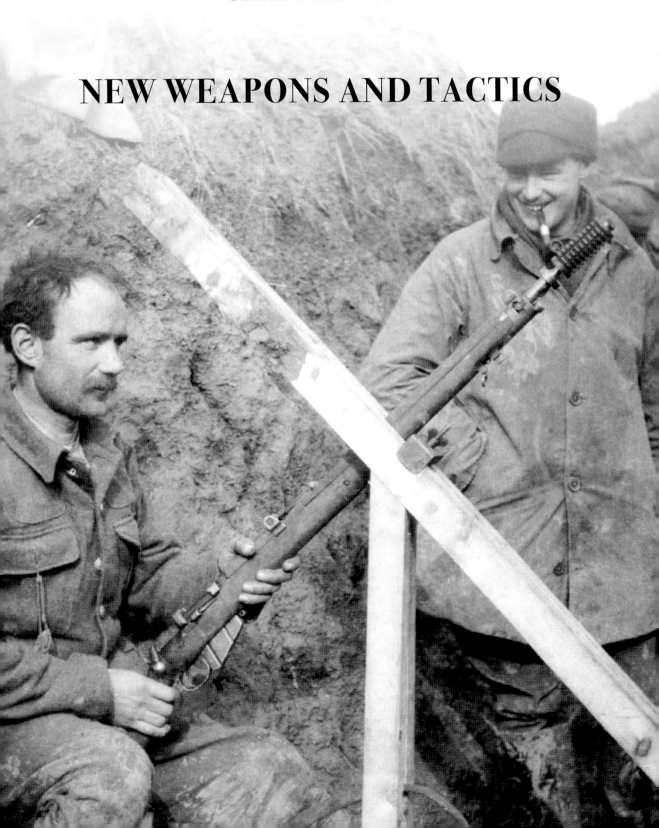

CHAPTER FOUR

NEW WEAPONS AND TACTICS

The commonly held belief that trench warfare and tactics remained much the same from late 1914 to early 1918 is entirely erroneous. Though casualties were undoubtedly high, advances frequently short, and lines often static, the way armies fought, and what they fought with, underwent many changes. Moreover innovations came surprisingly quickly, and were more often delayed by the need to produce new forms of matériel and retrain troops, than by a conservative mindset of command.

The realization that dense formations and failure to dig in quickly were cardinal errors in the face of artillery and machine guns was instantaneous. Henry Williamson recalled that on arrival in France in November 1914 his battalion practised trench digging and 'artillery formation' daily – and in any weather. Artillery formation was described by *Infantry Training*, 1914, as 'Small shallow columns, each on a narrow front, such as platoons or sections in fours or fives … on an irregular front'. Yet within weeks, if not days, it was recognized that 'artillery formation' was nothing like sufficient dispersal. As one general officer explained in *Notes From the Front*, Part 1, of 1914:

> The choice of infantry fields of fire is largely governed by the necessity for avoiding exposure to artillery fire. A field of fire of 300 to 500 yards is quite sufficient… An advance should not be made in rigid lines, but with clouds of skirmishers – 5 or 6 yards apart – thrown forward according to the ground and available cover.

A few months later a new edition of *Notes* was recommending 'loose elastic formations', which were adapted to the ground, discouraging 'rigid lines', and suggesting a distance of '8 or 10 paces' between individuals. On the other side of the line pre-war German regulations had already concluded that when 'platoon rushes' became difficult 'half platoons' and squads might be found more handy. Now, in the face of heavy casualties, orders were issued to decrease the density of attacking formations. Those of Fourth Army appeared as early as 21 August. Nevertheless this was easier said than done where reservists lacked the latest training, or there were attempts to overwhelm the enemy by sheer numbers.

Because trench lines were dug explicitly to defend the occupants against rifle fire, and a static soldier, with his rifle securely rested, had a huge actual and psychological advantage over a soldier moving in the open – who probably could not even see his enemy – the problem of attacking fieldworks came to the fore very quickly. Three answers presented themselves: to cover the approach of the attacker; to attack in new formations; or to use new weapons. All of these ideas had merit, and eventually a new combination of all of them would bring about a revolution in infantry tactics. Progress was swift, but sporadic, and often met with innovations by the defence which would mean that heavy casualties remained the order of the day. In this context, however, it is well worth observing that the greatest slaughters of World War I on the

Western Front occurred in periods that were characterized by 'open' rather than 'trench' warfare. On the German side clear peak casualty figures were reached from August to November 1914, and again from March 1918 to the end of the war. French losses were at their worst in 1914. To this extent British statistics are exceptional, as the army was small in 1914, and July 1916 was catastrophic. Nevertheless British forces also experienced heavy losses from August to October 1918.

Covering the approach of the attacker could mean one of two things: concealing him from view, or physically protecting him from the enemy's bullets. Of these concealment from view proved easily the most useful – night raids and attack around dawn or dusk were soon common, and smoke and fog were both used. Protection from bullets was far less satisfactory. 'Sapping', or extending trenches gradually closer to the enemy, had been practised for centuries and still formed a part of military engineering instructions, where it was seen especially useful as an aspect of siege warfare. Sapping was widely used in trench warfare, and sometimes the diggers were given the additional protection of screens or sandbags. *Feld-Pionierdienst*, 1911, provides an example in which pioneers erect a sandbag breastwork just ahead of, and to the vulnerable side of, a sap. Saps created useful sniping posts or 'jumping off' points, but were a narrow and problematic means to enter an enemy trench system as they would attract fire during their slow forward progress. *Feld-Pionierdienst* also suggests that advancing troops could carry

A Stosstrupp or 'assault squad' from 40th Fusilier Regiment, festooned with stick grenades and materials to create a 'trench block' or reinforce a captured position. The man in the centre of the picture carries a pick and spare sandbags on his assault pack, which consists of a shelter half-wrapped around his mess tin. The soldier on the right carries a gas mask in a soft container, a type later replaced by the familiar squat cylindrical tin. Ammunition bandoliers and a loophole plate are also to be seen in other frames from the same sequence of pictures. Here the leather Picklehaube is worn without its distinctive spike in accordance with regulations of late 1915. (Author's collection)

filled sandbags with them, preferably under cover of darkness, and throw up a small breastwork as the first stage of cover.

Metal shields were used early in the war, some of the first being detached from German machine guns. *Der Spatenkrieg* even suggested that in the attack some cover from bursting shrapnel could be given to a prone soldier by the blade of the entrenching tool, when its handle was inserted between the pack and body. Such methods were superseded by a variety of small shields, often with prop stands to the rear. The British Munitions Design Committee was still considering 'portable shields for infantry' in 1916. Medieval-looking defences on wheels had been used during the Spanish-American War, and were used again, at least experimentally, on the Western Front. Such ideas lingered for a long time but were rarely efficacious for a number of reasons. Perhaps most obviously, to be truly bulletproof a shield had to be tough, fairly thick, and at least large enough to cover a prone man's head and shoulders. Experiment suggested that 5mm of German armour plate was required to stop a British rifle bullet at 110 yards: a decent shield therefore weighed upwards of 44lb. This weight slowed attackers, who had to be prone to take advantage of the cover, and shields attracted more fire than individuals attempting to hug the earth. Naturally the manufacture and transport of shields in large numbers would have required considerable resources. Most of this effort was later redirected towards the provision of static loopholes.

The widespread use of heavy artillery against fieldworks had been thought unlikely before the war – but developed rapidly. The only real problem was that, initially at least, heavy artillery and suitable high explosive shells and fuses were in short supply. Following shell scandals in 1915 when batteries frequently ran short this would be corrected – then the major issue was the co-ordination of infantry with artillery. Another method of trench clearance that was sometimes successful, if terrain allowed, was to move a machine gun into a flanking position, perhaps by night, then attempt to empty the enemy trench by weight of fire.

The option of giving the infantry a weapon that could be used against holes in the ground was swiftly addressed by the grenade. Grenades had been in use since the late medieval era, and remained in the hands of the engineers as a weapon of siege warfare. Both the French and Germans held some stocks of ball-shaped bombs with pull-type igniters at the outbreak of war, whilst the British had small numbers of a much more technically advanced, but more difficult to manufacture, 'No 1' stick grenade which exploded on impact. That grenade-armed pioneers might have a role in trench warfare had certainly been foreseen by the Germans by 1911, and soon after trenches were dug pioneers were allotted to the infantry at the lowest level, sometimes to the extent of adding a single grenade thrower to infantry platoons where night attacks might be expected. Nevertheless in all countries grenade demand outran current production many times, the result being a scramble for new design and manufacture. The new sources of supply would be threefold – new production from home factories; extemporized production in workshops behind the lines; and bombs which the troops themselves ran up from existing scrap materials and explosives already supplied to the artillery and engineers.

Amongst the early bombs made by the troops at the front two basic designs predominated: the 'Jam Tin' and the 'Hairbrush' (or 'raquette'), and there were

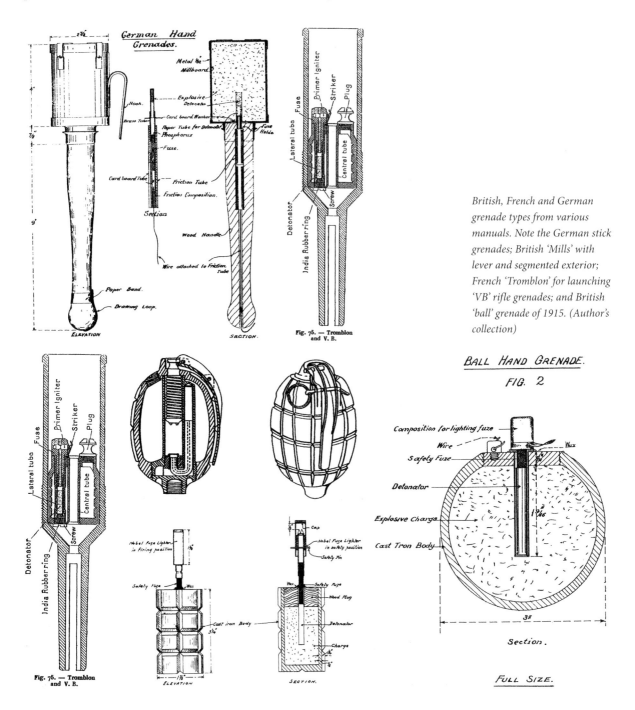

British, French and German grenade types from various manuals. Note the German stick grenades; British 'Mills' with lever and segmented exterior; French 'Tromblon' for launching 'VB' rifle grenades; and British 'ball' grenade of 1915. (Author's collection)

equivalents on both sides of the line. Amongst the British it was the Jam Tin – sometimes nicknamed 'Tickler's Artillery' after a well-known jam producer – that predominated. Basic in the extreme, it consisted of a tin can, packed with dynamite or gun cotton, with a detonator attached to a fuse that projected through the top. Fragmentation could be improved by adding pieces of scrap metal or fragments of barbed wire. The simplest fuses were lit with a match or cigarette; later some were provided with a compound to scratch against a rough surface – or a cap to be set off to ignite the fuse. *Notes From the Front* recommended practice with dummy bombs, and testing of fuses to determine burn time. Fuses were to be long enough that the bomb could be thrown, but not so long that an alert enemy could dive into cover or even hurl the missile back. Jam Tins were made in many different places, but one of the earliest venues that could claim the title 'factory' was the village of Gorre behind the Givenchy–Festubert sector where the sappers and miners of the Indian Meerut Division were ensconced from November 1914.

According to *Notes From the Front* the British improvised 'Hairbrush' was about 20 inches in length, with a slab of explosive surrounded by metal fragments within a sacking cover, attached to the wooden handle, again with a fuse and detonator. An Imperial War Museum variant has a tin attached to the backing board. French examples, from the Les Invalides museum, and seen in photographs, vary in detail. Some have nails tied around the explosive, others feature a slot in the wooden handle by means of which they can be slung from a rope around the bomber's body for easy carriage. The German emergency grenades were commonly known as *Behelfsmäßige Handgranaten*. Two models, approximating to the Jam Tin and Hairbrush, were depicted in the 1915 *Dienstunterricht des Deutschen Pioniers*. The tin type was about 4 inches in diameter, closed with a wooden lid, and contained fragments of iron weighing about 0.2oz. The German Hairbrush type was 20 inches long with a large slab of explosive.

Another type devised in the winter of 1914–15 was the British 'Battye' or 'Bethune' bomb, produced in army workshops in France. Named after its inventor, Major Basil Condon Battye RE, it consisted of an externally segmented small cast iron cylinder filled with explosive, a detonator and an igniter, usually of the 'Nobel' type. It was delivered in wooden boxes of 30. Battye was also celebrated for his efforts in bringing electric lighting and heating to dugouts. The so-called 'Mexican' grenade – later known as the 'No 2' – was a type of British explode-on-impact stick grenade seen in small numbers. Its strange name came about because it was being produced for a commercial contract for Mexico by the Cotton Powder Company of Faversham in Kent at the outbreak of war.

Though *Feld-Pionierdienst* had envisaged that grenades would be used in the clearance of fieldworks, quite how the grenadier would achieve this in practice was not immediately apparent. Grenades were quickly used in raids, and grenadiers were put in the front line ahead of attacking infantry, and another tactic used at a very early stage was to open rapid fire with other weapons, so allowing bomb throwers to creep forward: but none of these methods yet exploited the grenade to its fullest potential. Only when groups of grenadiers worked together would it be possible to develop new tactics, and this had commenced by the beginning of 1915. In *Notes on Attack and Defence* it was recommended that attacks should always be well supplied with bombs, and that there should be 'an organised plan' to keep the defenders 'of a captured trench amply supplied with these missiles'.

By May 1915 an ideal 'Trench Storming Party' had been devised by the British. This was to comprise upwards of 14 men commanded by an NCO. The men of the party would be divided into four distinct tasks: 'bayonet men' to cover the group and take the lead in winkling out the opposition; grenadiers; grenade carriers; and 'sandbag men' whose duty was to follow up, block side entrances, and finally form a barricade in the trench at the furthest point of the advance. To provide manpower for these storming parties the 'very best, bravest and steadiest in an emergency' were selected for training – with a minimum of 12 NCOs and men per company taking part. By October ideas were further refined in *The Training and Employment of Grenadiers*, which noted that:

The nature of operations in the present campaign has developed the employment of rifle and hand grenades both in attack and defence to such an extent that the grenade has become one of the principal weapons of trench warfare. Every infantry soldier

British grenades, described left to right. A 'No 27' hand or rifle projected phosphorus bomb, capable of causing dreadful burn injuries and ideal for clearing bunkers or creating smoke. The 'No 34' Mark III, a small 'egg' type ideal for combating the longer range of similar German grenades. The 'No 36', an improved 1917 model of Mills bomb, suitable for both hand, or – with the base plate seen here – rifle discharger use. The cast iron cylinder 'Battye' bomb. A 'Jam Tin', or, to be pedantic, in this instance 'Milk Tin' bomb. (Author's collection)

must, therefore, receive instructions in grenade throwing. It has been found in practice, however, that some men do not possess the temperament or the qualifications necessary to make a really efficient grenadier. For this reason in every platoon there should be a nucleus of one NCO and eight men with a higher degree of training and efficiency as grenadiers than the remainder. These men will be able either to work with the platoon or to provide a reserve of grenadiers for any special object.

A battalion 'Bombing Officer' and an NCO per company were to be allotted to assist in training and to organize the supply and storage of grenades. In the cavalry the basic trained element was to be one NCO and four men per troop. To carry the numbers of grenades needed for bombing duels various forms of grenade waistcoat, bandolier, bag and 'bomb bucket' were introduced. Flaming grenade bombers badges were initially worn unofficially, and confirmed officially by an army order of 11 October 1915.

That month the 'Grenadier Party' had a revised complement of nine: an NCO in command; two bayonet men; two grenade throwers; two carriers and two spare men. The bayonet men were selected from 'quick shots and good bayonet fighters', and were specifically ordered to advance with magazines charged and a round 'in the chamber' to protect the bombers 'at all costs'. The grenadiers were supposed to keep both hands free for throwing, and the carriers to keep closed up enough to pass the grenades or take the place of a wounded comrade. Spare men would carry up further supplies until required for other duties. As part of a bigger attack grenadier parties could follow one another, or be backed up by the remainder of their platoons, who would also carry grenades. Once an objective was reached it was thought best to drive the enemy an additional 50 yards to put him out of grenade range, and then establish two temporary barricades or blocks across the trench. The section of the trench wall between the two obstructions could then be pulled down to create a permanent block whilst the workers were covered by other members of the team.

By mid 1915 the powerful and distinctive side-levered Mills bomb (or 'No 5'), which would become synonymous with Tommy in the trenches, had entered service. The Mills bomb was an impressive performer: tests confirmed that anybody within 10 yards of its explosion was well nigh certain to be hit by its fragments, and that between 10 and 20 yards away there was a fair chance of injury. At 25 yards there was still a one in four possibility that a target would be hit. Weekly demand for Mills bombs was prodigious and apt to fluctuate wildly due to the strategic situation: half a million were wanted every seven days in July 1915, with 1.4 million being demanded in August 1916. Naturally it would be some time before such ambitious production targets were achieved, so the British Army struggled through 1915 with a whole phalanx of less efficient grenades making up the numbers.

Amongst these were not only factory-produced improvements on the 'Jam Tin' and 'Hairbrush' but oddities such as the friction pull 'Pitcher'; the 'Lemon', and the

'No 15' ball grenade. The Pitcher, light and heavy versions of which became known as the Nos '13' and '14', was widely accepted as one of the most unreliable and dangerous bombs of the war: even the official *History of the Ministry of Munitions* admitted that accidents were 'so numerous that they won for bombers the name of "Suicide Club"'. The Lemon bombs, Nos '6' and '7' were not as bad, and were delivered in boxes of 40 together with four haversacks. However, not many were produced and to activate them required such a Herculean pull that sometimes it was like removing a cork from a bottle, or even needed the efforts of two men working together. The 'No 15' was produced in numbers, and was much like the ball grenades of yore. Frank Richards of the Royal Welch Fusiliers called it the 'cricket ball'.[1] It was effective enough, but only if well stored away from damp. It was a staple of combat as late as the battle of Loos.

Parallel developments took place amongst the Germans, and grenadiers had certainly commenced working in concert by January 1915. During the course of the year orders were issued that 'all infantrymen and pioneers must be trained in bombing just as thoroughly as they are trained with the rifle'. Soon the *Handgranatentrupp* of half a dozen, or seven, men was being promoted for both offensive and defensive actions. In the attack the assault groups moved as small scattered parties, not lines, and entered the enemy works as swiftly as possible. Once there they rolled up the line, 'bombing' along the trench, throwing grenades over the traverses and forming 'blocks' using sandbags, shields, spades and anything else that members of the party carried with them. On the defence the *Handgranatentrupp* went into action immediately, and unbidden by higher authority, as was illustrated by orders issued to 235th Reserve Infantry in December 1915:

All men of the party carry their rifles slung, bayonets fixed and daggers ready, with the exception of the two leaders, who do not carry rifles. The latter may carry as many grenades as they can conveniently handle and should if possible be armed with pistols. The commander, similarly armed, follows the two leading men... The remaining three men follow the others one traverse to the rear; they keep within sight of their commander, and carry as many grenades as possible. When possible the grenades are carried in their boxes. The two leading men advance along the trench in a crouching posture, so that the commander can fire over them. The interval between traverses is crossed at a rush.

By early 1916 the *Handgranatentrupp* was further refined so that it comprised eight men plus a leader. The eight could be broken down into two subsections of four, with the lead portion of the *Gruppe* composed of two 'throwers', with two 'carriers' in support. When necessary all four threw grenades, creating short but heavy showers of bombs. The lead team carried daggers and pistols, the follow up rifles and bayonets plus fresh supplies of grenades and sandbags. To deal with a blockhouse or machine gun post two members of the team would adopt sniping positions, keeping down the heads of the defenders whilst the remainder worked their way around the objective using shell holes or any other handy cover. Finally they would rush the position from unexpected angles.

By the middle of the war many commanders on both sides were becoming concerned that their men had gone 'bomb mad' – by which they meant that they tended to use bombs rather than rifles even when the latter was obviously the correct choice. Injunctions were issued demanding that skills with the rifle should be strictly maintained. Being 'bombed' was an almost uniquely terrifying experience, and one which Lieutenant Symons of the 2/8th Worcesters barely survived when caught out in No Man's Land just before dawn:

> The first thing I knew about it was a rifle going off point blank and I turned round and cursed the sniper who was with me as I thought he had let off his rifle. As I turned I saw the earth at his feet kick up and then a bullet came at my feet and I looked and saw a Hun at handshake distance firing. Luckily they were either so flurried or such putrid shots that they did not hit us, anyway I was in a shell hole almost instantaneously. But the second I got in I saw a hand grenade just falling in my hole so I dashed off and got into another five yards further away. As I ran they threw six at me which burst in a shower all round and I felt my left hand go numb as I fell into the crater and when I looked at it there was only a red pulp with splinters of bones and tendons in it on the end of my arm… I got out my field dressing and poured iodine over the jelly and put on the dressings as well as I could and then bound my arm to my stick with my tie. As soon as this was done I ate my maps with all the HQs marked on them.[2]

Whilst grenades in the hands of small teams were the first weapons to find chinks in the tyranny of lines and trenches many devices were tried with greater or lesser success. Trench mortars, catapults and rifle grenades had all existed before 1914, and all developed rapidly during the first 18 months of the war. It was also true that all applied the same basic principle of lobbing a missile at high angle, so that it would fall into, rather than shoot across, defensive works. The rifle grenades of 1914 were based on a pattern devised by Englishman Frederick Marten Hale. The payload of the bomb and its detonator were contained in a cylinder on the end of a rod. The rod was slid into the barrel of the service rifle, which was loaded with a special blank cartridge. Any safety device, such as a pin, was withdrawn, and the rifle fired at high angle. The pressure behind the rod forced the grenade out of the rifle at speed and the grenade shot off towards the enemy. Being nose heavy the end bearing the percussion device hit the ground first and exploded the grenade. The German rifle grenades were the models 1913 and 1914 and the main British type the 'J' Pattern, later known as the 'No 3'. Though such grenades were fairly local in their effects the impact could be increased by firing them off in volleys, perhaps from stands set to predetermined angles within the trench system. The 'No 3' was powerful enough to dissolve into a cloud of fragments on detonation likely to cause serious injury or death to anyone within a circle 10 feet in diameter, and quite a few injuries well beyond that range. Many other rodded designs, adapted for greater simplicity and ease of use, followed.

By 1916 Mills bombs were adapted for rifle projection, first with the addition of a rod, and finally by means of a cylindrical 'discharger'. The French, Germans and Americans all adopted rifle grenades projected from dischargers or cups later in the war. The French model, also used by US forces, was the 'Vivien Bessière'. Named after its inventors, Jean Vivien and Gustave Bessière, it was a small grenade fired from a muzzle attachment or '*tromblon*'. The cartridge used to launch the bomb was a bulleted round which passed through a channel in the grenade and ignited its fuse as it was launched. Though it was not adopted by the British Army the 'VB' grenade received its UK patent in January 1916. The German *Wurfgranate* of the late war period worked on the same principles.

MORTARS, CATAPULTS AND FLAME-THROWERS

The mortar was a weapon of surprising antiquity, having been in existence, primarily for siege operations, since about 1500. Interest in the development of modern 'trench mortars' stemmed from the Russo-Japanese War of 1904–05 and the battle for Port Arthur. It was the Germans who were most alert to the possibilities, noting how mortars might be applied to French fortifications in the future. A specification was therefore issued for the development of a *Minenwerfer* throwing a demolition charge of 110lb or greater; capable of accurate fire to at least 330 yards; plus combining compactness with the least possible weight. The first heavy trench mortars were deployed with German pioneers in 1910. Despite this lead even the Germans could field only 190 weapons at the outbreak of war. The result was the rapid development

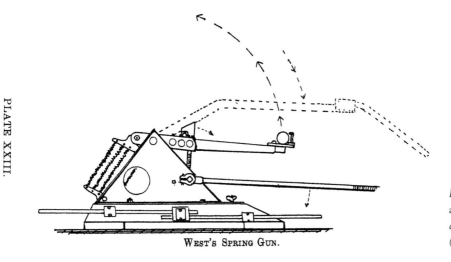

PLATE XXIII.

WEST'S SPRING GUN.

From the Australian Grenades and their Uses, *1916, showing a diagram of the West spring gun.* (*Author's collection*)

and deployment of several different stopgap mortars. These included the so-called 'Earth Mortar' which was a tube buried in the ground for lobbing a 52lb sheet steel projectile; the *Albrecht* with its wooden tube made in three calibres, and the *Iko Flügelminenwerfer*. The *Iko* was a particularly unwieldy smooth-bored beast with a massive base plate, throwing a 220lb projectile about 1,090 yards. At the other end of the scale was the little *Lanz* mortar capable of projecting 9lb shells about 440 yards.

Being on the receiving end of 'Minnie' fire was a terrifying and occasionally surreal experience. The mortar was usually concealed in a pit, and the sound of its discharge was less impressive than the bark or roar of ordinary artillery. The bombs were predominantly large but, being projected at high trajectories and relatively low velocities, could sometimes be seen tumbling or wobbling towards the ground through a serene arc. The blast created by large missiles was prodigious. Captain Hitchcock recalled that one blew his candle out, even in a dugout 20 feet below ground. For destroying all but deep dugouts and collapsing sections of trench nothing but the heaviest artillery could equal the effect. As George Coppard of the Machine Gun Corps recalled, 'men just disappeared and no one saw them go'.[3]

German soldier Karl Josenhans was uncomfortably close as he watched *Minenwerfer* bombs fall onto the French lines:

> One murderous instrument with which we have the advantage is the big trench mortar. They hurl huge shells about a thousand feet into the air and they fall almost vertically… Earth and branches are flung into the air to the height of a house, and although the shells fell 80 yards away from us, the ground under us shook. During the explosions I was looking through a periscope into the French trench opposite and could see terrified men running away to the rear. But somebody was evidently standing behind them with a revolver, for one after another they came crawling back again. This war is simply a matter of hounding men to death, and that is a degrading business.[4]

By 1916 German efforts focused on three standard models: a light 7.5cm, medium 17cm and heavy 25cm mortar. The following year it proved possible to replace whatever mortars were then held by the infantry with four 'new model' 7.5cm light *Minenwerfer* per battalion. All were capable of being shifted in wheeled carriages, though trench conditions meant that they were often dismantled and carried in pieces. In 1917 the light model *Minenwerfer* was also fitted with a flat trajectory carriage that allowed it to be used as a close support weapon, or even an anti-tank piece.

British trench mortars got off to a comparatively slow start, and not until October 1914 did Field Marshal French make a specific request for 'some special form of artillery' suitable for trench destruction. So it was that the British struggled for almost a year with inadequate numbers of inefficient, and often dangerous, stopgaps. The 5inch 'Trench Howitzer' that materialized in December was dismissed as both unwieldy and inaccurate, and a better Vickers Pattern, accepted in March 1915, was available only in pitiful numbers. Such efforts were supplemented by obsolete 19th-century French mortars, and some fashioned locally from piping.

Dramatic improvements commenced in mid 1915 with the first arrivals of the 2inch 'Trench Howitzer', colloquially known as the 'Toffee Apple' bomb-thrower. True to its nickname the key to the weapon was its projectile, a large spherical bomb mounted on a steel 'stick'. The bomb weighed 50lb and could be thrown 500 yards. By the time of the offensive on the Somme about 800 of these mortars were in use. An interesting refinement seen on some of them was a periscope attachment that enabled the firer to see the target from within the safety of a pit. A devastating salvo of Toffee Apples was witnessed by Wyn Griffith of the Royal Welch Fusiliers:

> A pop, and then a black ball went soaring up, spinning round as it went through the air slowly; more pops and more queer birds against the sky. A stutter of terrific detonations seemed to shake the air and the ground, sandbags and bits of timber sailed up slowly, and fell in a calm deliberate way. In the silence that followed the explosions, an angry voice called out in English, across No Man's Land, 'You bloody Welsh Murderers'.[5]

Ammunition for the 2inch trench mortar, or 'Toffee Apple' bomb thrower, being brought up on the Somme, Acheux, 28 June 1916. The projectile heads are seen being picked up from the large dump and carried on blocks with a harness across a waterlogged ditch, which has been bridged using wooden 18pdr ammunition boxes. The metal projectile 'sticks' or tails were fitted to the explosive heads prior to firing. (IWM Q747)

At the end of 1915 the French 9.45inch heavy 'flying pig' design was also added to the British inventory. Parallel work in the UK also led to the development of the remarkable Stokes mortar, brainchild of Wilfrid Stokes of Ipswich. The Stokes was simple, consisting essentially of a barrel and pair of legs, and a bomb that slid into the mortar tail first. It met four vital criteria: simplicity, speed, lightness and ease of setting up. Despite teething difficulties it was introduced in 1916, and within a year had proved its efficiency. Its basic design has informed that of mortars the world over, ever since.

The trench mortars of both friend and foe were distinctly unloved by the front line infantryman, not least because one of their most favoured tactics was to displace before any retaliation occurred. As C. J. Arthur put it:

> The trench mortar batteries used to come up and let off a few rounds, then go back. We were left to patch up the trenches after the usual replies from the 'minnie' brigade. Those *Minenwerfers*! I shall never forget their soul-destroying qualities. To be hit by something you could not see was not too bad, but to see something coming, sufficient to blow a crater of 15 feet diameter and not know which way to go to avoid it, was enough to destroy the nerve of a suit of armour. You can imagine, therefore, how decidedly unpopular the trench mortar batteries became.[6]

It is perhaps surprising that the catapult, siege weapon of the ancients, should have gained a new lease of life early in World War I. That it did was due at least in part to the early lack of more modern equipments such as mortars and rifle grenades. Like the ancient weapons many of the new catapults worked on two basic principles – the sprung arm and the bow. One built by the Cambridgeshire Regiment in Ploegsteert Wood was indeed a direct copy of a Roman machine, inspired by the classical scholarship of a Cambridge professor. A few others depended on elasticity, being not unlike overgrown schoolboys' catapults. Most threw some form of grenade, or an extemporized Jam Tin. In addition to being relatively easy to produce these catapults had the not inconsiderable advantage of being comparatively quiet. Conversely they were not always easy to mount and conceal, had relatively short range, and were quickly outclassed by better weapons. In British official nomenclature they were 'Bomb Engines'; in the German, *Wurfmaschinen*, or 'Throwing Engines'.

Some catapults were local improvisations or patented inventions that never got much beyond the experimental. Various French devices using the leaf springs of lorries and assortments of bicycle parts would seem to conform to these descriptions. Nevertheless certain types saw widespread use. Amongst these were the French Sauterelle, and the Leach catapult and West spring gun in British service. The Leach, devised by C. P. Leach of South Kensington in 1914, was a large fork, rubber springs and a sling to hold the projectile. It was also known as the 'Gamage's' catapult, since the famous London store was co-patentee, and the production version of the device was built in their factory. Amazingly Leach catapults were issued on a scale of 20 per division in 1915.

The West spring gun, issued on the same scale as the Leach, relied on an arm whose vicious forward and upward flick was powered by a battery of steel springs. Downward pressure on a cocking leaver by two or three men set the mechanism. It could be carried into position by stretcher-like handles, and required sandbags on its base to prevent it bucking crazily on discharge. Guy Chapman thought that the West was likely to decapitate its user, and its dangerous reputation was certainly confirmed by a November 1915 report in the 144th Brigade War Diary:

Lieutenant Schwalm, 6th Glosters, Brigade Grenadier Officer, was killed whilst firing the West bomb thrower, his foot slipped and his head was hit by the arm of the machine, after the spring had been released. This is not the first accident which has occurred with this machine, a very cumbersome one from which the results obtained are no means commensurate with the dangers incurred by the user and the difficulty in manoeuvring it.

A series of drawings from the French Platoon Leader's Manual, *1917 showing a grenade throwing sequence. (Author's collection)*

Fig. 10 *bis.* — Tearing the safety-pin out of the igniter.

Fig. 11. — Aiming at the objective *with* extended left arm, the grenade being held in the right hand.

Fig. 12. — Left arm kept in the direction of the objective. Right arm carried back.

Fig. 13. — Left arm without change, right hand back, arm extended. Look at the grenade and see that nothing will hinder its throwing.

Fig. 14. — Look again at the objective. Describe with right arm an arc in a vertical plane.

Fig. 15. — Let go the grenade, right shoulder and body following right arm movement. Left arm follows left shoulder which is refused. The grenades will go in the direction aimed at with the left arm

Experimentation with the weird and wonderful continued even after the demise of the West and Leach. In June 1916, for example, the Munitions Design Committee looked at a 'Rotary Apparatus for Throwing Grenades' designed by a Sergeant Day. This operated on the centrifugal principle, and once cranked up to speed the user consulted a 'speedometer' which indicated how far the bomb would fly on release. Though the machine was deemed portable, and a test determined that grenades could be flung fairly accurately to 150 yards, it was decided that the weapon was 'unsuited to the service'. Another eight-armed centrifugal device designed by a Mr Bonnafous was also rejected by the same sitting of the Committee.

Flame weapons had existed since classical times – but a portable, practical, device for the battlefield had only been perfected in Germany in the years leading up to war. The first *Flammenwerfer* attack was made against the French at Malancourt in February 1915.

Before long 'liquid fire' was also turned on the British at Hooge. In part the flame-thrower was a terror weapon – since it was very short range and for many it was totally demoralizing – but not all were daunted. Captain Hitchcock reported that the Leinsters were taught to aim specifically at those carrying the *Flammenwerfer* tanks, who had a heavy burden to carry, and could on occasion ignite with 'a colossal burst'. Later the 2nd Royal Welch Fusiliers were treated to a demonstration with a captured flame-thrower, which they found more amusing than expected because, 'its premature operation scorched some of the staff'. An eyewitness of a flame attack was Guy Chapman at Third Ypres:

> The enemy were attacking under cover of *Flammenwerfer*, hose pipes leading to petrol tanks carried on the backs of men. When the nozzles were lighted, they threw out a roaring, hissing flame 20 or 30 feet long, swelling at the end to an oily rose, 6 feet in diameter. Under protection of these hideous weapons, the enemy surrounded the advance pillbox, stormed it and killed the garrison.[7]

Remarkably the German flame attack soon generated its own very specific *modus operandi*. As outlined in late 1915 the textbook assault began with the blowing of charges to create holes in the barbed wire, then on the sound of a siren or whistle the discharge of large static flame-throwers. The conflagration from these fixed devices was vicious, but lasted only a minute, at the end of which the attackers would swarm from their trenches – often up short ladders that had been specially positioned. Taught that small amounts of burning fuel left on the ground posed no serious threat they would hurry on before the defenders had a chance to react. The first wave were the 'assaulting party' with man pack flame-throwers,[8] grenades, rifles with fixed bayonets and engineers with charges for blowing strong points or stubborn wire. The men would be dressed in 'assault order', and have with them at least two grenades and 200 rounds of ammunition. These were followed by a 'consolidating party' whose job was to hold the trenches captured. In the rear followed a 'carrying party', to bring up grenades, ammunition and other stores, and the 'communication trench construction party' whose much longer and laborious task was to connect the works captured with existing saps. As the attack unfolded artillery and mortars would open fire, shelling selected positions – thus supporting the assault as it unfolded rather than giving the enemy prior warning. Captain P. Christison of 6th Cameron Highlanders faced the peril of the flame-thrower at Passchendaele:

> There was no immediate counter-attack, but towards dusk one came in – headed by flame-throwers to add to our misery. This was a new one. Our rifles and light machine guns were now useless, being gummed up with mud, and we had to hurl grenades and use pick handles in close combat. One had no time to feel frightened it all happened so quickly. I saw a large Hun about to aim his flame-thrower in my direction and Company Sergeant Major Adams with great presence of mind fired his Verey pistol at the man… The round hit the flame-thrower and with a scream the man collapsed in a sheet of flame.[9]

In terms of producing flame weapons the Allied response was patchy. Arguably the French learned the techniques most quickly, and a patent for a French portable flame-thrower was lodged by March 1915. The British concentrated on fixed flame projectors. An American devised a bizarre 'flaming bayonet', which, perhaps fortunately, appears never to have reached the battlefield. As so often happened response then met with counter-response as the Germans issued instructions that their own artillery should be concentrated wherever possible on enemy flame projectors, whilst the infantry focused on attempting 'to shoot the men carrying the small apparatus', whose dangerous burdens would then become a hindrance to the men around them.

An MG 08 deployed on an improvised wooden based 'trench mount', 1917. The standard mount of the MG 08 weighed 70lb – not counting any armoured shield, cooling water, spare barrel or ammunition. Attempts to increase battlefield mobility led to the use of many different lightweight mounts, and eventually the introduction of a tripod, though this was never a universal issue. Finally the '08' was replaced in the attack by the somewhat lighter 08/15 with shoulder stock and bipod. This team, wearing 1915 type gas masks, are led by an NCO (right) with the oval arm badge of the MG 'Sharpshooter' detachments. These independent Scharfschützen units were allocated wherever circumstance demanded rather than tied to an individual infantry regiment or battalion. (Author's collection)

LIGHT MACHINE GUNS

Perhaps more than anything it was the development of the light machine gun that helped free the infantry from pedestrian tactics – and whilst the Germans could claim leads in the fields of the grenade, mortar, light weight artillery and flame-thrower the British had a definitive head start in this area. The Lewis gun, initially referred to by some as an 'automatic rifle', was first designed by an American before the war and was under production in Birmingham by August 1914. It weighed about 29lb, against the 90lb of Vickers gun and tripod. The immediate priority was that the air-cooled Lewis should be adapted for use for aircraft, but before the year was out demand for machine weapons of any type – and a growing realization that lightness had advantages – saw its experimental introduction with the infantry. A gradual build up in Lewis gun numbers allowed the heavy Vickers guns to be withdrawn from the infantry and placed together into the companies of the Machine Gun Corps, which was founded in October 1915. Thereafter Lewis gun numbers continued to increase in the ranks of the infantry, to two per company by the Somme, and to at least one per platoon during 1917.

Whilst it had long been realized that Lewis guns had greater flexibility to be hidden or rapidly redeployed in and around the front line trenches, and the long range of the Vickers suited it better to flanks or positions further back, the organizational separation of the two hastened tactical reassessment. A key instruction in this development was *Notes on the Tactical Employment of Machine Guns and Lewis Guns*, issued in March 1916. This drew a clear distinction in tactical roles. Lewis guns complemented heavier machine guns, but could not entirely replace them, nevertheless:

> Owing to its lightness and the small target that it offers, the Lewis gun is of great value in an attack. It is particularly adapted for providing covering fire from the front during the first stage of an attack. Lewis gunners, under cover of darkness, smoke, or artillery bombardment, may be able to creep out in front and establish themselves in shell holes, ditches, crops, long grass etc., where it will be difficult for them to be detected, and where they will be able to fire on enemy machine gun emplacements, loopholes and parapets generally, and so assist the infantry to advance. Covering fire on the flanks of the attack, must, however, be provided by machine guns as they can keep up a sustained fire from stationary platforms on previously considered objectives.

At this stage, however, it was thought that Lewis guns should not be in the forefront of the attack proper – an opinion that was later modified.

The withdrawal of the Vickers guns from the infantry to the companies of the Machine Gun Corps was not met with universal approval, but this mass of heavy firepower did allow more imaginative long-range saturation tactics. Machine gun 'barrage fire' was defined by *The Employment of Machine Guns*, Part 2 as, 'the fire of a large number of guns acting under centralised control, directed on to definite lines

or areas, in which the frontage engaged by a gun approximates [to] 40 yards'. Commonly guns would be concentrated in 'batteries' of from four to eight machine guns, and anything up to 24 guns in several batteries would make up a 'group'. The wall of bullets thus generated could be used for a number of different purposes: preventing enemy troop and supply movements; destroying morale; preventing the operation of working parties; creating a protective screen of fire; general harassing, or suppressing enemy fire. Machine gun barrages could also supplement artillery barrages, being worked progressively over areas or adding a surprise element at intervals. By regulation a 'slow' barrage was 60–75 rounds per minute per gun (in bursts of 15–25 rounds); 'medium' 125–150rpm; and 'rapid' 250–300rpm. It may thus be seen that a full size group firing a 'rapid barrage' was capable of dropping over 7,000 rounds per minute into a relatively confined space.

Interestingly, the French had quickly come to the conclusion that light machine weapons would be useful for 'walking fire', in which a two-man team could fire on the move – or rather more practically go prone from time to time during the advance. Unfortunately it was some time before the 1915 model French Chauchat could be made in quantity, and worse, the gun itself proved unreliable, unergonomic and intolerant of mud. The concept of carrying light machine guns into the forefront of

A selection of automatic weapons from the trenches. Left to right: German 08/15 light machine gun; Bergman 'MP 18' Maschinenpistole; British Lewis gun; and French Chauchat model 1915 or 'CSRG' machine rifle. The MP 18 was the first true sub-machine gun, firing a 9mm pistol type round from a 32-round magazine. Designed for trench clearance and mobile attack it came too late to have a significant impact on events. (Author's collection)

the attack remained, however, and sooner or later all the major armies included a sling with their weapons.

The German MG 08/15 light machine gun was much more reliable than the Chauchat, but also took time to bring into production, and was actually quite weighty at 43lb. As Georg Bucher recalled:

> I wasn't at all enthusiastic about that latest type of gun – in the first place I was unable, with the best will in the world, to understand why the clumsy things should be called 'light', and secondly, the old heavy gun was my favourite weapon because of its reliability and precision.[10]

Nevertheless the introduction of the 08/15 was one of the things that allowed the German infantry to adopt more flexible 'self supporting' tactics in the latter part of the war. German Sixth Army instructions on the use of the new gun recommended three-man teams, who were to carry carbines for close protection, or in the event of mechanical failure of the machine gun. Initially it was intended that the weapon be positioned near to the platoon commander, and that the battalion commander keep a reserve of these guns in hand for use in counter-attacks. Ideally the 08/15s, which were highly suitable for flanking fire, were to be 'posted in the first line, in shell craters, or in other available places which have been reconnoitred in advance'. Where possible two different guns were to be able to cover one piece of ground. As the 08/15 was not suitable for overhead fire direct lines of sight to the targets were needed, but it was ideal for 'mobile defence' and bursts of 'harassing fire' in short surprise volleys.

German MG 08/15 team. Devised in 1915, but not reaching the front in large numbers until 1917, the new 'light' machine gun was still water-cooled, belt fed, and weighed about 43lb. Nevertheless its widespread issue down to small unit level made possible much more flexible tactics in which machine gun support could be carried forward at the pace of the infantry platoon. Note the use of the weapon's distinctive wooden shoulder stock and the 250-round metal ammunition boxes shown here. Some guns were fitted with a detachable drum magazine. (Author's collection)

As the German manual observed:

It should not be forgotten, however, that the precision of the 08/15 machine gun is limited and that this fact must be taken into account in regulating and utilisation. The gun must never completely take the place of infantry, but on the contrary, the infantry must have clearly in mind that for them the 08/15 machine gun is only a means of increasing their firing capacity. By reasons of imperfections of a technical order the 08/15 model does not serve entirely to replace the 1908 machine gun.

The initial American approach was summed up by the document *Notes on the Use of Machine Guns in Trench Warfare*, issued in March 1917:

In trench warfare as it exists in Europe, automatic machine rifles, popularly called machine guns, find their greatest use. Besides the trench, the essential elements of the trench line consist of a depth of wire and a front of machine guns. The tremendous stopping power of machine guns enable them to replace a large number of riflemen along

German booty captured by the South Staffordshire Regiment on the Somme. The weaponry includes nine MG 08 machine guns, a bayonet and a G98 rifle with special 20-round 'trench magazine'. Towards the centre are boxes of communications equipment. In the foreground are spiked helmets or Pickelhauben *from Baden and Bavarian units; steel helmets; and a trench club. (IWM Q162)*

The archaeology of a mortar pit: Vimy Ridge.

On the battlefields of the Western Front, even those now preserved as memorial parks, trenches and shell holes can often appear as surprisingly gentle or shallow features. In some areas this may be because of high water tables which impeded deep excavations – but more usually it is due to 'solifluction', or soil flow. Observed over time soil may act more akin to a liquid than a solid, creeping to restore uniform levels. This phenomenon is more pronounced, and may occur more rapidly, in sandy or muddy conditions – indeed, geomorphologists commonly divide movement into 'wet mud flow', and 'wet' and 'dry' sand flow. The following illustrations show such effects on a German mortar position constructed according to standard plans.

A) Mortar position schematic from the latter half of the war. The oblong cavity is framed with timber and accessed from the rear by five steps down. Overhead cover is of a sandwich construction, which includes baulks of wood, concrete and sand. This arrangement is designed to burst shells before they can penetrate the pit and absorb shock and fragments. The high angle of outgoing fire means that the embrasure is effectively a large, steeply sloping slot in the ground, presenting no direct target to the enemy. (Author's collection)

B) Inter-war photo of a preserved sandbagged pit within the Canadian memorial park at Vimy, c.1930. A medium Minenwerfer, together with its accoutrements and a helmet, is correctly positioned with a circular traversing base on the floor of the pit, its muzzle pointing up through the steeply sloping port. However, soil flow has already commenced, as can be seen from the vegetation pattern. (Author's collection)

C) Author's photo showing the same structure in 1988. Over just half a century almost a foot of soil has flowed in through the aperture, burying the weapon so that the deep base plate is now flush with the ground level. The lintel over the pit embrasure, some of the cement sandbags, and all the small artefacts, have disappeared whilst the mortar has been broken from its mount. Rather than re-excavation to conserve the monument poor restoration techniques have included blocking up the embrasure with an additional three courses of sandbags in a vain effort to prevent flow, and the placing of an anachronistic concrete 'duckboard' to keep visitors' feet clear of the mud. The impression created is of a very shallow concrete bagged pit, quite unlike the original. (Author's collection)

D) Contemporary photo showing how the medium Minenwerfer was disassembled for movement over rough terrain, with the heavy barrel slung between four of the crew. (IWM Q23723)

E) An extemporized battlefield variation on the textbook mortar pit showing how the medium Minenwerfer was muzzle loaded, an operation requiring particular care as the barrel was rifled, and the shell weighed 110lb. It could be fired at a maximum speed of one round per minute. The range of the 17cm medium Minenwerfer was about 985 yards, and the projectiles included high explosive and gas munitions. According to Notes on German Shells, 1918, explosive rounds of this calibre were likely to create shell holes 5 feet deep and almost 10 feet across in clay; even larger holes were blown in other types of soil. (IWM Q56544)

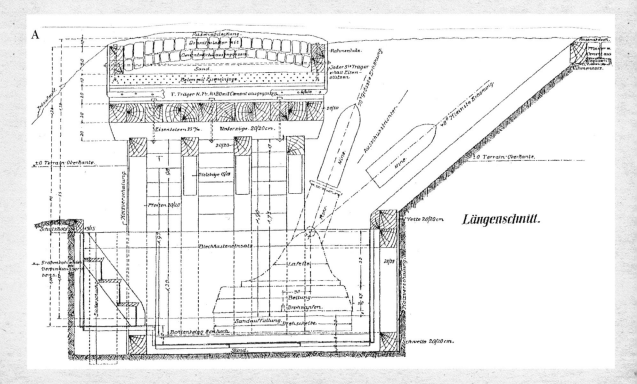

this line, reducing to a minimum the men employed in actual defence, thereby leaving a large part of the force in reserve for use in the counter-attack, or for the assumption of the offensive at another part of the line. Their use also reduces the daily wastage due to sickness, and prevents the offensive spirit of the infantry from becoming impaired.

Somewhat optimistically this manual claimed that the US Benet-Mercie model 1909 gun could fulfil all of the roles of both the machine gun proper and the machine rifle. Sadly this proved to be an exaggeration of its capabilities, and in fact American forces used a number of different types of machine gun depending on availability and which ally they were fighting alongside.

American instructions took particular note of the painful lessons that had been learned in offensives prior to 1917:

Experience in Europe has been that some machine guns and crews have always survived, ready to emerge and open a flanking, annihilating fire against the enemy's advancing infantry and the more oblique has been this cross fire the greater has been

The German 7.6cm 'new type' light Minenwerfer. *This rifled mortar fired a 11lb shell to a range of over half a mile, and could be used with both high explosive and gas munitions. At the beginning of 1917 four of these weapons were directly attached to each infantry battalion, replacing obsolete models and providing immediate fire support. Pictured in September 1918 with men of a* Landsturm *infantry unit this mortar is in a low-trajectory mounting on a wheeled travelling carriage. (Author's collection)*

Arguably the oldest of the Irish regiments, the origins of The Royal Irish Regiment date back to 1683. The regiment fought for William III in Ireland at the Battle of the Boyne, and in 1695 was honoured with the title of The Royal Regiment of Ireland becoming the 18th (The Royal Irish Regiment of Foot in 1751. In 1881 it became The Royal Irish Regiment.

1914 - 1918

Four new service battalions were raised in 1914 as well as two reserve and two garrison battalions and served with a range of divisions throughout the war. The 5th formed part of the 10th (Irish) Division at Gallipoli, while the 6th fought with the 16th (Irish) Division at the Somme and later absorbed the 7th Battalion into its ranks. The 1st Battalion served in the Near and Middle East while the 2nd Battalion served on the Western Front and later became part of the 16th (Irish) Division.

First World War Battle Honours include:

Mons, Suvla, Somme, Serbia and Messines.

The Regiment was disbanded in 1922.

On pourrait affirmer que 'The Royal Irish Regiment' est le plus ancien des 'Irish Regiments' (Régiments Irlandais) puisque ses origines remontent à l'année 1683.

Certains bataillons de ce régiment combattirent au sein d'un grand nombre de divisions au cours de la première guerre mondiale, notamment la 10ème Division irlandaise à Gallipoli et la 16ème Division irlandaise sur le front de l'ouest.

Le régiment fut dissous en 1922.

British 2inch 'Trench Howitzer' or 'Toffee Apple' bomb thrower in the visitor centre at the Ulster Tower, Thiepval. A suitable riposte to the German Minenwerfer, *the Trench Howitzer packed a heavy punch. During the Somme these weapons were in positions just a few hundred yards from this display example. (Author's collection)*

its effect… Emplacements in front of the firing line are made by digging narrow trenches of the same depth as the firing trench to the front, 15 or 20 feet, and then turning them to the right or left and then widening them out to accommodate the guns and crews. The gun rests solidly on the ground at the end of this cul de sac, which is sunk just low enough below the natural ground to conceal it when in position… Where opposing trenches are close together and machine guns would be subject to capture by raid if placed in the front line trench or in front of it, this danger can be avoided by emplacing them behind the parados of the firing trench. This position will give a better field of fire, and, owing to the feeling of safety which this position inspires, the men will work their gun with more coolness and judgement than if the gun were sited in the parapet or in front of it.

Though it was appreciated that the machine gun officer was required to handle gun with 'boldness and cunning', US instructions did not immediately recognize that automatic weapons had a role in the spearhead of the attack. The initial theory was that machine weapons should be in the 'fourth wave'. When moving forward it was stated that 'the machine guns should mix with the infantry and try to disguise their identity as much as possible'. Combat experience and acquaintance with the woeful Chauchat made many in the US Army realize that both equipment and tactics needed swift and drastic revision. If anything the later American version of the French automatic rifle was worse than the original since it was modified to fire the more powerful .30 cartridge. This, and rushed production, tested the already dubious Chauchat beyond its capabilities. However, at the eleventh hour, and in a complete reversal of fortune, US forces received what was arguably one of the best light support weapons, the Browning automatic rifle, or 'BAR'. Weighing 22lb it was lighter than the Lewis gun, and fired from a modern-looking 20-round box magazine. It has been criticized for production problems and lack of great accuracy, but this was not the point – it was capable of going where platoons and squads went, at much the same speed, and when it arrived in the summer of 1918 it was more than a match for anything else used in this role.

Opposite:
Men of 1st Cameronians using a Vermorel spray for gas dispersal within a trench, May 1915. One man directs the nozzle, the other demonstrates the pump mechanism on the liquid 'hypo solution' reservoir. The device could also be operated by one man wearing the reservoir strapped on his back. Both men wear masks with eye protection. (IWM Q51647)

CHAPTER FIVE

GAS

That poison gas might be used in war was appreciated in the late 19th century, and in 1899 an international convention at the Hague committed its signatories not to 'deploy projectiles the sole use of which is the diffusion of asphyxiating or harmful gases'. Though well meaning the exact form of words would come back to haunt the nations attempting to avoid the worst horrors of chemical warfare. For the convention did not outlaw all gas, or its development, though it did appear to curtail the most likely delivery systems. The result was that the major nations continued to experiment with tear gases, which were not considered to cause long-term harm, and after the outbreak of war research with other substances was intensified. Small-scale and ineffective early usage of irritants by both the French and Germans went unnoticed, whilst Britain developed a substance known as 'SK', or 'South Kensington', named after the location where trials were made.

In April 1915 these Lilliputian efforts were suddenly overtaken when the Germans, working to methods devised by Professor Fritz Haber, employed the brutally practical expedient of opening large cylinders of chlorine gas at their own front line and allowing the billowing yellowish green contents to drift across to the enemy. So was born the gas 'cloud' or 'cylinder' attack. Launched at Ypres on 22 April by men of Pioneer Battalion 35, Operation *Disinfekt* came as a surprise to its victims. It should not have done, as an enemy prisoner named Auguste Jäger had recently been captured in possession of a respirator, and had mentioned gas cylinders. Elsewhere Belgian Army intelligence had corroborated his story. Lance Corporal Keddie of 48th Royal Highlanders of Canada was witness to the attack, whose worst effects fell on French colonial and territorial troops:

> My company was in the reserve trenches … we noticed volumes of dense yellow smoke rising up and coming towards the British trenches. We did not get the full effect of it, but what we did was enough for me. It makes my eyes smart and run. I became violently sick, but this passed off fairly soon. By this time the din was something awful – we were under a crossfire of rifles and shells, and had to lie flat in the trenches. The next thing I noticed was a horde of Turcos making for our trenches behind the firing line; some were armed, some unarmed. The poor devils were absolutely paralysed with fear.[1]

As it turned out fear was justified, for chlorine was fatal if enough was inhaled, killing by irritating the lungs so badly that they flooded with fluid, effectively drowning the victim, who fell to the ground starved of oxygen, choking, face turning blue. About 4,000 were killed or injured that April afternoon. The French fled, in one famous German description, 'like a flock of sheep'. Only with difficulty did the Canadians block the breach. Sir John French would call this attack 'a cynical and barbarous disregard of the well known usages of war … as a soldier I cannot help expressing the deepest regret and some surprise that an Army which hitherto has claimed to be the chief exponent of chivalry of war should have stooped to employ such devices against brave and gallant foes'.[2] W. A. Quinton of 1st Bedfordshires – who was gassed in another attack not long afterwards – described the experience as like having his 'lungs burnt out' and needles thrust into the eyes.[3] Often the first impulse on getting a whiff of gas was to run, but all too often this involved leaving the relative safety of the trench to become a target for bullets.

Dramatic and dangerous as this debut of chemical combat was, post battle analysis would ascertain that gas was not a wonder weapon ready to win the war. First and foremost it was unpredictable – it required careful preparation to make an attack, but there was no guarantee that weather conditions would oblige. Wind in the wrong direction blew gas back across the attacker's own forces; wind too strong would dissipate the fumes before they had a chance to reach their target. Moreover wherever it went gas would not discriminate between friend and foe, and it took organization to get sufficient troops to follow up close enough to the gas clouds to take good advantage of their disabling effects.

Naturally those on the receiving end now gave gas protection measures the highest priority. The very next day the Paris municipal laboratory was set to work, as simultaneously British headquarters issued its first anti-gas instructions. These were pretty desperate, and included the idea of rolling a handkerchief into a ball, putting it into the mouth and breathing through it. Prolonged exposure was to be combated by a 'piece of flannel' tied around the head and breathing in through the mouth and out through the nose. Within a few days the British and Canadians were

German soldiers in a firing position wearing the 1915 model rubberized fabric or 'gummi' type gas mask, with detachable filter. The NCO nearest to the camera demonstrates the action of the standard G98 Mauser rifle, showing how the cartridges are loaded into the five round integral magazine from the top, with the bolt open, using a charger. The trench is lined with planking and has both a fire step and duckboards standing clear of the earth floor. (Author's collection)

battling in gas with a variety of improvised protections varying from cloth dipped in urine to face pads with tapes run up by the nuns of Poperinge. Failing all else marginal relief was sought from cotton bandoliers dipped in water. Soon alkaline solutions were being produced specifically for gas neutralization, and masks impregnated to much better effect. Thereafter there was a race between those developing more deadly gases and better ways to deliver them, and those devising new methods of protection. New gases were inevitably followed by new gas masks, or new filters to be fitted to existing masks. This struggle would last until the end of the war. In the process gas would demonstrate its horrible potential as a weapon of debilitation, fear, injury and 'neutralization', but it would never become as deadly as high explosive, nor – since both sides used it – could it ever give one side anything like a war winning advantage.

Firing gas shells from artillery pieces became increasingly common from mid 1915, and quickly gained favour with German tacticians who saw this method of delivery as ideal for maintaining surprise and effective targeting of specific points. British theorists were less sure initially because the volumes of gas delivered by shells were relatively small, and if cylinders released gas, then guns were free to fire high explosive and shrapnel. Nevertheless shell delivery became increasingly significant with time, and many types of artillery weapon and mortar were eventually matched with a gas projectile. Gas shells came as a considerable surprise, hitting targets that were previously regarded as invulnerable to gas attack. In July 1916, for example, 1/8th Worcesters were working on a communication trench when they were suddenly bombarded with a new type of gas shell. Only eight men avoided some degree of gassing – and 400 were still unfit some time later. Gradually, however, gas 'shoots' became more familiar, and troops learned to recognize the distinctive sounds of the arrival of chemical munitions. Some projectiles opened with a 'plop', far quieter than high explosive; others a double bang.

Also in mid 1915 the Germans introduced a new lung irritant known as *K-Stoff*. Phosgene, much more virulent than chlorine, and more difficult to detect, was in use before the end of the year. On the downside phosgene was lighter and had greater tendency to dissipate, and was therefore often mixed with chlorine to produce a lingering toxic cloud. Various other toxic gases, including the so-called 'arsenical compounds' were introduced, but 'blistering agents' were arguably the most significant gas development of the latter part of the war. The most famous of these was initially identified simply as 'H. S.' or 'Hun Stuff', but, owing to its distinctive smell was soon known as 'mustard gas'. The key point about 'mustard', also known as Yperite, or 'Yellow Cross' from the markings on German shells, was that it affected not only the respiratory system and eyes, but any part of the body it came into contact with. Soon after introduction it was causing more casualties than all the other German gas munitions combined. As the regimental history of the Liverpool Scottish explained:

German gas Pioniere *prepare cylinders for a 'cloud' gas attack, 1915. The containers are partly dug into the firing step of the position for stability and partial protection against shell splinters, forming a* Flaschen *(bottle or cylinder) battery. The pioneers wear the 1914 Dräger type* Selbstretter *or oxygen re-breather apparatus. The insert shows a soldier of 245th Reserve Infantry Regiment with the gas protection current for other troops in April 1915, the* Reichpäckchen *pad with tapes, which was stored in a rubberized bag on the uniform when not in use. (© Richard Hook, Osprey Publishing)*

It was impossible to avoid casualties in a heavy concentration of this gas. The box respirator protected the throat and eyes but the dense fumes which hung about shell holes attacked the skin – especially the softer parts of it – and caused painful sores. In these circumstances the kilt is not an ideal garment.

'Mustard' also lingered for a week or more depending on weather conditions, and both sides used it to hamper movement, or deny areas of the battlefield to the enemy. Private Dolden of the London Scottish had a narrow escape:

Opposite:
Bombers of the 1st Scots Guards
in 'Big Willie' trench at Loos,
October 1915. The open Mills
bomb box shows how they are
packed: six at either end with a
tin of igniter sets in the middle.
A 'key' for removing the base
plugs of the bombs was included
under the lid of the tin. One of
the guardsmen, left, wears his
'PH' gas helmet rolled up on his
head; others carry them in bags
on straps over the shoulder.
(IWM Q17390)

We came to a shell hole in which there was an unusual kind of yellow powder, and a peculiar smell. I took a good sniff and declared that there had been gas in the shells. This was something new… Robertson took a sniff and said it was not gas, and a long argument ensued during which we both took a few new sniffs and then went along to the dugout to call the Gas Corporal… He took a mild sniff and then chased off like mad yelling 'Gas'… I was very lucky to get away with that 'packet' as lightly as I did, for I must have taken quite a lot of gas into my lungs with the many sniffs that I took. The ground had become so impregnated with the gas that all the troops were ordered out of the area, and the trench was put out of bounds. I was unwell during the morning, and had a shocking headache, and completely lost my voice… The next day Robertson was worse, and had to be led to the aid post with a bandage round his eyes, for he could not bear the light on them. There was a continuous stream of water running from my eyes, and they were very inflamed and sore. I was in chronic pain, as my head, throat, eyes, and lungs ached unmercifully. In addition the mustard gas had burnt me severely in a certain delicate part of my anatomy.[4]

Dolden's story sounds incredible. Nevertheless those exposed to mustard gas for any length of time tended to lose their sense of smell, making them more vulnerable. Moreover concentrations could build up gradually, and a delayed effect, particularly where the gas was encountered in limited quantities, was a well-known phenomenon.

Some idea of the injuries caused by gas can be gleaned from the pages of the British official *Medical History.* Here are described the suffocating effects of chlorine and phosgene, and the terrible burns of 'mustard'. Blister casualties might be virtually flayed or blinded, and some types of gas – like the 'arsenical compounds' – produced psychological as well as physical symptoms. Yet gas, for all its terrors, remained surprisingly non-lethal. According to 1915 British statistics, of 12,792 personnel treated for gas symptoms, only 307 died, and almost all of the others returned to duty. Of a sample of 23,626 treated for 'gas poisoning' in the latter part of the war 93 per cent were eventually fit to return to duty, and just over 3 per cent died. By contrast, statistics from 1917 showing casualties from all causes suggest that roughly half of bullet wounds were categorized as 'serious', and that in general almost 10 per cent of wounded men died. In short, if you could get medical help the chances of surviving a 'gassing' were very high, and a decent gas mask, and instruction on how to don it at the first sign of trouble, were correctly identified as the best way to combat the problem. Paradoxically, the evil reputation of the insidious menace of gas would be upheld over coming decades by the numbers of men who were gassed but survived. Larger numbers who were hit by shells and bullets never left the battlefields.

Considering the numbers needing to be equipped and the continual discovery of new gases, the invention, manufacture and distribution of new protection was surprisingly quick. In May 1915 the British brought in the so-called 'Black Veiling' respirator, which, although only a crude pad, was soaked in a 'hypo' solution,

PASSCHENDAELE

From the Zonnebeke sheet, 28 N.E. 1, 1:10,000, corrected to 30 June 1917. 'Passchendaele' – now popularly synonymous with the entirety of the muddy Third Battle of Ypres, which commenced on 31 July and continued until 10 November 1917 – was actually two specific engagements within the larger campaign whose main objectives were to expel the enemy from the Belgian coast and relieve pressure on Britain's allies. Thus it is the 'First Battle of Passchendaele' commenced on 12 October, with a second starting on 26 October. The German defensive line *Flandern II* ran south and west of the village, but by this time the emphasis was less on narrow continuous trench lines – which were in any case very difficult to maintain in this waterlogged terrain – but on wide zones, strong points and concrete works. Even by the time of the First Passchendaele the village had virtually ceased to exist. Its demise was witnessed by the war correspondent of *The Times* in a report printed on 13 October:

> Nearly six weeks ago I described the village of Passchendaele, which stands on the summit of the ridge, as even then we could see it, with its many red roofed buildings still more or less intact among the uninjured trees. Since then it has changed. Our shells have stripped and splintered the trees, and only here and there bits of pink roofs remain over the area of tumbled masonry. While our men are fighting in the awful swamp region directly under and before this edge of the ridge, to the right the topmost ridge is in our hands … there is no possible question that our men are fighting with desperate determination to do all they set out so to do, and if they fail in any detail it will be the weather and the mud that stop them.

Mobility was achieved only with the most extreme difficulty over ground that in many places was now impassable even for tanks. A modest walking speed was maintainable only on duckboard tracks, which were easily destroyed and tended to channel movement. Maintaining direction also became difficult even with a map, because most things had disappeared. As Captain Glanville of 2nd Royal Dublin Fusiliers put it, 'Mud awful, no trenches, no shelters, no landmarks'. Perhaps most important was the problem of moving artillery, supplies and ammunition, without which attacks could not even be attempted.

Passchendaele from the air, before and after the 1917 offensive that virtually obliterated the village. In the second photograph the only structure readily identifiable is the church, completely wrecked, but still maintaining its distinctive outline at the centre of the village. Now restored it incorporates memorial windows to 66th Division and the arms of Lancashire towns. (IWM Q42918A)

The Harvest of Battle by C. R. W. Nevinson, 1919. Together with Sargent's better-known work Gassed this painting was a commission for the Hall of Remembrance. It was based on sketches that the artist made at Passchendaele. In a letter Nevinson described the picture as a 'typical scene after an offensive at dawn. Walking wounded, prisoners and stretcher cases are making their way to the rear through the water-logged country of Flanders. By now the infantry have advanced behind a creeping barrage on the right, only leaving the dead, mud and wire; but their former positions are now occupied by the artillery. The enemy is sending up SOS signals and once more these shattered men will be subjected to counter-battery fire. British aeroplanes are spotting hostile positions.' (IWM ART 121)

and undoubtedly saved lives. Almost immediately this was followed by the 'Hypo' or 'Smoke' helmet invented by Cluny MacPherson, a medical officer with the Newfoundland Regiment. The Smoke helmet was a flannel bag enveloping the whole head, soaked in hypo, and fitted with a mica window. The French, with a larger army and a longer front line, were a little slower to begin distribution of new masks – but soon they had their own equivalents. About 50,000 French 'helmet' types were distributed in late May, and a million 'C2' *Compresse* face pads were issued by mid August 1915. Not everyone received the new masks sufficiently quickly, and new German gases were soon testing the old face pads beyond their capabilities – but it was enough to blunt the full effects of the assaults in the spring and summer of that year.

In the summer scientists at the Royal Army Medical College in London actually sought to get a head start on the gas weapon technologists. Having identified 70 possible gases that might be used, they set out to redesign the Smoke helmet to take account of the most likely possibilities. The result of this was the 'Tube' helmet, which had a mouthpiece valve for the wearer to breathe out; a double thickness bag of cotton flannelette; and two eyepieces. These were manufactured rapidly enough for every British soldier to be given one by mid November 1915. Improvement though they were, Tube helmets were hot and uncomfortable. Some, confused by the smell of chemical impregnation, even ripped off the mask prematurely in battle. They could also be the subject of ribaldry, as anybody failing to use the tube properly could cause the bag to inflate on his head, or let out extraordinary noises whilst struggling to exhale.

Captain F. C. Hitchcock of the Leinsters described his men's first experience with Tube helmets:

> It had talc eye pieces and a rubber breathing tube for the mouth; the ends of the respirator had to be tucked under the jacket collar. They were all drenched with a solution of hypo, and were very sticky, messy gadgets. We then marched the men off to watch a gas demonstration, a section of the Belgian defence trenches were covered over, and turned into a gas chamber. The gas was pumped out of a large cylinder... When we came out of the chamber our buttons were blackened and our watches had stopped.[5]

The British launched their own first gas attack at Loos on 25 September 1915, a 'violent and continuous action' in co-ordination with French forces, intended to drive the Germans out of their existing trench lines in this sector and cut their communications, so that they would be driven into a retreat. The operation would be heavily reliant on the shock and surprise of gas, but only a little more than half of the quantities first envisaged were available. Only by releasing the chlorine along with periods of smoke generation would it be possible to maintain the illusion of a large and continuous gas attack. In the event matters would go seriously awry, as was reported by Lieutenant A. B. White of the Royal Engineers' 'Special Companies' tasked with the discharge of gas:

At first the gas drifted slowly towards the German lines (it was plainly visible owing to the rain) but at one or two bends of the trench the gas drifted into it. In these cases I had it turned off at once. At about 6.20am the wind changed and quantities of the gas came back over our parapet, so I ordered all gas to be turned off and only smoke candles to be used. Punctually at 6.30am one company of the King's advanced to the attack wearing smoke helmets. But there was a certain amount of confusion in the front trench owing to the presence of large quantities of gas. We experienced great difficulty in letting off the gas owing to faulty connections and broken copper pipes causing leaks. Nearly all my men suffered from the gas and four had to go to hospital. Three out of five machine guns on my front were put out of action by the gas. Very little could be seen of the German line owing to the fog of smoke and gas. Our infantry reached the enemy wire without a shot being fired, but they were mown down there by machine gun fire or overcome by gas.[6]

A scene in an Australian front line trench at Croix du Bac, near Armentières, 18 May 1916. The soldier is adjusting a wind vane, which would serve as a direction indicator in the event of a gas attack. Note the 1907 type bayonet and helve for the entrenching tool worn at the soldier's left hip. A spare bayonet, often used – against regulation – as a hook for equipment, is pushed into the parapet. A plank forms an alcove for munitions at bottom left of the picture. (IWM Q585)

German machine guns and errant gas put paid to many, but there was clear evidence that lack of experience with gas in the offensive was a contributory factor. Some panicked, believing they were gassed when they were not, and medical personnel had difficulty distinguishing gas symptoms from shock and fatigue.

A British Vickers machine gun team of the Machine Gun Corps, firing near Ovillers during the battle of the Somme. The crew wear 'Tube' helmets against gas, and the gunner wears the special padded short waistcoat for carrying the gun over his shoulder. Though mounted on a full-sized tripod this weapon also has a light 'auxiliary mount' attached under the water jacket for rapid deployments. A full 'gun detachment' was six men: usually two manned the weapon; others brought up ammunition or acted as spares, and were able to take cover a short distance away when under fire. (IWM Q3995)

Whilst Loos demonstrated how much was yet to be achieved, organized gas drills in defence of trench lines gradually improved both survival and confidence. Typical of the directions given to trench garrisons were those in force for 124th Brigade in late 1915 and early 1916. All ranks were to carry two Smoke helmets and have instruction on their use: helmets were to be inspected at Stand To. At the first sign of gas, whether detected by sight or smell:

> the sentries will sound the gas alarm gongs and bells which are hung up at intervals throughout the trenches. On hearing this alarm every officer and man will at once adjust his Smoke helmet and fall in on his alarm post. Nobody will remain in dugouts. To make certain of the warning reaching everybody, the order 'put on Smoke helmets' will be passed from man to man throughout the trenches held by the division.

Officers in the trenches opposite to the enemy discharge were to send an 'SOS' call to the artillery, which was to commence rapid fire on the enemy line. When the gas cloud was thick enough to hide the enemy's front parapets, machine guns and rifles would also open fire 'in short bursts on fixed lines' with the intention of breaking up any forming attack, causing casualties and piercing gas tubes. Even when not firing,

Illustrations showing a variety of Allied gas masks 1915–16.
1) British Barley mask,
May 1915.
2) British Hypo helmet,
Summer 1915.
3) British Large Box Respirator,
June 1916.
4) French P2 mask,
October 1915.
5) French M2 mask,
summer 1916.
6) Russian Koumant Zelinski respirator, 1916.
(© Adam Hook, Osprey Publishing)

rifle bolts and machine gun crank handles were to be worked back and forth occasionally to prevent corrosive gas from impairing the mechanism. Gas 'gongs', often made from old shell cases or requisitioned bells, were largely superseded by the latter part of 1916 by the 'Strombos' horn, a specially issued, and mightily loud, device reminiscent of a ship's horn.

As well as protecting individuals from gas there were also attempts to sanitize the trench environment. 'Gas curtains' across dugout entrances were a good first line of defence, as Captain Christison of the 6th Cameron Highlanders explained:

The Germans mixed gas shells with ordinary shells and so compelled us practically to live wearing our respirators. We rigged anti gas blankets on frames at the entrances to our dugouts and behind each blanket was placed a flat tin containing chloride of lime; the men stood in this, crossed a further anti gas blanket and could then remove masks and get food and rest. Unfortunately, heat generated gas out of men's clothing and some got gassed even with all precautions.[7]

Later in 1915 fans and sprays were also in use. The most commonly encountered spray in Franco-British service was the 'Vermorel', a backpack device with tube and handheld nozzle from which neutralizing chemicals could be sprayed in solution. Edmund Blunden described the Vermorels, not inaccurately, as 'simple machines such as were used in Kent to wash cherry trees with insect killer'.[8] Fans were far less effective than lighting fires which shifted gas by convection, warming bodies of air and thereby raising and dispersing the gas. Moreover, once properly ignited a brazier required little attention from troops who could then concentrate on their own personal protection. Nevertheless fans were seen, and the most infamous of these was the 'Ayrton'. Designed by Hertha Ayrton, the Ayrton fan was effectively a piece of fabric on a stick with which the user flapped the gas away. Many landed up in the braziers.

Many photographs from early 1915 show German soldiers carrying a small wallet attached to one of their jacket buttons, and in this was contained a small pad type gas mask, but from the latter part of that year a much better sort of gas mask was deployed. This comprised a light rubberized fabric face piece with eyepieces, and a screw fit cylinder on the front containing the filter chemicals. Once a filter had been exhausted a new one could be fitted. Folds in the mask enabled the wearer to clean the eyepieces without removing the mask. Held tightly to the face by elasticated tapes, the mask could also be supported by a tape around the neck when hanging loose. Initially the new mask was carried in a canvas belt bag, but later in a small, distinctive steel cylinder. Soldiers with full beards or spectacles were warned that either of these might compromise the seal of mask to face. Solutions included whole or partial shaving and the wearing of special glasses with tapes rather than arms. A general issue of the new mask was completed on the Western Front at Christmas 1915.

General German instructions of July 1916 emphasized early warning, but allowed somewhat more flexible approach in terms of reaction:

The behaviour of men in the trenches must be governed by the local and tactical considerations. Shelters which are unoccupied during a gas attack must be made as air tight as possible. Those in which men remain during an attack are best closed by means of wetted curtains, which however must not interfere with easy egress. On the gas alarm being raised, every man puts on his mask as rapidly as possible, mutual aid being given to ensure correct fitting. If possible, arms should be wiped over with an oily rag. The Oxygen Breathing Apparatus and the reserve cylinders are to be laid out ready for use, so that oxygen may be given to any who are gassed. Everyone moves to his proper post. Moving towards the rear is always dangerous, as one thereby remains in the gas cloud. To stay in dugouts without masks is also dangerous, as the chlorine gas tends to remain in dugouts. Horses should be removed from the gas zone as far as possible… Once the gas cloud has passed and any hostile attack has been beaten back, the trenches and dugouts must be purified of any gas that remains. Men wearing masks are detailed to open the doors of empty closed shelters and dugouts, to produce ventilation … by lighting stoves.

An observation post of the 1st/7th Sherwood Foresters in a communication trench, Cambrin, 16 September 1917. The observer uses a telescope concealed amongst foliage. The position also serves as a gas alarm point and is equipped with a metal triangle and a mighty 'Strombos horn'. The Strombos was to be used only in the event of a major event such as a cloud gas attack. (IWM Q6019)

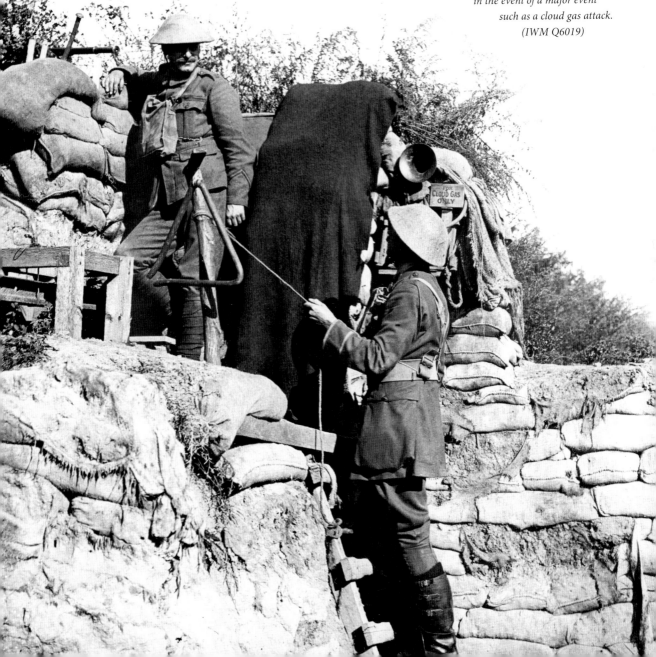

FOR CLOUD GAS ONLY

French gas defence lagged somewhat behind the other powers in the middle period of the war, and consisted essentially of different types of goggles and impregnated pads. As late as February 1916 there were orders for a new 'M2' type pad, though this was at least much larger and incorporated eye protection. Later in 1916 an improved version appeared, and though this was capable of providing several hours' protection, it was difficult to breath through and the eyepieces quickly misted up. The French *Appareil Respiratoire Spécial* or ARS mask, which was effective and had an appearance superficially similar to that of the German masks, was not distributed until 1917 when the first examples were issued to the artillery. Not all French troops had the latest mask until May 1918. Just how important gas defence, and indeed gas awareness, had become was underlined by a sample of 120 French gas casualties interviewed after a German chemical attack at Nieuport in June 1917. Of these 39 attributed their incapacitation to being surprised or their own carelessness; 15 to their removal of their mask too soon; 62 to an ill-fitting mask, or one which became displaced; and four to having an inadequate or obsolete mask. In short the vast majority of gas casualties were now avoidable if up-to-date, well-fitting masks were supplied to men who received warning of the attack, and put on their masks promptly and properly and kept them on.

The final types of British gas mask were the 'box respirators', the development of which commenced in 1915. These were a significant advance on what went before, because although made somewhat bulky by having a separate face piece and 'box' filter connected by a tube, they had a capacity to resist gas for long periods, and were fairly easy to upgrade with the addition of new filters to the existing box. Moreover the soldier did not carry the whole weight of the mask on his face, as was the case with the German 'gummi' mask, since the box rested in a satchel with a strap around the soldier's neck and shoulders.

The first of the box types was the 'Harrison's Tower' or 'Large Box' respirator, devised by Edward Harrison, chemist Bertram Lambert and John Sadd. The 'box' was created from a water bottle in which were three layers: lime-permanganate granules, fragments of pumice and fragments of bone charcoal. A corrugated flexible rubber tube ran from the box to a fabric facemask and a metal mouthpiece, which the wearer gripped in his teeth. With the 'Large Box' separate goggles were worn. As the latest word in gas protection this model was issued first to the 'Special Companies' of the Royal Engineers charged with gas warfare, and between February and June 1916 it was also supplied to machine gun and artillery personnel, who might well have to stay alert at their positions for long periods during gas attacks. From the 'Large Box' was developed the SBR or 'Small Box' respirator. This was more compact, included minor improvements to the valve system, and also incorporated the eye protection into the mask. This meant that the whole contraption was easier to handle, and if the bag was open on the chest and headgear removed, could be effectively donned in one fairly swift movement. The face piece of the SBR was made in four sizes. It was progressively issued to the entire British Army in the second half of 1916.

German gas protection measures:
1) The Atemschützer, *a mask covering the nose and mouth issued in August and September 1915. Worn with nose clip and goggles this was issued with bottles of hypo solution for soaking the mask.*
2) *A paper fibre and gauze mask for messenger and rescue dogs c.1918.*
3) *Gas-proof pigeon box incorporating air filters.*
4) *Horse respirator. First issued in 1917, and made in three sizes.*
5) *Mask designed for the wounded, made of leather and shaped like a hood.*
(© Richard Hook, Osprey Publishing)

American forces were given different types of Allied mask including limited numbers of the French 1916 model 'M2' pad. Nevertheless they were much more impressed with the performance of the SBR, and from October 1917 also manufactured their own version, which was dubbed the CE (or 'Corrected English') Box respirator. US production alone totalled about 5 million masks. Eventually the French and Americans would also lead the way in the development of gas-proof clothing to prevent skin contact with 'blister' gases. The Americans also issued their own anti-gas instructions,

French gunners on the Oise in the latter part of the war firing off a heap of shells. The gas mask worn is the latest ARS model, but the gun is that old war horse, the '75'. (Author's collection)

generally developed on British and French lines. Those of 1917 suggested that machine gun teams were key to successful defence under gas attack, and these had two main options. The first of these was to open fire on the enemy trench. This interrupted any enemy infantry attack, raised morale of friendly troops, and kept gun mechanisms free and less likely to be fouled by the action of the gas. The other possibility was to reserve fire until enemy infantry actually appeared. This was good for its surprise effect, but the guns had to be sprayed with decontaminant and the mechanisms tested by hand to make sure they did not become inoperative.

By 1917 gas defence had become almost second nature in well-trained units. Equipment checks were carried out daily; wind vanes were watched for unfavourable conditions; gas alarms positioned, sometimes duplicated, so that their warnings could be heard as far as brigade headquarters. At listening posts not only were ears used to detect the distinctive sounds of gas shells and hissing cylinders, but noses sniffed gently for ominously distinctive aromas. In the British instance respirators were worn in the 'alert' position ready to be slipped on.

The final and arguably most effective gas delivery systems were the gas 'projectors'. The first of these was the British 'Livens', the development of which commenced as early as the summer of 1915, with Captain W. H. Livens working in collaboration with his father, F. H. Livens. The first use of a prototype came at Thiepval in September 1916, and they were in use in numbers by Easter 1917. The perfected Livens projector was a crude-looking wide-bored tube, planted in the ground at a 45 degree angle, into which was loaded a propellant charge and a gas 'drum' projectile. Electric leads activated the propellant, and the round arced somewhat inaccurately in the general direction of the enemy. Night firing added considerably to the morale and surprise effects of the gas projector, and it was also possible to fire an oil incendiary round from the Livens. A round was similarly devised to scatter Mills bombs, much in the manner of modern 'sub munitions'.

Though at first glance the weapon appeared of dubious utility it was in fact a masterstroke, since Livens projectors were used in batteries, and large amounts of gas could be made to drop suddenly and simultaneously. The formation of very high concentrations on a target before the enemy could take precautions offered a significant advance. It mattered little that the tubes were not very accurate, since many bombs would still fall within a predictable area, and gas was essentially an area weapon. In its debut just before the opening of the battle of Arras, 2,340 projectiles were fired from 31 locations, dropping 50 tons of gas in one brief barrage. The result of this and subsequent attacks influenced the Germans to issue new instructions that troops should carry their masks 'in the alert position' ready for immediate use, whenever within 2 miles of enemy trenches. By July 1917 German troops were instructed to sound the gas alarm as soon as 'a loud report like a mine is heard 1,000 to 1,500 metres away', and to make good use of the 'several seconds' they might have before impact in putting on their masks. British projector tactics included the disguising of the gas shoot by conventional barrages and machine gun fire, and other ruses. At Mural Farm in August 1918 a genuine gas bombardment was followed a few days later by a dummy one, and during the confusion that ensued the position was rushed and taken.

Though the Livens gave the British an advantage, as with so many new inventions of the trench war, it was but short lived. By the autumn of 1917 the Germans had designed, built and deployed their own gas projector, and were using it on the Western Front by December. As was explained in the US manual *Defence Against Gas*, 1918:

Royal Engineers loading Livens projector tubes prior to a gas shoot. Electric leads had to be attached, and the large bombs slid into the tubes. The use of multiple barrels and rapid or simultaneous discharge meant that an area could quickly be deluged with large concentrations of gas. This increased effect and limited the chance for the enemy to react so men were often caught without their gas masks on. (IWM Q14945)

At the approach of hostile aircraft, men of an anti-aircraft section rush to their guns on the outskirts of Armentières, March 1916. The guns are 13-pdr 'Quick Firers' on a Mark III motor lorry mounting. The rapid developments of aircraft met with immediate counter-responses in the air and on the ground. (IWM Q460)

A British observation balloon ascending to observe artillery fire near Locre, 1916. Aerial observation added another dimension to the battlefield, but was not new, having existed from as early as the 1780s. What was new was that balloons were the target of enemy aircraft, and that those being observed now took many different measures to camouflage themselves. Many observers escaped death by taking to parachutes, the main type of which was the 'Guardian Angel' stowed in a tube and attached to its user by a rope and harness. (IWM Q449)

A 9.2inch howitzer of 55th Australian Siege Battery in action at Voormezeele, 13 September 1917. The four men to the rear of the gun lift the shells to the piece in a metal frame. An overhead net provides concealment from the air. (IWM E.AUS.964)

Captain Albert Ball VC DSO MC (1896–1917). Ball volunteered for service with the Sherwood Foresters early in the war, but learned to fly privately and went to France to join the Royal Flying Corps in 1916. With 44 confirmed victories he became one of the best known aces – yet was only 20 years old when killed in May 1917. The precise circumstances of his death are unclear, but his final downing was claimed by Lothar von Richthofen, brother of the more famous Manfred. (Author's collection)

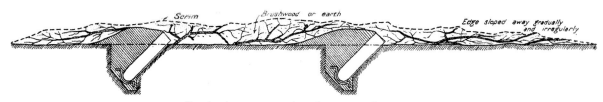

Projectors on level ground.

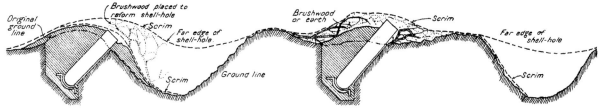

Projectors on shelled ground.

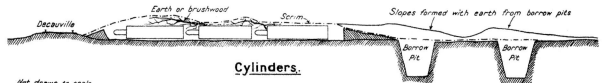

Cylinders.

Not drawn to scale

Illustrations from Work of the RE in the European War, *showing the positioning of Livens projectors. (Author's collection)*

The enemy makes use of 'gas projectors' having a range of about 1,500 meters and in the case of the new rifled projectors of about 3,000 meters. By this method a large number of projectiles, each containing about 16.5 pounds of liquefied gas are simultaneously shot from smooth-bore or rifled iron tubes dug into the ground or set in wooden racks. The propelling charges are varied according to the range desired. The electric current for firing the charges is generated by hand-driven magnetos called 'exploders', each of which fires about 25 projectors. On impact, or by means of a time fuse, the projectiles are exploded and the gas volatilized. By this method, the enemy is able to generate a cloud of gas within our lines. His tactics are not so dependent upon weather conditions as when cloud attacks are made. Projector attacks call for the highest degree of gas discipline among the troops affected because of the surprise which is often secured and the instantaneous formation of an extremely concentrated and deadly cloud of gas.

Opposite:
Sniper of the London Irish Rifles, Albert, August 1918. Equipped with an SMLE rifle with offset scope, he also wears trousers cut down to shorts. This particular patrol was a disaster: of seven taking part one was killed and three wounded. (IWM Q6902)

CHAPTER SIX

RAIDING AND SNIPING

Trench raids were first attempted at a surprisingly early stage, and the British *Official History* claims that the first mounted by British troops took place on the Aisne on 4 October 1914, just east of Troyon factory road. Here the enemy had dug a sap, and it was decided that this should be seized and destroyed by a party of the 1st Coldstream Guards under Lieutenant Beckwith Smith. The guardsmen rushed across a hundred yards of No Man's Land, and took two lines of trenches at bayonet point, but belatedly discovered yet another trench giving covering fire, so it was not possible to fulfil the objective. A wounded Beckwith Smith received the DSO. According to Corporal Sidney Amatt of the London Rifle Brigade some of the earliest German stealth techniques were almost laughably simple:

> They would pick out big, strong, physically fit men and arm them with clubs – long handled clubs about twice as long as policemen's truncheons and with weighted ends. They would black out their faces and crawl through our wire. Then, without making any noise at all, two of them would bodily lift out one of our sentries … and drag him over to their lines. When we got wise to that sort of thing we doubled the sentries.[1]

By early 1915 all parties were frustrated by lack of progress, fearful of poor morale, and often suspicious of enemy plans. As a result, and perhaps in some instances as a substitute for full-scale offensive action, raids and patrols became increasingly frequent and more organized. Small patrols might include a single officer accompanied by anything from one to half a dozen other ranks. Typical objectives included intelligence on enemy wire, troops and reliefs, or, more aggressively, the capture of an enemy patrol or the recovery of identification discs. Some raids were larger, as was that mounted by 2nd Royal Welch Fusiliers on 12 March 1915:

> After the word had been passed down the Cameronian companies that a party of RWF was going out, we crept over at 10 o'clock in two parties; Lieutenant Mostyn, myself and ten men of 'D' Company in one party, Lieutenant Fletcher and 11 other ranks of 'B' were the other, 10 yards on our left. Approaching the German line we ran into a known listening post. The two, perhaps three, occupants, fired, but when we made a rush for them they hopped it and got away. We pushed on to their line. Fletcher spoke in German to try to put the garrison off, telling them we were Germans, but they were ready for us when we started bombing. There was nothing for it but to get back as best we could. A blast of Mostyn's whistle broke off the action, and a flash of his torch let Hill know. Again we were between two fires, and our guns were barraging our flanks at 50 yards distance – as Mostyn insisted, for the gunners wanted it to be 100 yards.[2]

Scurrying and worming their way back guided by lamps in the British trench the raiders came under heavy fire; one man was lost and five wounded – not a few 'left pieces of clothing and flesh on the wire'.

As one officer bitterly remarked, this raid – and not a few like it – achieved little, because little was aimed at. Nevertheless early raids did build up experience, contribute to the development of minor tactics, and create a repertoire of clothing and equipment suitable for night and close combat. Gradually a blackened face, cap turned backwards, and rifle with fixed bayonet were supplemented by grenades, revolvers, trench daggers, coshes, knobkerries, knuckle-dusters, pullovers and muffled boots. The Royal Welch Fusiliers added the nice touch of knee protectors cut from old socks, and, on occasion, bill hooks as the raiding weapon of choice.

By the latter part of 1915 it was generally expected that each brigade would mount some sort of patrol every night. Instructions of 124th Brigade reminded its officers that patrolling and constant observation of the enemy line were 'the best security against attack'. Patrols would therefore take particular trouble to investigate the enemy wire to ensure that no gaps had been cut ready for troops to move through. Likewise friendly wire and parapets were to be checked for security. The usual method to find men in this brigade was to identify a company, then make up two small patrols of an NCO and three men each. These four-man patrols would go out sequentially, thereby ensuring some kind of patrol activity over a protracted period. The patrols were to cross the friendly obstacle zone by means of 'two or more zig-zag paths' through the wire. On returning the patrols were instructed to halt outside the wire, whilst the

A party of the 1st/8th (Irish) Battalion, King's Liverpool Regiment, on 18 April 1916. One officer, centre, is wearing a pullover, balaclava, gloves and face blacking and is carrying a revolver. Many of the men have soft caps and rifles with fixed bayonets or trench clubs. Other headgear shown includes captured Prussian spiked helmets and a service dress cap turned backwards. Turning the cap backwards had several useful effects during night raids: there was no peak to obscure vision; the cap was less likely to be knocked off; and from the front the general appearance was more like the German peakless Feldmütze. (IWM Q510)

patrol commander advanced to be challenged by the sentry guarding the entrance. Once identified the leader would bring his men through the gap.

A big raid chosen as the ideal model for future action was that by 5th and 7th Canadian battalions on the Douvre River on 16 November 1915. The raiders comprised two 70-man groups, and within each were sections devoted to different tasks, as for example wire cutting, bombing, blocking, supporting and reserve. Artillery co-operation on the day of the raid included targeting known enemy machine gun posts and wire. Despite minute preparation one of the Canadian groups drew fire prematurely and was forced to withdraw. The other achieved total success, stabbing a sentry before bombing dugouts, taking prisoners and retiring according to plan – total Canadian loss was one man accidentally killed and one wounded. Such was the ideal, but it should also be noted that there were many bloody fiascos. A raid by 86 men of

Tommies wearing a variety of 'liberated' headgear, including a German Guard Hussar busby, Garde du Corps helmet, various Pickelhauben *and a French steel helmet. One of the men, centre, has a German* Tornister, *or backpack. (Author's collection)*

the Dorsets, which advanced under cover of a mine explosion, led to four dead and 17 wounded because the enemy withdrew and promptly called down fire on their old position. A 55th Division raid near Blaireville Wood was caught by massive fire before it reached the enemy line, and 60 of its 76 participants were killed or wounded.

In March 1916 general instructions for raids and patrols were distributed under the title *Notes on Minor Enterprises*. This document sharpened the focus considerably. Objectives were to be 'limited and definite', and the choice of target influenced by any covered approaches to the enemy line, any lack of vigilance identified, and the ability of the enemy to reinforce or cover various parts of his trenches. Preparation of a week or more was recommended for each operation. Experience suggested that patrols of from two to eight were often successful in entering the enemy lines to secure information, whilst 'raids' with or without artillery co-operation might be almost any size from 80 to a whole battalion. Artillery was deemed particularly useful for cutting wire before a raid, or forming a barrage around the point of attack. Gas and smoke could be used to divert the enemy's artillery fire, or to form a barrage to one flank.

ZONNEBEKE

From the Zonnebeke sheet, N.E. 1, 1:10,000, with German defences in red, corrected to 30 June 1917. This area was one of the toughest nuts encountered during the 1917 offensive, with the Zonnebeke Ridge which ran from the village in the direction of St Julien infested with machine gun posts. Broodseinde was fought over twice by British 7th Division – once in 1914 and again in October 1917. The German defences are linear in only a few places, being mainly zones of bunkers and shell holes, some of which are disclosed by the presence of the tracks used to reach them. Maps of September 1917 show the main fire trench running south from Zonnebeke as 'Docile Trench', with 'Desmond Trench' continuing the front uninterrupted north of the road in the direction of 'Thames'. Further north still the 'D' theme of the British names was continued with 'Dabble Avenue', 'Dab', 'Dagger' and 'Dad' trenches.

Naturally there are now Canadian monuments in the vicinity, but probably the locations of greatest interest nearby are the Memorial Museum, Passchendaele – which is actually in Zonnebeke and was reopened after substantial renovation in 2004 – and the vast Tyne Cot Cemetery, which actually lies on the old 'Dabble Avenue' about a mile north of Broodseinde. Tyne Cot is the largest British and Commonwealth cemetery in Europe, and now also boasts a small visitor centre tastefully tucked away to one side. In the midst of the cemetery the customary 'Cross of Sacrifice', which was designed by Reginald Blomfield and appears in most Commonwealth war graves cemeteries, is built over a German blockhouse, an arrangement which it is said was suggested by King George V during a battlefield pilgrimage in 1922.

Finds from the trenches at Zonnebeke. Amongst the detritus are parts of rifles and a Lewis gun, German grenades, bayonets, ammunition and personal items. Evocative as such material undoubtedly is, creating a professional museum display of this type poses problems of both safety and long term conservation. (Author's collection)

German Pickelhauben at the Memorial Museum, Zonnebeke. The distinctive spiked helmet was introduced as early as 1842, and widely copied. The example foreground is of the Prussian Guard infantry; that with a ball finial is an artillery example. The grey pieces have bodies made of pressed felt, a wartime emergency measure. (Author's collection)

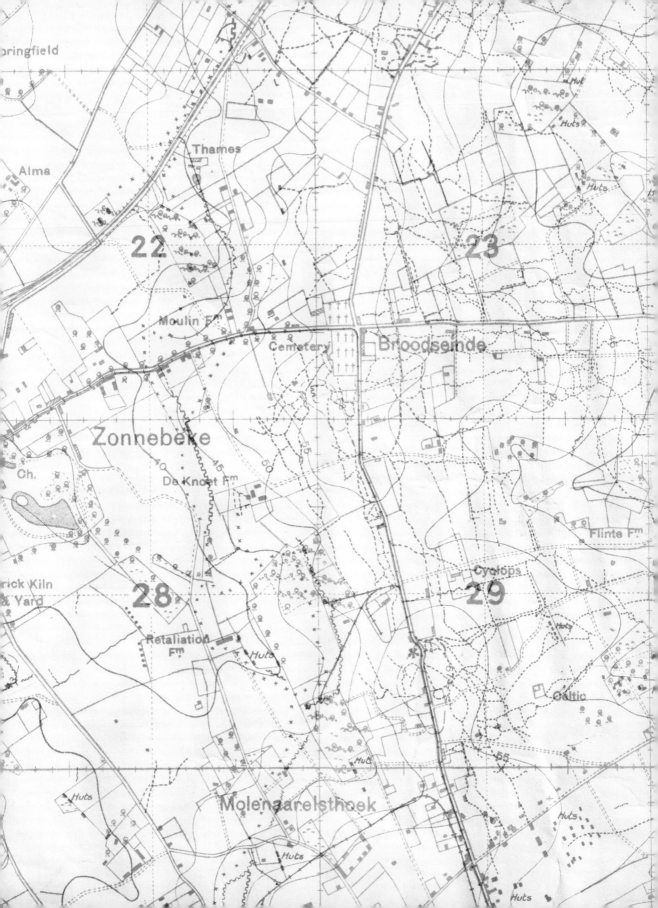

Not giving away more information than one was able to gather was naturally a key consideration. To this end every precaution was taken against taking documents and insignia on a raid, as an American report, citing British instructions, stated:

> Officers in charge of parties will be held personally responsible that all under their command are stripped of all identifying marks. Particular attention will be paid to ensure that the following articles are taken from the men and deposited in sandbags to be left at the regimental transport lines: cap badges, sleeve patches, pay books, regimental buttons, numerals, identity disks, shoulder badges, letters, roll books etc.

Individual schemes were prepared at unit level, but checked at brigade or divisional level. Reconnaissance and observation was an integral part of the planning process. Types of information to be looked at included aerial photographs, patrol and weather reports, prisoner statements, trench log books, and the reports of snipers and artillery observers. Recommended raiding wear now included woollen caps, gloves which might be discarded on reaching the enemy line, and a distinguishing mark that could be seen by friends when crawling but was not obvious to an enemy observer. Though revolvers, clubs, daggers and an issue of two grenades per man were still recommended another trick now advocated was using black insulating tape to attach an electric torch to a rifle. This was 'found useful for men detailed to clear dugouts'. When Ernest Parker took part in a raid with 2nd Royal Fusiliers he recalled that 'plain' service dress was worn, with burnt cork as face camouflage. Though the party included at least one Lewis gun many of the team relied on revolvers, with grenades and torches stuffed into pockets for dugout clearance. These were backed up by knives and clubs, and 'empty sandbags for souvenirs'. In Parker's case these would include some 'scraps of paper' picked from a dugout, and German shoulder straps from corpses. All was later gratefully received by the battalion intelligence officer, who turned out in pyjamas when the team reported back to HQ behind the line.

A not untypical raid described by Captain F. C. Hitchcock near Vimy on 5 October 1916 consisted of two assault groups of 14 and 13 men respectively, each led by an officer; a 'covering party' of 20 with an officer; and ten men to carry and operate 'Bangalore Torpedoes' – these last were a new trench warfare device consisting of a long tube packed with explosive for blowing a path through wire. These efforts in wire cutting were supported both by trench mortars and by scouts with wire cutters, both of which had been operative over the last few days. The attackers carried rifle and bayonet, grenades and 'knobkerries' based on entrenching tool handles. These may well have been the type with a metal 'cog wheel' head made up especially by the Royal Engineers. Hitchcock explained:

> When the enemy opened rifle fire, we judged that the raid was in 'full swing'. A few of our own wounded crawled back, but they didn't prove very informative. There was now

a good deal of bombing, which showed that they were meeting with opposition. Then some more wounded came back, and were followed by a small party escorting one slightly wounded Hun. Within a half hour from zero all the raiders had returned to our lines. Our casualties were six men wounded. The raiders had a great scrapping in the Hun trenches, and accounted for at least six enemy killed. It was a most successful enterprise… The prisoners, on being given some whisky, became very communicative, and talked of machine gun and trench mortar emplacements, reliefs and casualties.[3]

Such triumphs were balanced by dismal failures. One such, later described by Rudyard Kipling, was mounted on the Somme on 2 July 1916. It comprised 32 all ranks drawn from 2nd Irish Guards, plus three 'gas experts' – who were tasked to locate enemy gas equipment – and an officer of the Royal Engineers. At first, and despite the lightness of the night, all went well with 20 minutes of supporting bombardment. Thereafter everything that could go wrong, did. Alert German gunners returned fire on the British front line, and as the raiders emerged the gunners' efforts were backed up by machine guns from the enemy second line. Two of the gas team were wounded in No Man's Land. When the raiders reached the first trench they were checked by bombing and patches of uncut wire. Sergeant Austen was hit and fell into the entanglement. Thereafter many did get into the German line and Lieutenant Pym succeeded in knocking out a machine gun. Bombers now attempted to work their way along the trench, resulting in a 'general bomb scuffle', whilst the remaining gas scout discovered nothing. Some documents were picked up, but the man carrying them was killed and the booty lost. As the barrage grew heavier Pym sounded a horn, which was the signal to retire. The Guardsmen scrambled back into

Men of the York and Lancaster Regiment are briefed by a sergeant before starting out for a raid, Roclincourt, January 1918. A variety of crawling suits and camouflage robes are worn – 'boiler suit' designs were more popular for raiding as they were less of an impediment when crawling. The men also wear hoods, one of them modified for better hearing. (IWM Q23580)

the fire with four prisoners – there had been five, but one had been shot when he proved 'unmanageable'. Two of the remaining four were killed by German shells, as were some of the raiders. Lieutenant Pym was missing near the enemy line, believed killed, and Lieutenant Synge very badly hit in the British front trench. The Engineer officer, theoretically in charge of demolitions, was hit twice before he could achieve anything, but managed to get back. No useful information was gained – it was 'heroic failure'. The brigadier congratulated the survivors on their 'gallant behaviour in adverse circumstances'.[4]

Though well planned, an enterprise by 2nd East Lancashires in the early hours of 9 September 1916, also on the Somme, similarly achieved very little. This foray, organized mainly to investigate the opposing line and glean identifications, comprised 50 other ranks divided into three sections each led by an officer and provided with mats by means of which they were supposed to cross the enemy wire. It commenced well enough with the attackers crawling up to their start positions just 40 yards from the German parapet. At 2.15am the British artillery laid a 'box barrage' around the target zone, and the raiders attempted to storm the trench:

> The right party placed their mats but the enemy were on the alert, and the party was unable to force an entry into the trench and after a bombing fight, which lasted for some ten minutes, the party withdrew, firing a green Verey light as it did so. The centre party, under Captain Dowling, entered the trench without opposition, and worked along it to the right and left, bombing dugouts but seeing no Germans. When the green light went up from the right party, Captain Dowling waited for some minutes, and then sounded a Klaxon horn, which was the signal for withdrawing. The left party also entered the trench without opposition, and captured a prisoner. He could not, however, be induced to leave the trench, and had to be left. There was a good deal of fighting with bombs and revolvers, in which Sergeant Brenton distinguished himself considerably: but the party withdrew on the sound of the Klaxon horn without prisoners.[5]

The raiders lost six men, three wounded and two missing. The gallant Sergeant Brenton was killed by a grenade in No Man's Land.

By the middle of the war raids could be very large indeed, and were sometimes more like small attacks than pinpricks as part of general reconnaissance. One British raid on the night of 12 February 1917 employed a whole battalion, of whom 162 all ranks became casualties, though 160 enemy casualties were also claimed – plus destruction of 41 dugouts and 52 prisoners taken from a Bavarian Reserve Infantry regiment. Their captors noted that these were of good physique and 'appeared generally very intelligent'. A more obscure observation was that 'cotton underclothing' was worn by all the prisoners: this was probably taken to indicate that the unit had been recently re-supplied, or were new arrivals at the front.

Those on the receiving end of an enemy raid were not supposed to await their fate passively, and orders were often issued accordingly. Some such were disseminated to the company commanders of 1st/5th South Lancashires in early 1917. Captain Dickinson copied them into his *Correspondence Book*:

> Dispositions in Event of Raid
>
> This would be preceded by a heavy bombardment, In this event all men retire to dugouts except two men at each sentry post. A sentry armed with bombs will be posted at the door of each dugout. Immediately fire lifts from the trench everyone will come out [and] take up firing positions. During the bombardment NCOs (including Platoon Sergeants), also Platoon Commanders will be in dugouts either with, or very near, their men. This is important, Sergeants are not to remain in their usual dugouts but to be actually with their men. Grenadier party will be told off for each listening post – an additional grenadier party will be told off now, so as to be ready for use for each platoon. Every man to be acquainted with this – This supercedes the method of edging away to each flank.

Adopting such precautions was not always possible. The 1st South Wales Borderers were caught in the act of conducting a relief in the Maroc sector when struck by a German raid. They were 'still encumbered with packs and greatcoats and had not yet taken over when a tremendous bombardment began'. The other battalion 'cleared out', leaving the SWB to fight off the Germans, some of whom were hit by a machine gun whilst making their escape. Nonetheless the battalion suffered several casualties including a sergeant killed. Lieutenant Davidson had hardly gained his place in the trench before the enemy hauled him away as prisoner.

Raiding techniques were naturally modified to suit the new types of defence as they were brought into use. Eric Hiscock of the Royal Fusiliers described a raid just before dawn against Flanders concrete works, consisting of ten NCOs and other ranks led by an officer:

> Lieutenant Clarke, the Company Sergeant Major, and the two Sergeants, carried revolvers. The rest of us carried bandoliers full of cartridges, short Lee Enfield rifles, and small sacks hanging from the shoulder full of Mills bombs… We were to hurl our Mills bombs, then follow up the explosions by dashing round the rear of the pillboxes, entering, and seizing at least one prisoner.

On 1 November 1917 a carefully co-ordinated night raid was mounted by 7th King's Own Lancaster Regiment in the 'Bitter Wood' area: it comprised two officers and 28 other ranks, organized so that groups could attack individual dugouts. Its departure from friendly lines was covered by Lewis guns, and two men with a whistle were left near the jumping off point so that any stragglers could be attracted back to safety. As the battalion War Diary reported:

The raiders crossed the Beek in small parties at ten minute intervals and by 7.50pm had successfully worked their way into a position of assembly about ten yards west of and parallel with 'Rifle Road' – about 80 yards from their objectives. At 8.20 our barrage opened on the whole chain of dugouts which were not being attacked. At 8.24 the barrage lifted 150 yards east of the northern group and each party rushed forward to its objective. Dugouts 1, 2, 3, and 5 were found to be unoccupied. Dugout 4 was defended by a machine gun section which in its endeavour to escape was driven by Corporal Woods and his party into the barrage and probably suffered casualties. Lieutenant Holmes went for dugout 6 and found an entrance on the far side guarded by two sentries. These he promptly shot and they fell back blocking the doorway. The occupants of the dugout were firing through the entrance and prevented our men from getting in. A bomb was therefore thrown in. A machine gunner who opened out through the loophole was shot through the loophole by one of the men. Corporal Storey in the meantime was dealing with dugout 7. Lieutenant Holmes went to his assistance and eventually six prisoners were extracted. A further attempt to clear dugout 6 was made by Lieutenant Conheeny but he was held up by fire from within.

A British officer stands with a bullet-riddled steel loophole plate, July 1916. The modern rifle bullet was remarkably powerful, particularly at close ranges. Though some loop plates were left partly exposed as deliberate decoys, they were most effective when integrated into earth or sandbag defences and carefully camouflaged. Such work was best undertaken at night or otherwise screened from the enemy. (IWM Q120)

The object of the raid having now been accomplished, Lieutenant Holmes sounded the signal to withdraw and the whole party were safely back across the Beek with their prisoners by 8.40. Our casualties were nil.

Some of the weirdest patrols of the war were undertaken by two battalions of the East Lancashires at the northern end of the Allied line, where their positions butted against a canal in September 1917. Here intermittent shelling and gas were the order of the day:

Conditions in the front line were accordingly unpleasant, and such of the men and officers as were strong swimmers found themselves in the disagreeable situation of being detailed for swimming patrols. These patrols, clad in nothing but their skins and a waterproof bag containing a revolver slung around their waists, were assigned the unenviable task of descending from the British lines to the muddy edge of the canal, swimming the two hundred yards width of the canal to the German side (in itself no mean task, considering the run of the tide) and then of wandering, naked and shivering, on the enemy side to try and ascertain at what distance from the bank lay the occupied German trenches – there being certain trenches shown on field maps quite close to the edge of the water which proved to be unoccupied. No information of value was ever ascertained by these patrols other than the fact that the trenches referred to were unoccupied, but it speaks volumes for the spirit of the troops concerned that on one occasion a non-commissioned officer of the 2/5th Battalion who was a famous swimmer in his home town, once swam, not only across the Yser canal, but out to the end of the jetty or pier protruding into the sea from the enemy side and there affixed a small Union Jack…[6]

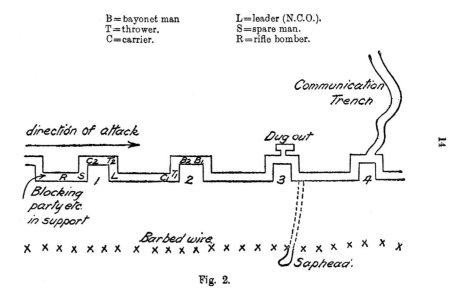

B = bayonet man
T = thrower.
C = carrier.

L = leader (N.C.O.).
S = spare man.
R = rifle bomber.

Communication Trench

direction of attack

Dug out

C2 T2

B2 B1

7 R S , L

C1 T1 2

3

4

Blocking party etc. in support

Barbed wire.

x x x x x x x x x x x x x x x x x x x x x x x x x x x x x

Saphead.

14

Fig. 2.

Line drawing from Instructions on Bombing, *1917, showing the tactics of the 'Bombing Party'. (Author's collection)*

Perhaps the ultimate summary of British raiding methods came in the December 1917 manual *Scouting and Patrolling*. Now the principal duties of scouts and patrols were recognized as essentially 'pre' and 'post' attack missions. Before offensive action scouts were to reconnoitre enemy wire, locate machine guns and snipers, and generally provide intelligence. Patrols were to achieve 'complete mastery' in No Man's Land. In a post-offensive situation scouts were to locate the enemy's new positions, attempt to ascertain his intentions, and act as guides. Patrols were now to follow up the retreating enemy and 'seize tactical features'.

As before much of the work would be done at night and was likely to focus around operations to gain information; kill, capture or harass the enemy; or protect vulnerable areas. Patrols were not to move until they had become accustomed to the dark, and at least one man was to remain listening whilst the remainder were in motion. Basic formations were described for patrols from two to nine men, and 20 was the recommended maximum for a 'fighting patrol'. In the largest patrols the men formed boxes around a Lewis gun for firepower, whilst a five-man patrol was ideal for two bombers thrown forward with three riflemen behind, through which they could retire. Men on patrol work were to go lightly equipped:

> A cap comforter is least visible, the face and hands should be darkened and gloves may be worn. Each man should carry two bombs, a bayonet or knobkerrie, and a revolver or rifle. A revolver is more convenient, but men so armed must be expert in its use. The rifle is the best weapon for purposes of protection… Scouts going out on patrol should have nothing on them which would assist the enemy if they were captured.[7]

Training for patrol work now included night exercises in which men were taught to differentiate the sounds of digging, marching, wire cutting, talking, whispering – and how far such sounds travelled under differing conditions of wind and weather. They also learnt various tricks to distract attention, and quiet movement, crawling and communication. Groups were instructed how to maintain contact with each other by touch, means of string, signals, white badges and even 'luminous marks'. Special 'Crawling Suits' also made their appearance during 1916 and were in widespread use by the following year.

By now patrol reports were expected to follow a standard form, with the information requested being the most important part and therefore forming the first section. To this was to be appended a map reference sheet; a list of personnel with names, ranks and numbers; time and place of departure and return; and a list of casualties and any details of how these occurred. The whole was to be signed and dated at a given place by the author. The task of patrol report writing, often not welcomed by the exhausted, was made slightly easier in some units by the provision of a standard 'Patrol Report' template. That of 42nd Division from early 1918 consisted of boxes for 'composition', 'task', times and places of exit and return, and a

KNOBKERRIE HEAD
FOR
NTRENCHING TOOL HANDLE

Measurements in millimetres.

Diagram from Work of the RE in the European War, *showing the Knobkerrie head for entrenching tool. (Author's collection)*

space for a sketch map. The main body comprised a brief chronological narrative. Interestingly it was now assumed that the person leading a small patrol, and hence writing the report, might be a sergeant.

Heart stopping as raiding and patrolling might be there were at least a few who preferred it to other possibilities. P. H. Jackson of 6th Manchesters recalled for example that in his battalion scouts were exempted from fatigues or inhabiting the front line trench unless slated for a patrol. The scouts formed a self-contained group of four, occupying a hut near battalion headquarters, and one man would remain behind to attend to rations whilst the other three were on patrol. Nevertheless by the end of the war there was an expectation that patrolling would be a normal part of the soldier's experience, not a specialized skill. As *Hints on Training* explained in May 1918, 'Patrolling must be done by roster and not on the voluntary system; every man in the company should be used for patrolling.' Moreover the ideal patrol was not only one with specific objectives, but one so organized that sections participated under their own section commanders. In any case there was a point of view that in the trenches danger and fear were perfectly natural. As Lieutenant Colonel J. S. Y. Rogers, Medical Officer to 4th Black Watch, opined:

> I think every man, no matter how brave out at the front, has experienced fear. You cannot avoid it with the various things that are going on. A man in the front line is under constant stress of excitement. He does not know when he is going to be shelled or sniped or undergo the dangers of patrol duty. He may be mined underneath; he does not know when the mine is going up. He has a fear of gas… They are not cowards.[8]

SNIPING

At first glance one might be forgiven for thinking that there was no connection between the rough but noble engagement of 'minor enterprises', as raids were called in official publications, and the 'dirty' game of sniping. In fact the two were soon intractably associated, for both were seen as methods to interfere with the enemy, and to gain intelligence.

To begin with sniping was an ad hoc undertaking, with no special training, and haphazard provision of equipment – this being whatever came to the front on the initiative of individual officers who had been target shooters or big game hunters. So it was that the soldier was stalked like game, and shot with high-powered sporting rifles such as the Jeffreys .333, .416 Rigby and the .280 Ross. Indeed the reactions of men aimed at by the sniper's bullet were much the same as those of large animals. A near miss would often cause a man to pause for a fraction of a second before ducking, or moving sharply away. A hit caused an instant reaction with buckling knees, or instantaneous flinch. Fatal wounds often caused the victim to fall forwards and slip down – rarely did a man throw up his arms or fall backwards. Experienced shots would look out for such signs when wondering what retaliation might be due from the enemy line, and when to relocate.

Orders for scopes were placed with classic gun makers such as Purdy, Holland and Holland, Churchill, Lancaster and Westley Richards. Soon 'magnifying' or 'Galilean' sights were also employed – these being separate convex and concave lenses mounted atop the rifle. Yet for the first year the Germans had clear advantage. There were two main reasons for this, the first being that in Germany, as a land of forests, game, shooting clubs and military conscription, there were already numbers of men trained in the arts of field shooting. The second, less obvious, was that the optics industries of Europe were centred in Germany, and supplies of telescopic sights and binoculars were more easily obtained in Central Europe. As Major Hesketh Pritchard reported:

The Symien Sniper Suit.

An illustration of the Symien Sniper Suit from The Principles and Practice of Camouflage, *March 1918. (Author's collection)*

At this time the skill of the German sniper had become a byword, and in the early days of trench warfare brave German riflemen used to lie out between the lines, sending their bullets through the head of any officer or man who dared to look over our parapet. These Germans, who were often Forest Guards … did their business with a skill and gallantry which must be freely acknowledged. From the ruined house or the field of decaying roots, sometimes resting their rifles on the bodies of the dead, they sent forth a plague of head wounds into the British lines. Their marks were small, but when they hit they usually killed their man, and the hardest soldier turned sick when he saw the effect of the pointed German bullet, which was apt to keyhole so that the little hole in the forehead where it entered often became a huge tear, the size of a fist, on the other side of the stricken man's head.[9]

Moreover, as Major F. M. Crum of the King's Royal Rifle Corps observed, the 'Bosche' remained 'top dog' in 1915. Crum himself was first employed leading snipers in Sanctuary Wood:

We lie in wait for them from dawn to dusk; there are always some of them watching with their eyes glued to the telescope. They become each day more cunning, and have great duels with the enemy's snipers. Sometimes we disguise ourselves by wearing a sandbag, sometimes with a mask of brown or green gauze, or with grass and bushes, or it might be a common masquerading mask painted like bricks or stone… The German sniper has iron loopholes; you watch and watch, and at last you see the slot slowly opening, the muzzle of the rifle being gradually pushed forward. This is the time for your marksman to shoot, but sometimes he shuts up his porthole quickly, like a snail going back into his shell. Now that's the time for the elephant gun – a steady aim and bang goes the steel bullet through the steel plate.[10]

During the latter part of 1915 and 1916, however, British sniping was revolutionized, both by an influx of new equipment and by the establishment of 'schools' behind the lines and in the UK. Colonel Lloyd's X Corps School was set up in 1915, and the same year Major Hesketh Pritchard began an itinerant teaching mission around the Corps of First and Third Armies, bringing with him telescopes and rifles from the UK. In May 1916 a brigade, later army, sniping school was opened at a disused quarry at Acq, which included a dummy German trench occupied by instructors in enemy uniforms. XI Corps School was at Steenbecque under Lieutenant Forsyth of the Black Watch, and was one of the inspirations for the large First Army School near Linghem which instituted a 17-day course. The Fourth Army School was set against the huge natural backstop of a steep chalk slope at Bouchon, and eventually equipped with a prefabricated 'farm building' which could be moved about. The Northern Command School at Rugeley Camp in Staffordshire, operating under Lieutenant Colonel Fremantle, printed its own little textbook of notes for its instructors in December 1916.

From practical experience and training emerged a systematic approach. Each battalion was now to have a minimum sniper establishment of eight men (a figure which was later increased, and could be as high as 24 in some units). These were intended to operate as two-man teams, spread across the battalion front, usually with one man observing, preferably with a rested telescope, the other ready to take shots. Though naturally one of the team might be better at one task than the other occasional changes were useful to keep the team alert. Their work was co-ordinated by an officer who kept plans of the posts, took back reports of enemy activity – and made sure that his team were kept fresh by reduced fatigues. For consistency of shooting each man attempted to stick with one rifle and the same batch of cartridges, kept clean and corrosion free. On firing usual practice was to look in the general direction of a target, often found by the observer, then bring the scope up to the eye. Searching using the scope was a useful supplement to the observer, but not the best way to take a fleeting shot – which was often all that was presented by a gap in sandbags, or a wary working party. Sights were not usually adjusted in action, but left set at perhaps 200 yards. The sniper could then act swiftly, correcting his aim as he lined up the target, higher for more distant, lower for closer – slightly ahead of a moving soldier by 'aiming off'. As Colonel Lloyd observed, trench sniping was 'the art of hitting a very small object straight off and without the advantage of a sighting shot'.[11]

Contrary to popular belief most sniping was done at relatively close ranges, and moving targets in particular were not much engaged beyond 300 yards. Indeed one of the key, and most dangerous, sniper tactics was to move closer to the enemy, perhaps slithering out of a sap or tunnel at night, and into a firing position which enfiladed an enemy post, or took an unexpectedly low angle on a loop or fire step. A long wait might be rewarded by a single clear shot before another long wait and retreat to friendly lines. Such work was best done wearing a sniper suit or robe and hood painted to match the local background, or with a speckled 'domino' cape which was particularly suited to conditions such as light filtering through trees or foliage. Where crawling forwards was too dangerous or restrictive, some snipers preferred to crawl a few yards back from their own trench line – which lengthened range slightly, but might create a different field of fire.

By the end of the war the two main issue patterns of sniper garb were the 'Symien' sniper suit of painted scrim, and the 'boiler suit' type, both commonly used with scrim hood, rifle cover or camouflage, and gloves. Expert snipers rarely shot from an obvious loophole, but from tunnelled lairs, prone from amongst heaps of earth or rubbish, or from within some location in deep shadow. Where armoured loops were shot from, best practice was to have a multitude of them. As Hesketh Pritchard noted, the Germans often had numerous loopholes:

> Many steel plates were shoved up on the parapet in the most obvious positions. These were rarely shot through, but they were certainly sometimes used. The German argument

must have been that if you have thirty loopholes, it is thirty to one against the particular one from which you fire being under observation at that particular moment.[12]

The sniper post was addressed at some length in the Northern Command *Notes*. The ideal was a place that commanded weak points in the enemy line, overlooked the enemy wherever possible, but was well concealed. Mostly these would be within 100–700 yards of the enemy. Somewhere within the parados at the rear of a friendly trench was one possibility, but the corner of a traverse in the parapet was also handy. Posts that were bullet, rain and sun proof as well as reasonably comfortable were most suitable for long-term observation – with alternative posts for relocation. Ideally the muzzle of the sniper's rifle would not project out of a post, and where this was likely to occur a pipe or sandbags could be arranged to conceal it. Openings would be made less obvious by being irregular, and by placing different coloured sandbags at intervals; covering with gauze or rubbish would also help. Disguise could include dummy loopholes, perhaps with a dummy rifle, or a black lining and some broken glass inside, to mimic the reflective nature of optics at a distance. Posts were best worked on at night with disposal of any freshly dug earth elsewhere before dawn. Major Crum's ideal post was somewhat different, being a gently sloped alcove off the forward side of the fire trench, within the parapet, and lined with sandbags and other

Snipers of US 168th Infantry at battalion headquarters, Badonvillers, May 1918. The rifles are .30 bolt action, 1903 model, Springfields. The modern-looking, and very effective, camouflaged suits break up the human form with nondescript shape as well as by means of colour and foliage. Hands and faces, often apparent to an observer, are also obscured. (IWM Q65492)

NEUVE CHAPELLE

From the Richebourg sheet, 36 S.W. 3, 1:10,000, with trenches corrected to 22 December 1917. The battle of Neuve Chapelle, fought in March 1915, saw British First Army seize the village at a cost of 13,000 casualties – but German reserves rushed to this sector prevented any possibility of a breakthrough. The village later changed hands again. Two and a half years later the enemy was still barely 500 yards from what little remained of the settlement. Myriad drainage channels show that this area was no rest cure in wet weather.

The British trenches and thoroughfares, marked in blue, show an interesting history through their names. 'Baluchi Road' and 'Gurkha Road' are reminders of the presence of the Indian Corps in 1914 and the subsequent attack by the Meerut Division. An Indian memorial now stands at the La Bombe crossroads. 'Oxford Street', 'Liverpool Street' and 'Edgware Road' are all London inspired – 'Hun Street' was probably once an enemy trench. The British have given the German trenches in the 'S' area opposite a predictable theme – with 'Sandy', 'Sampson' and 'Solomon'. 'Molly' and 'Mitre' are associated with the 'M' area. At the northern edge of the map can be seen the distinctive symbols of mine craters – which, being in red, are currently in enemy hands. In 1918 the ruins of Neuve Chapelle were held by the Portuguese, whose military cemetery is also nearby.

German troops make emergency repairs to a front line trench. Both the elements and shells could cause maintenance problems for the trench garrison. If walkways were allowed to remain blocked the flow of reserves and supplies could be disastrously impeded, and fire positions go unmanned. Very heavy bombardments or repeated shelling over long periods filled in trenches, blocked entrances, damaged drainage and degraded obstacles. Conversely new tactical features appeared in the form of shell holes. (Author's collection)

'After Relief from the Trenches' – the appearance of one German Frontschwein (literally 'front line hog') after a tour of duty. This man has used sand bags and sacking to create both improvised cape and knee pads. Though many Germans sported beards, which cut down on the amount of personal grooming required in the front line, these were later discouraged, or cut back, to allow the proper fitting of full face gas masks. (Author's collection)

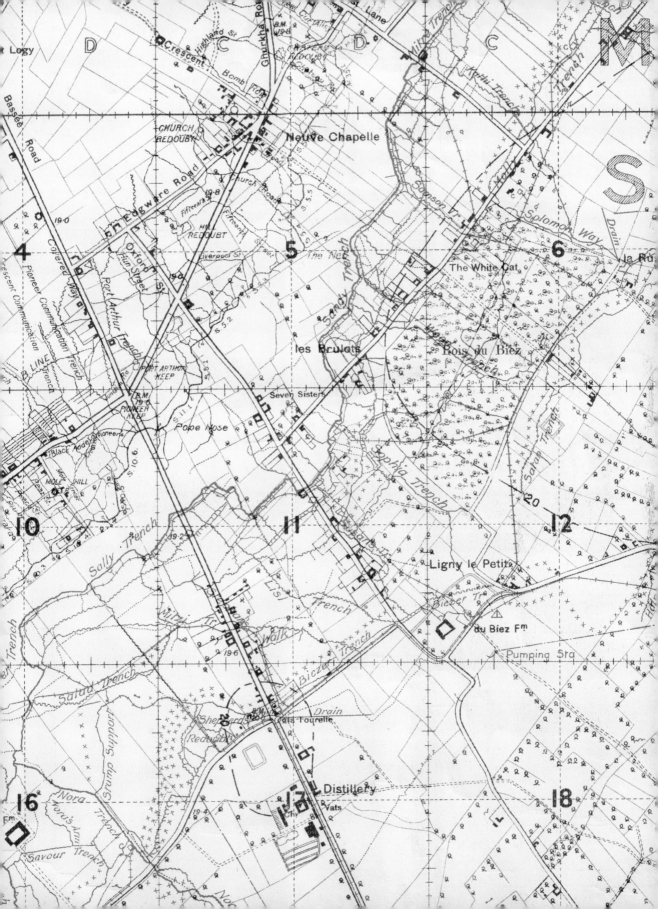

materials to allow the prone sniper to remain in comfort for some time. It was protected from the front by a loophole plate, but so positioned that the plate was within the earth, rather than outside. Sandbags filled with scrap iron could also be judiciously used for increased, but not obvious, bullet protection.

In December 1917 the role of the sniper was succinctly described in *Scouting and Patrolling*. Snipers were useful in both 'open' and 'trench' warfare. In the former they could be employed in both attack and defence, from concealed positions and as a counter to enemy snipers and machine guns. Additionally they could be used as a precaution against counter-attack when an enemy trench had been seized. From here they would creep a few yards further forward and occupy a shell hole or other suitable position whilst their comrades consolidated the trench. Picking off the first enemy to appear would deter counter-attack, and give alert to friendly troops. In static trench warfare a good network of snipers' posts could be arranged so that the whole of the opposing line could be kept 'under telescopic observation' and any enemy head showing at up to 300 yards brought under fire. Friendly casualties caused by rifle fire were to be investigated and snipers detailed to deal with the threat. The sniper posts were to be used for firing at 'live' targets only, whilst periscope smashing and firing armour-piercing rounds at loopholes were best done from elsewhere. Posts that had been discovered and fired upon by the enemy were to be put out of bounds for at least seven days, and preferably abandoned altogether.

As *Scouting and Patrolling* suggested:

The sniper should make use of veils, sniper suits, camouflage etc. when available and Scout Officers should keep themselves up to date with the latest ideas. The study of protective colouring is interesting and of value; but it must be impressed on the Sniper that, however well his disguise may conform with his surroundings, if he does not learn at the same time to keep still, or, move only with stealth and cunning, he is likely to disclose his position… Disguises may be improvised by using grass, leaves etc., and by smearing hands and face and kit to harmonise with surroundings. A regular outline of any shape attracts attention.

Opposite:
German tunnellers by the top of a mine shaft at the junction of Fernsprecher Weg *('telephone way'). One of the team, left, mans the cranking handle of the manual ventilator system, the large flexible pipe of which disappears into the mine. In the entrance of the working another soldier holds a miner's lamp: much safer than a naked flame where flammable gases might be encountered. The wood is to shore up the excavation. (Author's collection)*

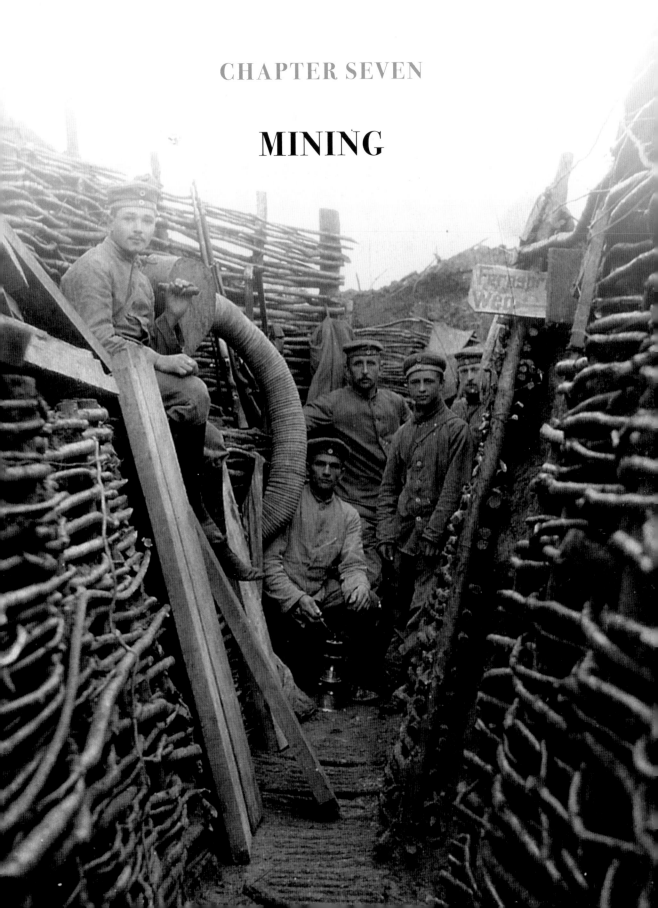

CHAPTER SEVEN

MINING

A static front with no obvious flanks presented a situation very much like that of the classic siege of old – and so it was that many of the techniques of the siege engineer were quickly brought back into use. Of these perhaps the most spectacular was the mine: a tunnel dug under the enemy lines, packed with explosives at its end chamber, and then detonated remotely, so blowing up a section of the enemy trenches. Such attacks had a history that went back to the medieval era, and were taught in the engineering branches of most modern armies. The Prussian manual of military mining dated back to 1866, and the German Army had practised mining in the field in the 1890s. In Britain an extensive tunnelling exercise had been conducted as recently as 1913 at Lulworth in Dorset. Before the end of 1914, mining had commenced on the Western Front – the first British mine being a relatively modest shallow 13 yards long tunnel dug near Festubert with the idea of supporting an attack by Indian troops. In the event enemy mortar fire intervened and this charge was never detonated, but the Germans launched their own underground war with a series of detonations in the same area on the evening of 20 December. Assault troops then succeeded in capturing sections of the line where they found some of the defenders still sitting, apparently unmarked and killed by concussion.

As a German VII Corps report explained:

Sap heads had been dug out from our line to within 3 metres of the enemy position. The enemy, who was very active in throwing hand grenades, had forced us to cover our sap heads. He himself made no saps in the region of the attack. From the ten sap heads in the zone of the attack, mines were laid under the enemy's trenches, each charged with 50kg of explosives. To ensure the ignition of the mines, the attack was arranged for 9am so that the leads could be tested by the company commander and his second in command, and that any improvement which appeared necessary could be made by daylight. A mine was also laid under a house, held by the enemy on the right front of the attack (*Quinque Rue*), and was charged with 300kg of explosive. All telephone communications were manned to ensure the neighbouring sectors commencing the attack simultaneously in the event of there being any delay in the explosion. Actually the explosion did not take place till 10.25 in the morning owing to special difficulties in the connection with one of the leads. When it was reported to the senior pioneer officer on the front of the attack that all the mines were ready, he had three signal flares fired simultaneously. This signal was only meant for pioneers, who then fired all the mines, including the one under the house in *Quinque Rue*.

At the same time a number of *Minenwerfer* directed their fire on the cover trench. The explosion was the signal for the attack, which was carried out as follows by the 2nd and 3rd Battalions, 57 Infantry, 2nd and 3rd Companies of the 7th Pioneer Battalion (less two sections) and the 1st Battalion, 19th Pioneer Regiment (less one Company). A storming party of half a section of infantry with 12 pioneers was in readiness in each of the ten saps. They rushed into the enemy's trench, searched it for mines, and cleared

The Morte Homme *memorial at the summit of Cote 295, near Verdun. It depicts a dead man holding a French flag, and the words 'They shall not pass'. Taken and retaken during the battle of Verdun the hill was so heavily shelled that it was described as 'erupting like a volcano'. Underground intensive tunnelling added another dimension to the struggle. (Author's collection)*

it with hand grenades and incendiary torches. A second storming party (in strength, a section of infantry between every two saps) rushed simultaneously across the open from their own position on both sides of the sap (sortie steps had been prepared for this), and reached the cover trench behind the enemy's position. A third party – a company from each Battalion – occupied our own trench in case of counter-attack. A working party in reserve – the remaining sections of the six attacking companies with pioneer detachments and material for providing cover (shields, sandbags etc.) – followed the attacking party into the enemy's cover trench for the purpose of reconstructing this into a new position facing West.

The ten mines were exploded simultaneously, and the attacking parties immediately rushed forwards with few losses. Amongst the booty seized by the attackers were six machine guns and 11 small trench mortars: there were 834 prisoners, and many more were claimed killed.

British efforts began with what were known as 'Brigade Mining Sections', usually small and rather ad hoc groupings brought under a Royal Engineers officer. Full-blown 'Tunnelling Companies' were formed in early 1915, the first units being designated as Tunnelling Companies numbers 170 to 178. Very rapidly mining was started at various sectors of the front including Hill 60, St Eloi, Ploegsteert, Houplines, Fauquissart, Givenchy and Cuinchy. Many of the early recruits were 'clay kickers', civilians who had worked on subterranean civil projects in the UK, brought together by Norton Griffiths, the Conservative Member of Parliament for Wednesbury – an early enthusiast of what he called military 'moles', who had the ear of Lord Kitchener. In the clay-kicking technique the man working at the head of the excavation rested on a wooden board or 'cross', and used a specially shaped spade, or 'grafting tool', with his feet. The spoil was removed by another man, and transported out of the tunnel in sacks, often in miniature trucks – known by German Pioneers as *Minenhund*, or 'mine dogs'. Often these trucks ran on narrow gauge rail tracks. The tunnel sides could be shored with props and boards. The smallest of the mines were the *camouflets* (or *Quetschmine*), which were designed to intercept and blow in enemy tunnels before they could reach their targets. As mine warfare developed, more sophisticated methods were applied including mechanically driven boring machines, clay cutters and coal mining equipment. Nevertheless skilled manpower was generally found to be most reliable. Electric and handheld power tools were also tested experimentally, but the noise they were likely to cause, plus the problems of maintaining power at the end of a long tunnel, ensured that they never entered general service.

Listening for enemy activity, from surface listening posts or underground galleries, became a vital skill in the tunnelling war. This began with periods of silence and the naked ear, simple measures such as tubes, and tins of water whose surface vibrated when diggers were near. 'Listening sticks', as used to trace leaks in water mains, were also procured from the Metropolitan Water Board. Other devices soon came into play. The 'geophone', of which several models were used by both sides, worked on the principle of amplifying vibration, or magnifying sounds through sensors and earphones. In the most popular British version the pair of wooden sensors contained mercury trapped between mica discs and the listener used a stethoscope. Moving the sensors to bring sounds into balance helped to indicate direction. Canadian tunnelling officer Lieutenant B. C. Hall recalled that on occasions it was not only possible to count the footsteps of enemy miners up and down tunnels, but, by correlating sounds from different points, to work out exactly where individuals were. *Mining Notes* gave useful tables of the likely distances different types of sound travelled underground. Perhaps surprisingly a pick on chalk was detectable with a geophone through solid rock at 300 feet – whilst at the other end of the scale talking was usually only evident from a yard or two away through the muffling effect of sand or loam.

Apart from keeping quiet there were various attempts to stifle underground noise, including soft footwear, blankets hung to deaden noise, and even rugs or carpeting on tunnel floors. There was also a specially designed single wheel barrow shod with a solid rubber tyre. One special trick mentioned in British literature was the use of dummy picks and shovels, which could be operated at a distance using a cord. Some struck at a surface, others scraped like a shovel, thereby misleading the enemy or covering the noise of real activity. Nevertheless lengthy listening vigils sometimes

German soldiers of 3rd Battalion, 15th Infantry Regiment demonstrate the magnitude of a typical mine crater, 1915. Many were much larger than this. Lochnagar Crater on the Somme is 300 feet across; Caterpillar Crater at Hill 60 still contains a small lake. (Author's collection)

yielded extraordinary results as, for example, when 181st Tunnelling Company actually holed an enemy gallery at the end of May 1916, and were able to hear the enemy at such close quarters that conversation was fully intelligible. For almost three days an intelligence officer, aided by an interpreter, was able to take notes on the German works, shift changes and other details 50 feet below ground level. The exercise concluded when the British tunnellers blew four 300lb charges and a raid was launched.

The plans of some of the earliest mines appear haphazard, dendritic, almost like the branches of trees heading out from the trench system, but later more organized layouts became the norm. In the fully mature British tunnel system access to underground works was usually from a shaft in the trench system, preferably from the forward lip of a trench which was therefore less susceptible to enemy shelling. Wooden rungs allowed miners to pass down the shaft, but usually winch and pulley systems were rigged for the lifting of spoil and the descent of materials. Where it was made necessary by poor ground conditions all or part of the shaft might be 'tubbed' – or fitted with tubular steel segments that were sunk using screw jacks and bolted together. From the bottom of the shaft a tunnel led to a 'lateral gallery' running roughly parallel to, and in front of, the trench system. This lateral gallery serviced the active tunnels, which led at right angles under No Man's Land out towards the enemy. Some of these ended in explosive chambers underneath the enemy trenches, and these were packed and 'tamped', or stopped up, prior to firing in order to focus the full effect of the explosion upward. Other tunnels parallel to the main mines might be used for listening, camouflets or as fighting tunnels to impede enemy work, and be further developed as need required.

In every tunnel lighting and ventilation were problems to be confronted. Lighting could be problematic since naked flame, put together with various forms of gas and explosive, presented a potentially lethal cocktail. Possible solutions included civilian type miners' lamps and sealed electric lighting. Canaries or mice in cages gave early warning of dangerous concentrations of toxic gases and lack of oxygen. In many tunnels mechanical ventilation systems were used, the earliest of which appear to have been based on bellows acquired from civilian smithies in the war zone. More complex devices included the British Holman air pump, with a lever that delivered airflow on both its forward and back strokes and rotary fans. In some cases where ventilation failed or gas gathered, full breathing equipment with cylinders might be worn, such as the British 'Proto' or German 'Draeger' equipments.

In January 1917 German mine warfare was examined as part of the document *Summary of Recent Information Regarding the German Army and its Methods*:

> A German mine usually commences with an incline, which terminates in a chamber from which a vertical, or almost vertical shaft is sunk. The depth of the system will vary with the nature of the ground and the scheme in hand. The enemy, like ourselves, locates the entrances to his mine system in the support trenches, or even further back.

Prior to blowing a mine the Germans would often attempt to induce enemy troops to gather in the danger area, perhaps by decoy patrols, or by bombardments on either flank of the mine area. Sometimes German mines were blown less for offensive than defensive purposes, as for example when a crater could be used as an observation point overlooking an area, or to form screened machine gun emplacements. Whilst early in the war craters had been rare and tended to attract a good deal of shelling, by 1917 they were common, and could often quietly be 'improved' without great danger from artillery. Often the technique was to 'sap' towards the crater and dig a trench behind the near lip, then gradually to take in the crater around the sides, using the far lip as the parapet of the forward position. These works could then be further linked to the main trench system. The British estimate was that the Germans had blown no fewer than 696 mines on their front in 1916 alone. The busiest month was June 1916, when an average of four mines per day were exploded.

There were certain places where mines and counter-mine craters finally overlapped to the extent that vast channelled features and areas of virtual moonscape were the result. At Vauquois on a relatively short sector of the Franco-German front near Verdun there were about a hundred mine detonations in less than a year. The 950-feet high Butte de Vauquois, once the site of a village, was transformed into a desert of craters and barbed wire. On a short section of the Cuinchy front trench maps recorded more than 50 mine craters, many of them interlinked. On the Hohenzollern south sector in the vicinity of 'Big Willie' trench there were a similar number of craters, the majority of which overlapped so much that they formed larger features, and eight were known collectively as 'Clifford Craters'. At Hill 60 the work incorporated an old French shaft now designated 'M3' – in bad condition with many changes of direction and level, and full of corpses – as well as new British tunnels. In places the section of the galleries to be negotiated was as little as 2 feet by 3 feet, which caused extreme difficulty when explosives had to be manhandled through such tiny spaces. Nevertheless, as the Royal Engineers history remarked with no little satisfaction, the mine literally 'blew out' the inside of the hill. Two overlapping craters, here 'M1' and 'M1(a)', formed a new feature 180 feet in length, whilst M3 created a hole 30 feet wide. At Hooge Chateau vast craters eventually encroached upon the German concrete bunkers, and today remain as a lake in the grounds of what is now a hotel. Biggest of all was the enormous Lochnagar Crater at La Boiselle, blown using 60,000lb of gun cotton on 1 July 1916 – the huge hole was 300 feet across and 90 feet deep.

Also on the Somme, the blowing of the mine at Hawthorn Redoubt was witnessed by cinematographer Lieutenant Geoffrey Malins:

> I looked at my exposure dial. I had used over a thousand feet. The horrible thought flashed through my mind, that the film might run out before the mine blew. Would it go up before I had time to reload? The thought brought beads of perspiration to my

forehead. The agony was awful; indescribable. My hand began to shake. Another 250 feet. I had to keep on. Then it happened. The ground where I stood gave a mighty convulsion. It rocked and swayed. I gripped hold of my tripod to steady myself. Then, for all the world like a gigantic sponge, the earth rose in the air to the height of hundreds of feet. Higher and higher it rose, and with a horrible, grinding roar the earth fell back upon itself, leaving in its place a mountain of smoke. From the moment the mine went up my feelings changed. The crisis was over, and from that second I was cold, cool, and calculating. I looked upon all that followed from a purely pictorial point of view, and even felt annoyed if a shell burst outside the range of my camera…[1]

By the time of the Somme tunnelling units were fully developed. There were now no fewer than 25 British, three Australian, three Canadian and one New Zealand company, so that well over 2,000 men were deployed on underground works. Along one particular sector, from the La Bassée canal to Hulloch, there was such activity that it was now possible to walk underground for almost 4 miles along the front. On the other side of the line in 1916 German tunnellers were reorganized into *Mineur Kompagnien* – or 'mining companies' – not so different from the British model. Eventually there would be more than 50 of these.

From Royal Engineers History, *showing the method of use of Geophone. (Author's collection)*

The Messines operations of June 1917 were arguably the most impressive mines of the war. The Hill 60 area had been mined several times already by the time 70,000lb of explosive was positioned under the Caterpillar in October 1916. The charge was placed a hundred feet underground, at the end of a gallery 1,380 feet in length. The 204th German Division holding the Hill 60 area lost ten officers and 677 men in the detonation of the Caterpillar and the adjoining Hill 60 gallery. The Caterpillar left a 'diameter of complete obliteration' 380 feet across, within which the actual crater was 260 feet wide. Large as the Caterpillar explosion was it was actually not the largest of the Messines mines, being somewhat dwarfed by the 91,000lb of ammonal at Spanbroekmolen, the 94,000lb of explosive at Maedelstede Farm, and two others of similar scale. The detonations of the Messines operations, which exceeded a million pounds of explosives altogether, were felt in London. As the florid description in the German *Official History* put it:

> Nineteen gigantic roses with carmine petals, like enormous mushrooms, rose up slowly and majestically out of the ground and then split into pieces with a mighty roar, sending up multi-coloured columns of flame mixed with a mass of earth and splinters high into the sky.

On some sectors the effect on the enemy was dramatic. In front of 19th Division the Germans ran forward to surrender, or back to escape. Three lines of trenches were captured, initially with surprisingly light losses, and altogether 140 officers and 7,000 men were captured. Most of the British casualties occurred on the objectives, after they had been taken.

What trench garrisons were supposed to do whilst mining was in progress, and how to react to the explosion of a mine, was sometimes covered in 'Trench Standing Orders'. The 1917 orders for the 63rd Royal Naval Division made it clear that mining operations were to be regarded as integral. No troops were to mention friendly mines, and brigades were to provide working parties to remove the bags of spoil, the contents of which were to be scattered on specified 'dumping grounds' – not left to block trenches and dugouts. When a British mine was exploded the garrison was to leave 'a clear space of 5 yards' on either side of the rear of the shaft, thus avoiding any back blast. Enemy mine craters were to be immediately occupied 'by the nearest troops', this order being made known to all ranks. According to the 1916 official manual *Consolidation of Trenches and Localities* the full drill was as follows:

> When mines are exploded by us in connection with an attack on the enemy's trenches, our object should be to seize and hold the whole of the mine crater or craters, or a line in front of them. The latter plan is usually best, and the craters to the rear can then be turned into strong points… When craters are formed as a result of an attack by the enemy on our trenches, or in the course of underground fighting, our object will

usually be to seize and hold the near lip of the crater. Parties must be rushed out at once to seize the lip. It may be impossible to open up communication to these parties till after dark. They should, therefore, take sufficient grenades, water etc., and must be prepared to hold on though isolated.

Wherever possible attempts to forecast the likely upshot of detonations were to be made and stores laid in accordingly for the consolidation of the void. Dugouts were ideally placed in crater slopes – not at the bottom where they might be prone to flood or burial – and trenches strutted for support, and dug into the craters at two or more points. Copious supplies of wire were also demanded, not merely for conventional linear defences but to be thrown into disputed craters to deny them as jumping off points to the enemy.

Apart from the ever-present danger of being buried alive one of the tunnellers' worst fears was underground confrontation with the enemy – and battles in dark confined spaces with pistols, grenades and daggers certainly obtained nightmarish qualities. During the major works entailed during the digging of the mines under Messines Ridge in late 1916 and 1917 one encounter was described by a Royal Engineer:

One day we broke into the top of an enemy gallery, and as the enemy were heard close by, an emergency charge of 15 pounds of gun cotton was tamped and fired near the hole. Actually, while the charge was being lit, the enemy were heard trying to enlarge the hole they had discovered in their gallery. After the charge had gone up and the mine was reported free from gas, an exploration party was organised and an advance was made into the enemy gallery. This gallery was lit by electric light and when the Germans heard our party advancing they turned on the light. But our officer had foreseen this danger. He had run forward and cut the leads of the lamps well forward of the party, with the result that the only part of the gallery occupied by the enemy was illuminated. Two Germans were seen advancing, one of whom was shot. Both sides then retired, and after two attempts to destroy the gallery with small charges we eventually placed a charge of 200 pounds in position and exploded it, with the result that the German gallery was entirely closed up.[2]

Interestingly, trench raids and infantry attacks could also have a mining dimension, as raiders might be tasked to attack works from the enemy end of the tunnel, perhaps with the intention of blowing them in. The Royal Engineers history contains reference to just such a scheme:

Following the explosion of mines under the German trenches on March 2nd, 1916, a raiding party of tunnellers accompanied the infantry attack. This party comprised an officer with two NCOs and eight men. The NCOs each carried a revolver, electric torch and hatchet, and the men with a 15lb box of guncotton, with 60 yards of instantaneous fuze.

A French Schneider tank blown open like a tin can after shelling. French industry did well to field armoured vehicles in numbers from 1917 but the Schneider was vulnerable to both artillery and armour piercing bullets.

The raiders located the entrance to the German mine inside an old crater, together with some of the tools used, and proceeded inside posting sentries behind them as they entered what turned out to be a complex of works already related to three craters. As indicated by draft, one of the galleries was still attached to the enemy-occupied trench system, so this was attacked with a charge which partially blocked the tunnel. Meanwhile the Germans counter-attacked, and reoccupied one of the craters. The British miners therefore responded by starting to dig a new connecting tunnel, and then prepared three further mines, up to 300lb in size, to cave in enemy access routes.[3]

Opposite:

German officers at the entrance to a deep bunker. The steps lead down from the forward lip of a trench for maximum protection. The trench itself is boarded, and a raised wooden lip at the dugout entrance is intended to reduce the amount of water or detritus flowing down. According to the 1916 manual Stellungsbau, *deep dugouts were unsuitable for the first line, being difficult to exit quickly. Further back, where cover 5 or more yards deep was advised for shell protection, bunker exits were to be unobstructed, and at least 1.5 yards from trench traverses. Two of the officers here wear the Iron Cross First Class. This was pinned directly to the uniform, unlike the Second Class type, which was suspended from a black and white ribbon on official occasions, and represented only by a piece of ribbon on combat uniform. Founded in 1813, and re-instituted at the outbreak of war, the cross patée shaped medal was awarded approximately 163,000 times in the first class, and 5,000,000 times in the second by November 1918. (Author's collection)*

CHAPTER EIGHT

CONCRETE AND *STELLUNGSBAU*

A s we have noted the first year of war saw the development of complex trench systems that became wider, and often physically deeper, with the passage of time. Early single lines with a support were soon supplemented by second, third and even fourth lines – critical points being reinforced with redoubts and strong points. Sandbags, wire and other materials were supplied more efficiently and in greater quantities. Defences were now often miles rather than hundreds of yards in depth. Led by German tactical analysis of the defensive battle, and an increasing emphasis on the role of the machine gun, there was a growing realization of the importance of posts and zones which formed a skeleton within the trench system. Progressively, and with a thinning of the trench garrisons, theorists laid more emphasis on the web of defence points, and less upon the ideas of linear obstacles and cover.

In 1916 *Stellungsbau*, the new German manual 'of the construction of field positions', became the engineering and defensive tactician's bible. The basic purposes of works remained the same: economy of forces; diminution of loss, and increase of loss to the enemy; and utilization of the ground so as to produce favourable conditions for combat. The way this was to be achieved had, however, changed out of all recognition since 1914. Now the first position was to be 'close up to the enemy', and was to consist of:

Below and opposite: Illustrations from the German Stellungsbau, 1916. Fig 2 shows a communication trench block. Figs 33 and 34 show shell-proof MG emplacement and enfilading wire while Figs 49–51 demonstrate different shelters. (Author's collection)

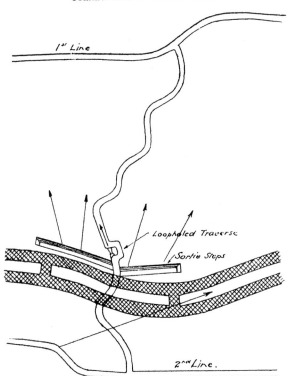

Fig. 2.

Communication Trench Block.

a trench system of several continuous but not parallel lines, at 150 to 200 yards distance from one another. The lines are to be connected by an ample number of communication trenches. Communication rearwards is ensured by approach trenches, which can never be too numerous. All the above trenches are to be so adapted to the ground, that, as far as possible, the enemy cannot see into them anywhere. A short field of fire is sufficient. Behind the first position at least one rearward position should be prepared. The same general principles hold good for this. It should be at such a distance that a simultaneous artillery attack on both is not possible. The distance will, therefore, vary from 4 to 10 kilometres.

Nor was this all, for each of the main positions would consist of at least three lines, and between the lines of each position, and behind the rear position, every spot was to be prepared for defence – with many 'strong points', 'holding points' and 'posts'. 'Strong points' were defined as defended villages, woods and the like, whilst 'holding points' might be smaller features such as shell holes, small trenches, ruins or thickets. The strong points were to be gradually joined up by fire trenches and

Fig. 33.
Section.

Fig. 49.

Shelter for reserves.

Section a–b.

(on concrete base).

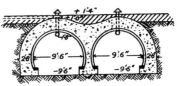

Fig. 50.

Section c–d.

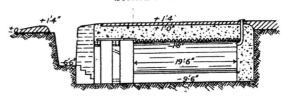

Fig. 34.
Plan.

Fig. 51.

Shelter for supports.

Floor space for 1 group (9 men) with 10·7 sq. ft. floor
space per man.

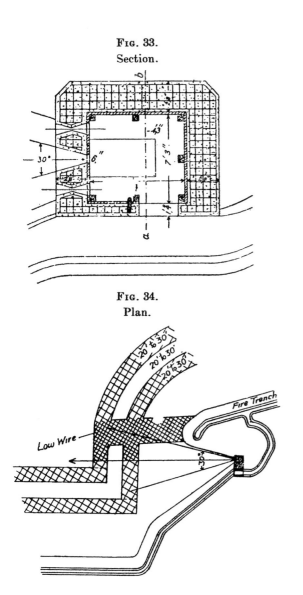

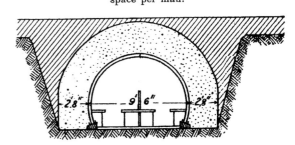

obstacles to create new lines, and blockhouses built in woods, thus creating 'a broad fortified zone'. Artillery observation posts were particularly crucial in the forward areas, and the defensive line itself was best placed on rear slopes, even if this entailed reduced fields of fire. In rearmost areas the most cost effective method was to fortify a few posts and dugouts but leave the intervening trenches until later – as extensive trench works required continual maintenance and would needlessly absorb resources.

The particular importance of posts in creating the skeleton was not overlooked:

Machine gun positions and dugouts form the framework of all infantry fighting lines. A hundred metres or less is sufficient frontal field of fire. Machine guns should be concealed in emplacements; they must enfilade the obstacles, the space in front of the

The Boyau de Londres – *London Trench – Verdun. This trench, parts of which survive, is a fairly late French construction intended as a communication trench to the forward forts. Unusually, parts of it are revetted with original prefabricated concrete panels. (Author's collection)*

obstacles, and the ground between different lines and positions from higher ground, if possible. They must, therefore, be scattered. The few guns used in the front line must endeavour to increase their power by mobility.

Interestingly, dugouts in the rear were to be stronger than those in the first line – presumably because the heavier enemy guns were usually trained on the more distant targets, and it did not matter so much if a rear area dugout took time to exit. The garrison of the forward defence was to be sufficient to deal with any 'surprise attacks', but the bulk of the troops were to be held back, being accommodated in the rear lines, ground between the lines, communication trenches and countryside behind the first position. As Hindenburg would later explain:

our defensive positions were no longer to consist of single lines and strong points but of a network of lines and groups of strong points. In the deep zones thus formed we did not intend to dispose our troops on a rigid and continuous front but in a complex system of nuclei, and distributed in depth and breadth. The defender had to keep his forces mobile to avoid the destructive effects of enemy fire during the period of preparation as well as to abandon voluntarily any parts which could no longer be held.[1]

Considering actual dimensions and details of works, *Stellungsbau* came to the conclusion that though narrow trenches gave best protection they were inconvenient for traffic and prone to blocking. For this reason narrow works were only of use as a temporary expedient, deep and broad trenches being generally preferable. Revetting was desirable where watery conditions might lead to collapse, but far less important than the construction of new works. Armoured and other loopholes were useful, but probably only required in every second bay of the fire trenches since major attacks would also be met by machine gun fire and general fire over the parapet. Communication trenches were ideally deep, sinuous and provided with recesses every 55 yards which served as cover from shrapnel and as posts for runners. Sortie steps were useful in places for quick entrance and exit. Communication trenches were similarly to be provided with the means to create a block, perhaps with a loopholed traverse and a barbed wire obstacle ready to be pulled into position. 'Splinter proof' dugouts were deemed of only marginal use, and fortification builders were urged to devote their efforts to 'shell proof' and 'bomb proof' shelters, these latter being defined as capable of providing protection from 'continuous' shelling from 21cm projectiles, and single hits from heavier guns. Concrete and deep mining could both give such protection, but the former was accounted best, as relatively tough shallow concrete works were easier to exit.

By the middle of the war German wire was usually thick and effective, and absorbed considerable labour. As the *Summary of Recent Information* explained in January 1917:

> Every defensive line, switch and strong point is protected by a strong wire entanglement
> on iron or wooden posts, sited, if possible so as not to be parallel to the trenches behind
> it. Endeavours are made to provide two or three belts, each 10 to 15 feet or more deep,

Concrete bunker, Hill 60, Zwarteleen, Belgium. Interestingly, Hill 60 is essentially manmade, being composed of spoil from the nearby railway cutting. As one of the few rises it was eagerly contested. The German works here were undermined, then assaulted by the West Yorkshires in June 1917. This bunker is a curious amalgam, being an Australian observation post (facing east) constructed atop an older German pillbox. It lies within a couple of hundred yards of the enormous 'Caterpillar' mine crater. (Author's collection)

with an interval between belts of 15 to 30 feet. These intervals are filled, if possible, with trip wires, pointed iron stakes, etc. and blocked by occasional bands of entanglement connecting the belts. Four different lengths of iron screw pickets are supplied, the longest, which has five loops, giving a height of 4 feet above ground. The distance apart of the pickets in an entanglement is intentionally irregular, but averages about 6.5 feet.

The use of concrete certainly aided the development of stand-alone strong points and bunkers, though it was first thought of merely as a more effective form of reinforcement. Reinforced concrete doorways were less liable to collapse, and layers of concrete, combined with earth and wood, were found to be more effective top cover for dugouts – as a 'sandwich' construction could burst the shell, and contain some of the shock by virtue of the different properties of the materials. Short sections of trench might also have concrete works built into them, as for example in 'under parapet' shelters. Though concrete was seen in pre-war fort construction its widespread adoption for fieldworks took some time. During 1915 the Germans began to organize transport of basalt and gravel using Rhine barges through the neutral Netherlands, off loading at points on the River Lys, thus supplementing the production of cement works nearer to the front such as those at Antwerp and Mons. An important realization was that concrete, especially with steel reinforcement, could make an effective protection without the need for very deep excavations. In Flanders, where deep digging was made difficult by the water table, concrete works would become crucial, and were in fact widely used by both sides. In German parlance concrete works were often known by the acronym MEBU, or *Mannshafts Eisenbeton Unterstände* – 'ferro-concrete personnel dugouts'. The term 'blockhouse' was already very familiar from the Boer War, and British troops also used the descriptive term 'pillbox'.

Though some concrete works had embrasures for machine guns and rifles, quite a few did not. First aid posts and rear area bombardment shelters did not need them, and perforation significantly reduced ballistic resistance. Even in the front line many bunkers were designed essentially as temporary shell protection for a section or two of troops, who would immediately emerge to fire over the top of the work, or disperse into nearby trenches and shell holes. German concrete structures appeared in numbers during 1916. By early 1917 the wide range of standard model works included observation posts incorporating rails for reinforcement; a bell-like iron reinforcement and aperture intended to be used with a mirror or stereoscopic binoculars; a machine gun post with side apertures for enfilading fire; a two-storey 'battle headquarters'; various command posts, ammunition bunkers, battery positions and shelters for supports. Some of these latter were designed as tubes, gaining additional strength from their shape. A nine-man *Gruppe* in such a tube obtained about 1 square yard of floor space per person. Perhaps the most frightening fieldwork was the 'low shelter', a coffin-like alcove 2 yards long into which a few men could squeeze themselves, but only when prone.

The yardstick conclusion of German engineers was that 30 inches of concrete was sufficient for a general 'shell proof' construction, half this being adequate 'splinter' protection. German concrete bunkers were constructed using both 'wet' concrete and prefabricated blocks. Designated 'mixing places' just behind the front line were used to make pouring concrete, with blocks manufactured further away as at the Wervik factory. On larger jobs light railways and tramways were used to move the materials. Standard fortification concrete was cement, sand and stone ballast in a 1:2:4 ratio, though this was reduced to 1:2:2 and the water content increased in reinforced structures to ensure that the mix flowed around the metal rods or joists. In block constructions the concrete bricks could be slotted together with rods on site to create a stronger structure. Though the works that remain today often appear very obvious cubes in the landscape most were originally well concealed. Some were deliberately placed in folds in the ground. Others were made to appear like agricultural buildings, or were built into genuine farms, and many were wholly or partially buried, or obscured with brushwood. The texture of the wet concrete was sometimes broken up with sacking and shapes concealed with netting.

Over 2,000 German concrete works were built around the Ypres Salient alone. As General Gough explained, this was 'a different system of defence', powerful and made more so by mud and drainage ditches, impossible to locate precisely from a

The German obstacle zone, near Arras, June 1917. Strictly speaking this particularly fearsome entanglement is not 'barbed wire' but 'razor wire', as it is formed of serrated bands cut from a steel sheet – not made by attaching 'barbs' to wire. Laid out in front of the trench system, belts of wire provided early warning, hindered attack and funnelled the enemy into the path of machine guns. Often obstacle zones were formed of multiple belts with gaps between: such elaborate obstructions were difficult to clear either by shelling or by teams equipped with cutters and explosives. (IWM Q2548)

PLOEGSTEERT WOOD

From the Ploegsteert sheet, 28 S.W. 4, 1:10,000, trenches corrected to 1 April 1917. In this map we see the eastern edge of the famous Ploegsteert Wood and the German trenches opposite. The village of Ploegsteert, known to Tommy as 'Plug Street', lay to the west and south of the wood, and often served as a reserve billet for troops manning the line. The British trenches, in blue, are shown only in outline, the enemy trenches, in red, in considerable detail. In this area the English names for the German trenches all begin with 'U' – hence 'Umpire', 'Umbria', 'Ultra' and 'Ulster'. 'Uncle' trench is the German second line. What passes for landmarks have been given names that bear mute witness to the destruction of war – 'Broken Tree House', 'Flattened Farm' and 'Dead Horse Corner' being just the most obvious. Mine craters, two held by the Germans, and three held by the British, are marked within a few yards of each other just to the north of Le Pelerin, close to the 'White Estaminet'. Remarkably another mine laid in this vicinity in 1917 lay dormant until it finally exploded – in 1955.

The wood was first taken by British cavalry in 1914, but part was later retaken by the enemy who were not actually driven back to the positions seen here until 1917. The next April it fell again during the Spring Offensive – and was only completely cleared by British 29th Division on 4 September 1918. 'Hunter Avenue' was one of the main thoroughfares through the wood, photographs of 1917 showing it as a roughly boarded 'corduroy' track passing through trees stripped of foliage. Both British and German concrete works from the latter part of the war survive on the fringes of the wood. 'Laurence Farm' – seen left of centre in square 27 – was sketched by Winston Churchill when he was here with the 6th Royal Scots Fusiliers.

British and German soldiers on the 11th Brigade front at Ploegsteert fraternizing on Christmas Day during the unofficial, but widespread, truce of 1914. The bearded smoking German, right, wears the spiked Pickelhaube with cover, and the early type regulation greatcoat with coloured collar patches. Several men have soft caps, scarves or pullovers against the winter weather. (IWM Q70075)

distance, safest from all but the very heaviest shells, and very much like a series of small forts.[2] Though battered and furiously fought over a majority of these bunkers remained usable even in mid 1918. Some had been bodily lifted or had subsided but remained intact. Reports noted:

> Most of the dugouts have been hit, and except for some in the front line, where the concrete appears to have been poor or the thickness insufficient, they have not suffered. One farm has been bombarded by ourselves and by the enemy for over a month, and is none the worse… The effect of shell fire on these structures has been practically nil, though the intervening ground is a mass of interlocking shell holes.

Often the combination of concrete and scattered 'defence in depth' worked all too well, economizing on troops and creating a very tough nut to crack. At Passchendaele in 1917, for example, the defences were arranged as a series of zones, studded with concrete. The foremost parts, along the Pilckem Ridge and western part of the Gheluvelt Plateau, were merely the 'outpost' zone of a 'battle zone' that covered the reverse slopes and ran back to the centre of the plateau. Beyond this were a third line and a rear zone. Further back had been created a 'Flanders I' line, and two further lines, 'Flanders II' and 'III', had just been laid out. Making progress through this would be expensive. Just one example from the battle was the advance of 1st Irish Rifles up Pilckem Ridge. The battalion followed a bombardment in an open 'artillery formation', but was not impeded so much by linear defence as by machine gun and sniper fire – much of it from a flank less affected by the shelling. The cost was 36 dead and 167 wounded and missing. The adjutant, Lieutenant Whifeld, was the only officer to survive the attack unscathed. As he later remarked, he was 'surprised to find so few dead' in the German line, 'showing that the enemy was evidently distributed in depth and that we should have a tough time'.

Though less enamoured of concrete British engineers were by no means ignorant of its use. In the La Bassée sector, for example, many tons of cement, sand and shingle were used as an antidote to swampy ground. Manuals of 1916, such as *Notes on Trench Warfare for Infantry Officers: Revised Diagrams*, did include reinforced concrete, most notably as a 'bursting course' in shelters designed against 15cm projectiles. There was also reference to a double-skinned concrete machine gun emplacement incorporating a blast-cushioning air space between the layers. Concrete had also been used for some time for 'hardening' specific points such as exposed observation posts and dressing stations. Similarly the Royal Engineers experimented with a front line concrete Lewis gun post, which was calculated to take 20 men 14 days to complete. Yet for two apparent reasons concrete was not widely used in the British front line. The first of these was that British forces expected to be on the offensive, and putting resources into fixed defences was not first priority. The second reason was the natural corollary of the first: for if the British attacked they moved forward, and, even if territorial gains were trivial, lines of fixed defences were quickly rendered useless. Interestingly British theory of

The Stahlhelm *worn by a pipe-smoking German officer. Designed by Dr Friedrich Schwerd the German steel helmet was trialled in 1915, and made a general issue during the course of 1916. It was not bulletproof unless fitted with a heavy brow plate which fixed over the distinctive side lugs, but was capable of stopping the small splinters and fragments which were the cause of many head wounds. Initially regarded with some misgiving it was soon a popular, even iconic, piece of equipment. (Author's collection)*

1916 suggested that, particularly in the front line, machine gun dugouts could be counterproductive, since any obvious work would attract artillery fire – which it was assumed would lead to their destruction. 'Bomb Proofs' were therefore only to be located where the enemy could not see them, and these were essentially cover during bombardments. Actual machine gun firing positions would be carefully concealed nearby, but might not be 'hardened' at all. They would be approached wherever possible by covered saps, tunnels or any other means presenting no obvious track way to give away their position.

Even so the toughness of the 1917 German concrete defences in Flanders undoubtedly came as a nasty surprise, and one that the Royal Engineers history readily admits caused a re-evaluation of the significance of such works. The result was a renewed interest in concrete, and a factory for blocks was opened at Aire-sur-la-Lys: a 'School of Concrete' was founded in early 1918. Though this would be too little too late to meet the German Spring Offensive, quite a few concrete pillboxes were erected towards the end of the war. These included not only conventional-looking boxes, but 'Moir' model machine gun posts and the Australian-designed armoured 'Hobbs' post with a revolving cupola.

Arguably the last official outline for a British First World War trench system was that presented in the booklet *Field Works for Pioneer Battalions*, originally produced in 1918, though many of the copies do not appear to have been printed until the following year. This set the context for trench defences rather more explicitly than earlier instructions. Now it was assumed that the 'general line of defence' would be dictated by the strategic situation and 'higher authority', whilst the siting of actual trenches would be determined by the need to retain 'tactical features' which would 'screen from the enemy's direct observation the maximum amount of ground'. The unobserved area would serve for the marshalling of reserves and artillery, ideally whilst denying similar cover to the enemy. The essential parts of the system were the 'Main Battle Zone' and an 'Outpost Zone', with an additional area for the reserve. The outpost zone alone was from 1,500 to 4,000 yards in depth. The distance between the main battle zone's front trench line and its support was to be a further 150 to 200 yards, and the distance from here to the rear reserve line about 500 yards. The whole system could therefore range from under 2, up to well over 3, miles in depth. In case of necessity a whole new system was to be constructed behind the first.

Detailed layouts were to be 'very irregular', with trenches taking advantage not only of natural cover and folds in the ground, but particularly any 'water obstacles' that might constitute a defence against tanks. In all instances the enemy view of the position was to be considered when planning. The outpost zone was to be lightly held, inconspicuous, and should not require 'continuous lines' or a high level of organization. Nevertheless 'artificial obstacles' and 'shell proof accommodation' were to be included in every zone. Trench lines were to be marked out first with tracing tapes, flags, pegs and pickets, the work being done by a 'tracing party' led by an officer and an NCO, with as many men as were needed to carry the equipment. Basic dimensions of trenches remained much the same as previously, but particular attention was to be paid to drainage, as it was not safe to assume that if pumps were included in an initial scheme it would prove possible to keep them working indefinitely.

Revetments were divided into two main types. The first were those intended to form a 'skin' against the face of earth, held in position by uprights. These revetments were likely to include corrugated iron, expanded metal, brushwood and hurdles, supported by pickets or frames. The second type of revetment was those that were built up like a retaining wall or dam, acting under their own weight. These included sandbags, sods and gabions. Where possible trenches would be dug to take standard

Captured German officers under guard outside a recently captured concrete bunker near Langemarck, 12 October 1917. The highland sentry wears a groundsheet as a rain cape. Heavily fought over in late 1914, Langemarck near Ypres was captured by the Germans in April 1915. It was recaptured by British 20th Division in August 1917; recaptured by the enemy in early 1918; then finally fell to Belgian forces on 28 September 1918. The sombre cemetery at Langemarck is now the main site for German burials in the Salient area. It contains over 44,000 bodies, including a mass grave of 25,000. (IWM Q3013)

frames, made at base workshops, which would also accommodate a duckboard with a drainage channel below. By 1918 the Royal Engineers' 'battalion dumps' usually contained two sizes of 'A' frame; corrugated iron sheets; duckboards, with spare slats for running repairs; revetting panels; and hurdles a standard 6 feet by 4. Sandbags were still held, but were regarded as mainly for sap heads and other special tasks. When completed lengths of trench were to be put under the eye of a designated 'warden', and immediate repairs would be done by the troops in occupation.

Interestingly, though pioneer battalions were to be particularly proficient in the construction of fieldworks, infantry were still expected to get themselves under cover by the swiftest means possible. Whilst formulas of men, per hour, per yard, were still employed, by 1918 the new system of 'intensive digging' was used in times of emergency. As *Hints on Training* explained, relays of one spade per three men, or one pick and two spades per nine men for hard ground, was the ideal balance between economy of weight and economy of effort. So supplied, all tools could be kept at work, at maximum efficiency, day and night – with one of the three-man team digging for all he was worth for a couple of minutes only, before handing the spade to the next. The change over being accomplished with 'lightning rapidity', the whole unit could be underground in a 6-foot deep trench in an hour.

Germans in a deep bunker from a work by Elk Eber exhibited at the Haus der Deutschen Kunst *in Munich. The original caption states that the subjects are sheltering from* Trommel, *or 'drum' fire. Note the use of a French bayonet as a candle holder. Deep cover saved many lives, but was not necessarily proof against super heavy projectiles, gas, collapsed entrances and surprise attacks, during which the enemy might attempt to bowl grenades down steps. Nerve-wracking bombardment might continue for days, and became a well nigh universal aspect of the trench warfare experience. By the latter part of the war it was usual to shelter troops in parties of one or two* Gruppen, *or up to about 20 individuals, reducing potential losses. (Author's collection)*

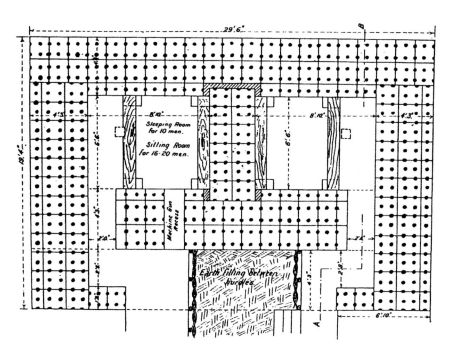

DUGOUT
CONCRETE BLOCK WALLS AND REINFORCED ROOF
ARRANGED AS DEFENSIBLE POST.
From Drawings found in MESSINES 17.6.17. by 12ᵗʰ FIELD Cᵒ AUSTRALIAN ENGᴿˢ.

E. in C. FIELDWORK NOTES.
Nº 31.
PLATE - 5.

Drawings found at Messines. showing a German dugout with concrete block walls. (Author's collection)

Sleeping Room for 10 men.
Sitting Room for 16-20 men.

Machine Gun Recess

Earth filling between hurdles.

PLAN (OF FIRST LAYER)

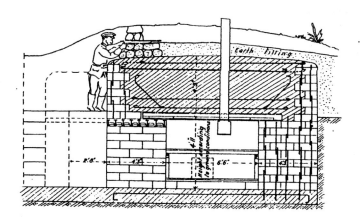

Earth Filling

CROSS SECTION A.B.

Whilst a full trench system was still regarded as an ideal, in quite a few instances Allied defensive zones – like the German – came to rely on a series of posts rather than a continuous line. In the case of the South Africans at Delville Wood on the Somme, for example, the first stage of hurried consolidation was the digging of mainly two-man rifle pits. Digging was rendered difficult by tree roots. Lewis guns were then brought up around the perimeter, and once in place supplemented by Vickers guns. Only then were the original pits extended to form continuous trenches, and support trenches dug in Buchanan Street, Princes Street and Strand Street. Finally strong points were constructed by the Royal Engineers. Colonel Tanner's original intention had been to hold the wood with machine guns 'with small detachments of infantry', but was overtaken in this design by immediate enemy counter-attacks which necessitated a larger garrison to resist.

CONCERTINA BARBED WIRE.

Nine pickets are arranged in a circle 4 ft in diameter

Four men sit round the circle and one guides the wire, uncoiling it off the drum till the whole coil is bound round the outside of the nine pickets.

Pieces of pliable wire about five inches long having been prepared each strand of barbed wire is bound to the next strand above it in the centre of every second space between the pickets.

There being an odd number of pickets, the result is a diamond pattern when the coil is stretched out.

When the coil is expanded and bound with pliable wire it can be lifted off the pickets. It is then secured by wire and tags are fastened to the two outside circles to enable them to be found with ease at night.
The coils are now ready to be carried to the site.

TO ERECT THE ENTANGLEMENT.
Erect a row of pickets at three to four feet interval. See that they are perpendicular and firmly fixed. Extend the Concertina and drop it over the pickets. Run a line of strong plain wire through the top loop of each picket; if screw pickets are used and the Concertina, giving the wire a double turn round the loop, so that if one bay is cut, the next will stand up. If other posts are used the plain wire should be twisted round top of each picket

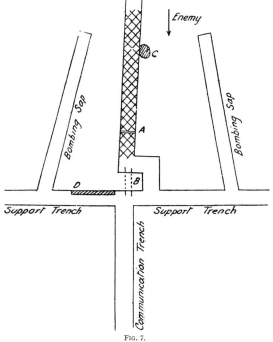

60   CONSTRUCTION AND EQUIPMENT OF TRENCHES.

BLOCKING GATE FOR COMMUNICATION TRENCH.
Placed at junction of communication and support-line trenches.
The gate "A" is made of expanded metal double sheets. It is an ordinary "shut-to" gate which is closed by two iron rails which slip into iron hooks on the doorposts.

FIG. 7.

At the gate the trench is wired over, close enough to stop a grenade from being thrown out of the trench.
At "C" there is a barbed-wire knife rest, which can be pulled into the trench to form an additional obstacle.
Bombing can be carried out from the saps on either side, and from fire step at "D."
There are two loopholes in the traverse at "B," which cover the gate and trench beyond it.

As early as November 1916 the forward positions of the 1st/4th Loyal North Lancashire Regiment at Railway Wood were noted as:

a certain number of sentry posts, each consisting of an NCO and, when possible six men – more often four – some posts being Lewis gun posts, others bombing posts, others riflemen only. This line of posts, weak as it is, is strung out between and in front of a series of strong points containing machine guns and an infantry garrison lodged deep in mines, while behind us is the support company ready to come up in case of need, and reserve troops further back; in addition we have the guns, which we can always switch on in a few seconds by telephone or sending up a rocket; all these things give us confidence, weak though we feel ourselves to be.

Opposite and below: Line drawings from the US Trench Construction and Equipment, 1917. The illustrations show concertina wire and entanglements, a blocking gate for a communication trench and the trench system for a battalion in the front line. (Author's collection)

Sometimes such discontinuity of the line was a conscious tactical choice, but often it was a function of either the terrain or movement that did not give time for a recreation of the ambitious works of the middle war period. British defences on the Lys canal, erected hurriedly in the face of the German offensive of 1918, were described by C. G. Chead of the Argyll and Sutherland Highlanders as:

small 'posts' a few yards distant from each other, each holding about half a dozen men. These 'posts' were actually strips of trench with a rather high parapet – open at the rear, made up with very little sand-bagging, protected in front with the usual rows of barbed wire.

Dugouts and shelters for the trench system of 1918 were divided into 'cut and cover', 'concrete' and 'tunnelled' types. Cut and cover models were not to exceed a capacity of 12 men, and not expected to be proof against anything bigger than a 15cm shell. The overhead protection of such a shelter was a five-layer sandwich consisting of a bursting course, cushion, distributing course, second cushion and a thin layer of hard material on the inner face, immediately above the roof to stop splinters. Concrete shelters were to be either of the poured or block concrete types, and to resist a 21cm shell a thickness of 3 feet 6 inches was recommended.

Tunnelled dugouts could be anything up to 40 feet deep, dug according to a number of standard plans, or

CONSTRUCTION AND EQUIPMENT OF TRENCHES.

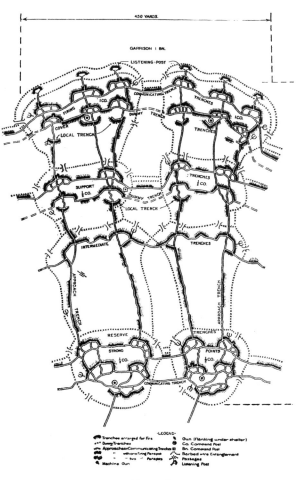

PLATE I.

195

Illustrations from Fieldworks
for Pioneer Battalions, *1918.*
(Author's collection)

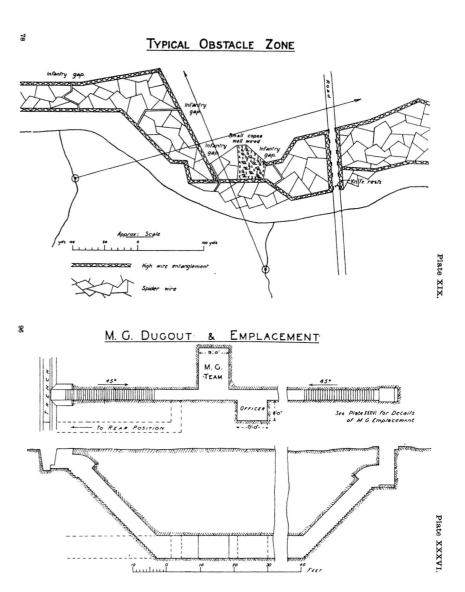

designed around specific circumstances. The standard plans included HQs, deep
shelters attached to MG emplacements, and personnel shelters. All could contain
bunked sleeping accommodation. Precise depth and the amount of timber needed in
galleries were to be varied according to ground conditions. The biggest tunnelled
dugouts were complexes capable of holding complete battalions, and might even be
linked to each other, or trench systems, by 'subways' – often at about 20 feet under
ground level. These subways were wooden lined corridors with a standard height of
6 feet 6 inches and a width of 3 feet 6. These dimensions ensured that all but the very
tallest troops could walk fully erect and if necessary pass each other without undue
difficulty. The standard subway design of the latter part of the war also allowed for
electric lighting with bulbs at intervals protected by expanded metal guards.[3]

Tunnelled dugouts had the advantages that they were easy to conceal and gave better protection. On the negative side they were difficult to exit. For these reasons they were to have a minimum of two entrances at least 40 feet apart. Nevertheless there were still accidents, such as that which overcame part of the 'Hedge Street Tunnels' complex of dugouts, south of the Menin Road, near to a location known as 'Tower Hamlets', in January 1918. Fire broke out underground, and 2nd Green Howards were forced to seal up part of the system to localize the conflagration:

> … when it was reopened some days later by the 20th Division the bodies of our men were found in the various bunks still wearing their gas helmets. Except where part of a man's body was lying in the main alley there were no marks of burning on the bodies, but everything in the main alley was charred up.[4]

The notion of multiple entrances to deep dugouts was sound, but sometimes two were not enough. At Turco Farm, for example, the enemy happened to succeed in landing heavy trench mortar bombs on both entrances of a large dugout simultaneously. Signaller Stanley Bradbury of the Seaforths was one of those entombed:

A photograph from the Royal Engineers' camouflage collection, showing a screen of canvas and 'fish netting'. The fish net proved effective and popular, and could be garnished with grass, raffia or canvas strips. In many instances it was simply thrown over stores or positions and pegged down. By August 1916 a standard portable kit was devised for the 18-pdr field gun, which included a 30 foot square net with dyed raffia, guy ropes and a light iron frame supported on four 'gas pipe' uprights. Almost 13,000 of these kits had been made by the end of the war, and the total output of fish netting was approximately 7.5 million square yards. (IWM Q17791)

The result was terrific. The whole of the heavy cement blocks crashed in burying those under and near them and the dugout was reduced to a heap of dirt and debris. The dugout had been full of men all sitting on the steps from the top to the bottom. We were blown amongst a heap of wreckage onto the floor of the dugout but beyond the shock had not suffered any injury although from the cries and groans of those who had been on the steps it seemed that many were terribly injured. A state of panic then existed as with intense darkness and the only entrance whereby fresh air could enter the dugout being completely blocked there appeared to be grave fear that we should suffocate.[5]

Eventually rescuers tunnelled in: of 38 occupants three were dead, and 32 wounded. The problem of ventilation in dugouts was difficult to solve, since lack of ventilation meant possible suffocation, whilst too much ventilation could lead to the ingress of gas, or present opportunities to drop grenades down ventilation pipes – for which reason vents were sometimes kinked or fitted with a trap. Where vents had to be created after the construction of a dugout or shallow mine gallery this was sometimes accomplished using the 'Wombat Borer', a giant two-man hand-cranked drill with which the operators bored upward.

Impressive as tunnelled dugouts became, the ultimate in underground accommodation were the caves of Arras. This town near the front line was built of a form of hard chalk, much of which had been mined locally, and the caves were discovered by the military in late 1916. They were found to extend up to 60 feet underground and were conveniently located between the town and front line. Soon it was decided that the caves should be occupied and connected to the front via subways, excavated mainly by the New Zealand Tunnelling Company. These 3 miles of subways contained not only electric lighting, but water mains and supplementary dugouts. There were nine major caves and a complex of mainly smaller ones, these latter being known collectively as the St Sauveur caves. Many had multiple entrances. The total capacity was reckoned at a staggering 11,425 men – or the better part of a division. The bigger caves were identified by suitably New Zealand-inspired names such as Wellington, Christchurch and Auckland, whilst the St Sauveur caves were named after British towns and Channel Islands, hence Crewe, Glasgow, London and Alderney.

Like concrete, camouflage and the associated art of screening also grew in sophistication and organization as the war progressed. The uniforms of many units had acquired dull hues as early as the 19th century, and foliage had been used for centuries, but it is claimed that one of the first real attempts to hide large objects in World War I came in September 1914 when French artist Guirand de Scevola conceived the idea of hiding his gun battery behind screens of painted canvas. An experimental French camouflage detachment was formed at Amiens in February 1915. Eventually this grew into an entire 'Camouflage Service' whose works included not only netting, screens, frames and painting but also more exotic devices such as concealed observation posts and dummy bodies of men and animals. A key adjunct was the use of 'Army Factories' and 'Base Factories' – the latter being mainly staffed by women and tasked with mass production.

In co-operation with the French the British professionalized their own camouflage efforts in the winter of 1915 to 1916, and a full 'Special Works Park' of the Royal Engineers was soon in operation. This was expanded to multiple establishments and depots later. Early efforts included disguised observation posts, which might appear to be trees or parts of parapets, and gun covers of painted canvas. Later the product range was extended to the concealment of almost anything, and in their turn American officers were attached to the British camouflage units to learn the trade. By 1918 there were five British camouflage factories under a 'Controller of Camouflage'. Some of the main British standard items of camouflage included canvas and scrim; wire netting; 'fish nets'; various types of observation post; concealed

Drawings from the French Platoon Leader's Manual, *1917, showing trench sections and gabions. (Author's collection)*

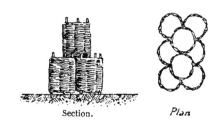

Fig. 39. — Splinter proof shield.

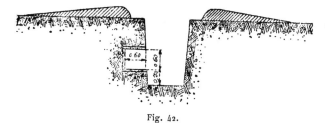

4° **Ammunition recess.**

Fig. 42.

5° *Boyau.*

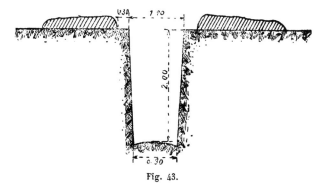

Fig. 43.

The concrete and armoured observation posts atop Fort Vaux, Verdun. This fort, which was effectively the north-eastern bastion of the defence, held on heroically until June 1916, and was recaptured by the French in November. On its outer wall is one of the oddest memorials of the conflict, a tablet recording the pigeon which carried the last message from Vaux by its commander, Commandant Raynal. (Author's collection)

periscopes; road screens; sniper suits and 'Chinese' figures. These last were wooden cut outs that could be raised suddenly to simulate an attack – though of course these only stood a significant chance of misleading the enemy if used in concert with a bombardment or poor visibility.

Though various aspects of concealment were dealt with in different publications such as *Notes on Camouflage* and *Notes on the Camouflage of Battery Positions,* the manual *The Principles and Practice of Camouflage,* of March 1918, was arguably the most important summation. This made it clear that all possible methods of observation and reconnaissance had to be taken into account, including not only eyes and binoculars but also aerial photography, flash spotting and sound ranging. Key concepts in the war against observation included light and shade, point of view, covering evidence of approaches and use, as well as the actual point or object, and shadows and pattern. In addition to standard items 'special manufacture' pieces could be ordered through the camouflage officer. It was also recommended that artillery pieces should be camouflage painted: as it was seldom possible to repaint a gun every time it was moved to match the new surroundings the 'next best thing' was to attempt to 'destroy its identity' so that it was difficult to recognize from a distance. The present scheme of three colour painting with green, cream and brown with a 'strong black definition between each colour' was calculated so that one of the three pigments would be likely to merge with the landscape, leaving the remaining areas a meaningless jumble of 'dissociated pieces' not readily discernible as a gun.

Opposite:

The male Mark IV tank 'Hyacinth', of 'H' Battalion, ditched in a German trench a mile west of Ribecourt, Cambrai, 20 November 1917. The infantry are men of 1st Leicesters. The Mark IV featured improvements including better fuel delivery and relocation of the petrol tank, smaller side sponsons and shorter gun barrels, and a better exhaust system. It also lacked the awkward wheeled tail of the Mark I. Entering the fray in mid 1917 the Mark IV had a maximum of 12mm armour and a crew of eight. Its top speed, on ideal ground, was 4mph, a fraction of this over a churned trenchscape. (IWM Q 6432)

CHAPTER NINE

THE TANK

Although armour, the gun and the caterpillar 'track' all pre-dated World War I the successful fusion of these inventions to create the tank was very much the product of trench warfare. Indeed the tank was introduced as an antidote to the trench, barbed wire and the machine gun. Interestingly, we still think of the modern tank in terms of its three basic original attributes, movement, armour and firepower – the 'armour triangle' – the increase of any one element being often at the expense of one, or both, of the others. As early as 1914 Major E. D. Swinton promoted the idea of a 'machine gun destroyer', and before long the notion had found influential backing from Winston Churchill, who urged the development of 'armoured caterpillar tractors'. Various models were eventually put forward to the 'Landships Committee' of which 'Little Willie' by Foster's of Lincoln was arguably the first practical design. In answer to War Office specifications further modifications were made, resulting in the now familiar rhomboid contraption which emerged as 'Mother' in January 1916. The name 'tank' was in fact a cover story intended to make the enemy think that the large riveted metal boxes were 'water tanks'.

The real problem now was how they should be used. Swinton's appraisal was that 'driblets' would ruin the shock effect, and that ideally tanks should be part of a big combined operation with infantry and gas and that at least 90 machines should be deployed on a 5-mile frontage. Field Marshal Haig would have liked to include just such an attack as part of the opening of the Somme offensive, but producing sufficient machines in the time available proved impossible. Only by mid September were anything like enough completed, and getting them to the battlefront – and beyond this to their starting points – proved difficult. Of 60 tanks, 49 were in working order on 14 September, and of these just 36 were able to join the action at Flers the following morning.

Navigation over a churned morass was so difficult up to the jumping off point that tapes were laid in advance to ensure that at least the tanks started from the right place. Lieutenant B. L. Q. Henriques was one of the tank commanders in the first tank action:

> Four [o'clock] arrived and we steamed ahead, squashing dead Germans as we went. We could not steer properly and I kept losing the tape. At five I was about 500 yards behind the First Line. I again stopped as we were rather too early. There was to be a barrage of artillery fire through which there was a space left for me to go. At 5.45am I reached another English trench but was not allowed to stop there for fear of drawing fire upon the infantry so I withdrew 20 yards and waited five minutes… As we approached the German line they let fire at us with might and main. At first no damage was done and we retaliated, killing about 20. Then a smash against my flap at the front caused splinters to come in and the blood to pour down my face. Another minute and my driver got the same. Then our prism glass broke to pieces, then another smash, I think it must have been a bomb, right in my face. The next one wounded my driver so badly we had to stop.

By this time I could see nothing at all, my prisms were all broken, and one periscope, while it was impossible to see through the other. On turning round I saw my gunners on the floor. I could not make out why. As the infantry were now approaching and as it was impossible to guide the car, and as I now discovered the sides weren't bulletproof I decided that to save the car from being captured I had better withdraw. How we got back I shall never understand, we dodged shells from the artillery. I fear that I did not achieve my object…[1]

If anything, things were worse in Lieutenant Huffam's tank:

On moving off we watched [tank] D14, it appeared to stop and immediately exploded. I went to my port side gunners to see why their guns were silent. They never fired again, both gunners were dead I believe, several bullets and small shells had penetrated

A Lewis gun post on the bank of the Lys canal, near Marquois, during the German Spring Offensive, 13 April 1918. The gunner fires through the bank using a wooden box type loop, whilst the sergeant stands ready with a fresh magazine. The team are dismounted tank crew and wear leather equipment; the secondary weapon of the gunner, a holstered revolver, is also visible. (IWM Q6528)

THE BAYERNWALD

From the Wytschaete map, 28 S.W. 2, 1:10,000, with German trenches in red, British in outline in blue, corrected to 1 April 1917. The Bayernwald – or 'Bavarian Forest' – was so called after the garrison who manned this sector of the Ypres Salient near Wytschaete, (known to Tommy as 'White Sheet'), which lies less than 2 miles away to the south. The local name for this woodland is 'Croonart', like the chapel here – or in French 'Bois Quarante'. Although less well known to English-speaking visitors this area is one of the most interesting on the Western Front, and is one of the places in which Adolf Hitler is known to have served. The defences consisted of a trench system which was eventually studded with concrete bunkers against bombardment.

Archaeological curiosity commenced early, and the site has a long history as a visitor attraction. Schoolteacher Andre Becquart excavated the four prefabricated block construction concrete bunkers here, though other plans show as many as ten bunkers in these woods. The bunkers are relatively shallow and exit direct into the trenches, the largest of them having two doors. In 1971 Becquart investigated 'Berta 4', one of the two mine shafts. In 1998 a new round of more systematic work commenced involving the 'Diggers' and the 'Association for Battlefield Archaeology' under the local council. Interestingly it now proved possible to demonstrate different phases of trench construction, beginning with wood and sandbags, and from 1916 a method of inverted 'A' frames at intervals connected by wattle. The Bayernwald reopened to visitors in 2004, though as recently as the summer of 2008 earth movers were again in operation.

Recently re-excavated trenches at the Bayernwald near Wytschaete (now Wijtschate), Belgium. Here is seen one typical German method of revetment, the sides of the winding communication trench being held by a system of posts and willow osiers, topped off by a course of sandbags. Though primitive in appearance this method of trench construction used local materials and benefited from the flexibility of the wood, which could survive relatively near misses and be simply repaired. (Author's collection)

A German concrete bunker at the Bayernwald. It can be seen that the shelter is built roughly flush with the surrounding ground surface, and entered via the trench. Note the construction, individual blocks of concrete having been cast off site and then used like giant bricks cemented together and reinforced with rods. (Author's collection)

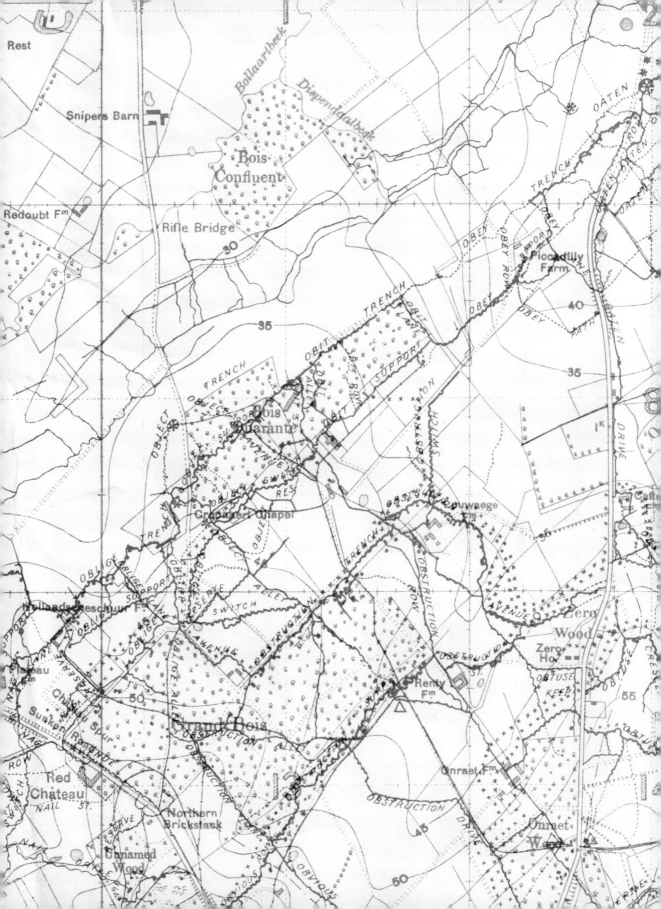

our armour plate, we were all in bad shape when we were hit by a larger shell, there was an explosion, then fire, and I came round to find myself lying on top of my corporal, his shins were sticking out in the air. I had already been issued with morphia tablets and I quietened him with these and bandaged him with first aid dressings from the others of my crew. We were close to the enemy lines, with my corporal in agony and all others damaged and shell shocked.[2]

The first tank attack had been at best a local success – but it was certainly a technical feat and a propaganda victory. Tank D17 'Dinnaken' under Lieutenant Hastie had made it into the village of Flers, putting the enemy to flight, a feat that made newspaper headlines. Field Marshal Haig was pleasantly surprised by their performance compared to a generally lacklustre background, remarking in his diary, 'Certainly some of the Tanks have done marvels! And have enabled our attack to progress at a surprisingly fast pace.'[3] This was enough to ensure orders for a thousand tanks – an extremely far-sighted decision considering the conservative tactical attitudes that had marked the opening of the Somme. Interestingly, improved armour was stressed as an immediate requirement of new production, and so, after day one of the tank's service life, the battle between the tank and the anti-tank weapon began.

Tanks were used again later in September and in November 1916, and 60 were at Arras in early 1917. At Bullecourt tanks went forward in a blizzard in support of the Australians against the Hindenburg Line. The results of this engagement were far from happy. Just 12 machines were deployed for this part of the operation, of which 11 started out spread out on a front of about 800 yards. Of these four attacked Bullecourt and two the Hindenburg Line nearby. The initial terror the enemy had felt when tanks were first deployed had begun to dissipate, and the dark lumbering monsters were outlined against the snow. According to German 27th Division reports one tank got stuck in thick wire and others became the focus of streams of armour-piercing bullets, direct artillery fire and trench mortar shells. The majority of the tanks were knocked out or damaged and just one passed the first line German trench.

As Major W. H. L. Watson recorded:

The first battle of Bullecourt was a minor disaster. Our attack was a failure, in which three brigades of infantry lost very heavily indeed; and the officers and men lost, seasoned troops that had fought at Gallipoli, could never be replaced. The company of tanks had been, apparently, nothing but a broken reed. For many months after the Australians distrusted tanks, and it was not until the battle of Amiens, sixteen months later, that the Division engaged at Bullecourt were fully converted.[4]

June 1917 was something of a watershed, for that month the British tank battalions, previously regarded as merely the 'Heavy Branch' of the Machine Gun Corps, now became a 'Tank Corps' in their own right. Pairs of battalions were brigaded together and old Mark I types were attached as supply tanks. At the same time the new Mark IV took pride of place as the main fighting tank. In many respects the Mark IV was similar to its predecessors, being of the familiar rhomboid design, having a six-cylinder Daimler engine, and a top speed of just under 4 miles per hour. It also came in 'Male' and 'Female' varieties – the former having two 6-pdr guns and a secondary four machine gun armament, the latter six machine guns only. Nevertheless there were numerous improvements, including relocated fuel tanks with greater capacity which increased the radius of action to 35 miles, and slightly thicker armour. Whilst tanks were still defenceless against direct hits from shells they were reckoned proof against 'all bullets'. Another innovation that appeared at about this time, and was reported to be the brainchild of Major P. Johnson, was the 'unditching beam'. This great Baulk of metal-shod oak was supported on rails atop the tank whilst progress was good, but when the machine got stuck in mud it could be chained to the tracks. As the tracks slithered they pulled the beam down in front of the tank and provided traction, allowing the tank to move forward.

Australian engineers of 4th Field Company carry a dummy tank near Catalet, September 1918. Some dummies were for training, but by 1918 the main use was as decoys to mislead enemy air observers. To advise on the camouflage of real tanks a Royal Engineers officer was on permanent attachment to the Tank Corps. (IWM E.AUS 4938)

Despite appalling conditions tanks were deployed at the Third Battle of Ypres. Amazingly they scored some successes even with mud and concrete added to enemy resistance. One such was achieved by Lieutenant Maelor-Jones in tank G9:

> At dawn on 31 July I proceeded with other tanks of No 3 Section, crossing over the enemy front line in a north-easterly direction for Kitchener Wood to the right of the Oblong and Juliet Farms. At the latter I waited for our barrage to lift, meanwhile filling up our radiator with water. I then steered for Alberta, leaving it on my left. Here I met some Hampshires retiring. With difficulty I persuaded a man to speak. He told me they were held up by some machine guns. I advanced towards a long blockhouse about six feet high where I observed a machine gun emplacement on which I drove the tank. On the other side I came on a machine gun and two men whom we shot and crumpled up the gun. Advancing we came to an old and strong breastwork manned by the enemy on which our gunners opened fire. The Hampshires then came on and cleared the trench, taking all prisoners.[5]

It has been said, with some truth, that the battle of Cambrai in November 1917 restored the credibility of tanks – and also convinced the infantry that they were vital to a new era of warfare. All nine battalions of the new 'Tank Corps', with 378 machines, took part with a 6-mile line of tanks led into action by Brigadier General Hugh Elles. Following a short and selective barrage the tanks advanced in three waves, dropping fascines into the three lines of trenches to create crossing points. Other vehicles were equipped with grapnels to shift barbed wire, and there were even nine tanks with wireless sets to provide mobile communication posts. Planned essentially as a three-day 'raid' the battle was initially a success that it proved impossible to exploit. The commander of 'H' Battalion left a graphic account of the working of a Mark IV in action:

> Shells were bursting all around us and the fragments of them were striking the sides of the tank. Each of our 6-pounders required a gun layer and a gun loader, and while these four men blazed away, the rest of the perspiring crew kept the tank zig-zagging to upset the enemy's aim. It was a hard job to turn one of these early tanks. It needed four of the crew to work the levers, and they took their orders by signals. First of all the tank had to stop. A knock on the right side would attract the attention of the right gearsman. The driver would hold out a clenched fist, which was the signal to put the track into neutral. The gearsman would repeat the signal to show it was done. The officer, who controlled two brake levers, would pull the right one, which held the right track. The driver would accelerate and the tank would slew round slowly on the stationary right track while the left track went into motion. As soon as the tank had turned sufficiently the procedure was reversed. Zig-zagging was therefore a slow and complicated business.[6]

A fighting section was now three machines. In the 'unicorn' deployment first used at Cambrai the advance was in a triangular formation with the lead tank pointing toward the objective, and the two rear tanks each leading a platoon of infantry.

By the end of 1917 the tank had proved its worth, and new regularized methods and training were brought forward. A 'uniformity' of doctrine was aimed at, based upon commanders training the tank troops they would lead into action. As explained in *Instructions for the Training of the Tank Corps in France,* aspirations were high:

> The object of all training is to create a 'Corps d'Elite'; that is a body of men who are not only capable of helping to win this war, but are determined to do so. It cannot be emphasized too often that all training, at all times and in all places, must aim at the cultivation of the offensive spirit in all ranks.

Tank battalion commanders were specifically tasked with keeping track of the efficiency of the unit and the 'mechanical efficiency' of the machines; detailed reconnaissance of the ground to the front; laying schemes for possible formations, routes of attack and co-operation with other arms; and concealment of the unit. Some elements could be delegated to company commanders, who would also supervise the section commanders in the selection of specific 'tracks' along the axis of advance. Battalion and company commanders would be trained specifically on conditions that battle would be likely to produce, the latest details of organization and equipment, and the practicalities of specific 'schemes', which were set as outdoor and indoor exercises. The models

A British Mark I 'male' tank of 'C' Company, broken down across a trench whilst on its way to Thiepval, 25 September 1916. The usual armament of the 28ton Mk I 'male' was two 6-pdr guns in the side sponsons and four machine guns; 'females' carried six machine guns. Top speed was less than 4 miles per hour, even on good ground, and a gallon of fuel was required for every mile; nevertheless, the Mk I could cross a trench 11 feet wide. The strange superstructure of wood and netting seen here is an anti-grenade precaution: bombs hurled on top of the tank will usually roll off before exploding. (IWM Q2486)

for these plans would be drawn from real actions of the past year. Individual tank officers were expected to learn orders and timings by heart and to 'locate all prominent topographical objects in the neighbourhood of the operations'. During the attack it would be their responsibility to see that 'a sharp lookout is kept for the enemy's machine guns, signals from our infantry, points where the enemy are holding out, and the progress of the infantry and of the neighbouring tanks'.

Individual 'schools' were used to teach tank skills using training machines on range areas containing trenches. The 'Gunnery School' covered the 6-pdr and Hotchkiss guns, which were now the key tank weapons, as well as revolvers, which were the emergency arms of the crews. The teams of the main armament were tried against targets at various distances from moving and stationary vehicles, and machine gunners practised against moving and disappearing targets. Revolver training encompassed not only simple accuracy and care of weapons but realistic 'trench practices'. In the 'Mechanical and Driving School' the trainees were grouped together as crews and taught not only maintenance and driving but night work, 'unditching' and camouflage. Instructors took note of the amount of driving each pupil completed, and at the end of the course graded the candidates as first- or second-class drivers, or failures. The failures were further screened so that some were recorded as able to repeat the course, others as 'unsuitable as a driver'. 'Wireless', 'Gas' and 'Compass' schools dealt with these specialist subjects as they pertained to tank crews.

By 1918 tactics had advanced beyond supporting the infantry into enemy trenches, knocking out machine gun posts and driving up and down the lines shooting up or terrifying enemy troops. Now there were aspirations to break out of and through, not merely into, enemy positions. This was made possible partly by the introduction of new types of machine. The Mark V, which was another conventional rhomboid design, first extended the radius of action to 45, and finally to as much as 67 miles in a version poised to take the field at the end of the war. At Amiens the 'Carrier' tanks, armed with just one machine gun, provided a valuable service in taking supplies across the battlefield – according to one calculation effectively replacing the efforts of 2,500 men who would otherwise have been required in old-fashioned 'carrying parties'. In the summer of 1918 a completely new 'Whippet' type also appeared. This was armed with machine guns only, but cut the number of crew required from eight to only four. At the same time it boasted ranges over 65 miles, and a top speed of about 8 miles per hour. It was initially hoped that Whippets could work in conjunction with cavalry and armoured cars, but with or without accompanying horses and other vehicles they managed to cover some impressive distances during their operations and pointed the way to what future armour might achieve.

Though Britain deployed the first tank it is sometimes forgotten how close on its heels came French armour. As early as 1914 a civil engineer called Frot had suggested building an armoured body onto a road roller, an idea that was tested, albeit rather unsuccessfully, the following year. Filtz and Bajac agricultural tractors with wire cutting devices were tried about the same time. Holt tractors with 'crawler tracks' were obtained by the Schneider company in May 1915, and one of these was soon armoured as a prototype 'machine gun carrier'. Eventually a co-operation between Colonel Estienne and Monsieur Brillié of Schneider came up with a design acceptable to the authorities, and a target date of November 1916 was set for the delivery of 400 vehicles.

Despite delays 132 Schneiders mounting short 75mm guns were committed to action on the Chemin des Dames in April 1917. This was a significant achievement, though the first French tank battle was extremely bloody: 76 tanks were immobilized on the battlefield and 57 of these completely destroyed – many of them burned out. As one French tank commander reported:

> A few machines were stopped by enemy fire; others, including mine, got into critical positions in shell holes and could only get out again after many attempts. For a few minutes, as I was second in the column, I was terribly afraid of blocking the other 79 tanks which in that spot had no way of getting through either on the left or right. One of my steering mechanisms was broken and all I could do was get out of the hole to clear the way… I cried with rage at our helplessness to repair the tank, and it was difficult for me to follow the stages of the battle; I saw tanks catching fire all over the plain and the first wounded men walking past my vehicle; some tanks were several kilometres ahead of me and pushing on.[7]

A rival Saint Chamond model was first used in May 1917 when a company of 16 machines, together with Schneiders, supported an infantry attack at Laffaulx Mill. The Saint Chamond mounted a 75mm gun in the bows, but its long body, which overhung the tracks, front and rear, had a tendency to ground. The Renault FT 17, a modern-looking lightweight with a turret, was introduced in early 1918, and large numbers were made before the end of the war. More than 2,000 tanks of French provenance were in service on 11 November 1918, some of the light tanks being with American units. Another 2,000 British machines were in service, giving the Allies total domination in armoured warfare. Little wonder that the Germans focused significant effort on methods to counter tanks in the last two years of war, including the deployment of single guns and whole batteries on anti-tank work, and the invention of the anti-tank rifle. The first 'AT' rifle was the Mauser T-Gewehr, introduced in 1918: this was effectively a huge single-shot rifle, firing a 13mm round.

Perhaps oddly, the Germans made least progress with producing actual tanks, partly due to an early underestimation of their eventual worth, and partly due to lack of industrial resources, over which artillery and machine guns claimed priority. The only German-made tank of the war was the monstrous A7V, whose key specifications were not laid down until October 1916. The first battle-worthy vehicle was produced

PILCKEM RIDGE

The eastern part of the ridge from the St Julien sheet 28 N.W. 2, 1:10,000, German trenches in red, corrected to 30 June 1917. The low-lying Pilckem Ridge north-east of Ypres was one of the enemy-held features that hemmed in the town, and stood directly in the way of the 1917 plan to break out towards the coast. The maze of fortification seen here is the German first line, and parts of the second – a third lay further back between Langemarck and Poelcappelle. On the British side these defence lines were dubbed 'Blue', 'Black' and 'Green'. The battle of Pilckem Ridge was launched at 3.50am on 31 July with all batteries from 12inch down to field guns firing in the darkness against pre-registered positions. Taking the 'Blue' and 'Black' lines would cost 30,000 casualties.

British topographers have excelled themselves in finding suitably Teutonic names for the features in this sector, from the 'Iron Cross' near the top of square 3, to 'Mauser Cottage', 'Essen Farm' and 'Krupp Farm' in square 14. Many buildings have been given the names of German generals, hence mentions of Hindenburg, Below, von Kluck, Francois and the like. A more satirical mind appears to have dreamed up the names 'Civilisation' and 'Kultur' for the farms in square 16. Being in area 'C' the trenches follow the letter – with such gems as 'Cake Lane', 'Cannon Trench' and 'Camphor Support'. What is less apparent and proved even more deadly to the attackers were the many concrete bunkers, some forming shelters within the trench systems, others flanking fire positions.

Above: A packhorse, with a gas mask bag secured to his head harness, is loaded with supplies near Pilckem, 31 July 1917. The long items on top of the burden are metal screw pickets to hold barbed wire in place. Screwing in metal pickets was usually quieter than banging in wooden stakes. (IWM Q5717)

Below: Men of the Irish Guards tend a wounded German prisoner during the battle of Pilckem Ridge, 31 July 1917. The trench is revetted with wooden stakes and wattle. At least two of the men wear 'Small Box' respirator bags slung on their chests, another, back to camera, has a 'Cruise Visor' hanging from his helmet which is worn back to front. The Cruise Visor was devised by Captain Cruise of the Royal Army Medical Corps, oculist to the King, and was a curtain of chain links for eye protection. It was said to produce dizziness when worn in front of the eyes, and was not popular. (IWM Q2628)

a year later, and only in 1918 were A7Vs committed to action. As finally fielded it weighed 33 tons and was equipped with one 57mm gun and six machine guns and a crew of 18. The total German tank arm in July 1918 was just eight detachments of five tanks each, and of these only three were composed of German-made tanks, the remainder being captured machines.

Given the lack of German tanks and the gaps between their battlefield deployments it was not until April 1918 that the first tank versus tank action took place at Villers-Bretonneux. A dozen German machines left the start line in three groups, under cover of fog, and following a fight with machine gun nests managed to assist their accompanying infantry into the British front line, capturing quite a number of troops. The 'Steinhart Group' of four tanks, however, quickly found itself confronted by British tanks – and what happened next depends on whose records are used. According to German sources one A7V accidentally overturned and its crew continued to fight dismounted, their tank being later blown up to prevent it being captured. The second German tank was set upon by eight British tanks, and forced one of these to retire, before receiving multiple hits, and itself retiring before being abandoned. The third, supporting the infantry, survived unscathed; and the fourth was in action with another group of seven British tanks. In the firefight between these no fewer than three of the British tanks were claimed put out of action by Leutnant Bittner, and the German machine eventually retired with a damaged main armament. A British counter-attack later retook the ground gained.

The British account of Villers-Bretonneux by Frank Mitchell, commander of number one tank, of 1st Section, A Company, 1st Tank Battalion, awarded the Military Cross for this action, was rather different:

> Suddenly a hurricane of hail pattered against our steel wall, filling our interior with myriads of sparks and flying splinters. Something rattled against the steel helmet of the driver sitting next to me, and my face was stung with minute fragments of steel. The crew flung themselves flat on the floor. The driver ducked his head and drove straight on. Above the roar of the engine sounded the staccato rat-tat-tat-tat of machine guns, and another furious jet of bullets sprayed our steel side, the splinters clanging against the engine cover. The Jerry had treated us to a broadside of armour piercing bullets!
>
> Taking advantage of a dip in the ground, we got beyond range, and then turning, we manoeuvred to get the left gunner on the moving target. Owing to our gas casualties the gunner was working single handed, and his right eye was swollen with gas, he aimed with the left. Moreover as the ground was heavily scarred with shell holes, we kept going up and down like a ship in a heavy sea, which made accurate shooting difficult. His first shot fell some fifteen yards in front, the next went beyond, and then I saw the shells bursting all around the tank. He fired shot after shot every time it came into view.

New Zealand artillery personnel in a captured German emplacement near Grévillers, 25 August 1918. The officers, foreground, are holding a German 'T-Gewehr' anti-tank rifle: other equipment, including packs and mess tins, can be seen scattered on the ground. (IWM Q11264)

Nearing the village of Cachy, I noticed to my astonishment that the two females were slowly limping away to the rear. Almost immediately on their arrival they had both been hit by shells which tore great holes in their sides, leaving them defenceless against machine gun bullets, and as their Lewis guns were defenceless against the heavy armour plate of the enemy they could do nothing but withdraw… We turned again and proceeded at a slower pace. The left gunner registering carefully, began to hit the ground right in front of the Jerry tank. I took a risk and stopped the tank for a moment. The pause was justified; a well aimed shot hit the enemy's conning tower, bringing him to a standstill. Another roar and another white puff at the front of the tank denoted a second hit![8]

Whippet tanks then came up and joined the fray getting amongst the German infantry. Three of seven returned, 'their tracks dripping with blood'. Whilst it is clear

Tommy (to Escort with prisoner wearing body shield) : " WHO'S YER FRIEND, MATE—JOAN OF ARC ? "
Escort : " DUNNO—BUT IF YOU'LL LEND ME A TIN OPENER, I'LL HAVE A LOOK AT ITS IDENTITY DISC."

W. Smithson Broadhead.

A cartoon from the Blighty Christmas Number, *1917, illustrating German trench armour. (Author's collection)*

that the A7Vs had been grossly outnumbered at Villers-Bretonneux it has to be acknowledged that many of the British machines deployed on that day were armed only with machine guns and not really capable of engaging tanks. Moreover, whether the German machines were mainly disabled by enemy shells or their own inherent design flaws mattered little. They were outnumbered, or outclassed, or possibly both. In the armour balance Germany was at a huge disadvantage from which she could not recover.

Opposite:

British stretcher bearers carry a casualty over the top of a trench in the ruins of Thiepval, September 1916. German grenades are scattered amongst the debris. Picture by Lieutenant E. Brooks. (IWM Q1332)

CHAPTER TEN

'OVER THE TOP'

Opposite:
*A fine study of a German
assault squad or* Gruppe,
*autumn 1916. Grenade bags
are worn around each shoulder,
and a shelter half across the
chest. Most of the team carry
a P08 Luger semi-automatic
pistol, grenades and a trench
knife or a bayonet, two each of
which are stuck into the ground,
centre foreground. Textbook
tactics also called for at least
a couple of the group to carry
a carbine or rifle to engage
more distant targets. About
1.7 million Luger 'Parabellum'
pistols were made by the end
of the war. The pistol's quickness
to load and fire, combined with
its well-calculated 9mm round,
eight cartridge magazine and
ergonomic handling, made for a
useful trench weapon – though
its effectiveness was sometimes
compromised by susceptibility
to dirt. (Author's collection)*

Despite what generations of school children have been taught the trench was not the soldier's nemesis but his friend. Sometimes it was also his grave; but more often than not it was where he hid successfully from shells and bullets, where he lived, worked and sometimes fought. It was not going into trenches that so often signed a man's death warrant, but leaving them, especially when headed in the direction of the enemy. Paradoxically, therefore, the ultimate terror of the trenches was getting out of them.

Actually full-blown attacks were a relatively rare experience: as Grenadier Guards officer and future Prime Minister Harold MacMillan put it, 'the thrill of battle comes now once or twice a twelvemonth'.[1] But when it did come it was often terrible and spectacular. As the diary of the German 153rd Infantry Regiment recorded of Loos in 1915:

> Dense masses of the enemy, line after line, appeared over the ridge, some of their officers mounted on horseback and advancing as if carrying out a field day drill in peacetime. Our artillery and machine guns riddled their ranks as they came on. As they crossed the northern front of the Bois Hugo, the machine guns there caught them in the flank and whole battalions were annihilated. The English made five consecutive efforts to press on past the wood and reach the second line position. Ten columns of extended line could clearly be distinguished, each one estimated at more than a thousand men, and offering such a target as had never been seen before, or even thought possible. Never had the machine gunners such straightforward work to do or done it so effectively. They traversed to and fro along the enemy's ranks unceasingly. The men stood on the fire steps, some even on the parapets, and fired triumphantly into the mass of men advancing across open grassland. As the entire field of fire was covered with the enemy's infantry the effect was devastating and they could be seen falling literally in hundreds.

Interestingly, quite a few who went 'over the top' regarded it not only as necessary, but also the vital duty to perform. The young Lieutenant Basil Liddell Hart, serving with the King's Own Yorkshire Light Infantry, and later one of the generals worst critics, referred to his possible demise in action as a noble death 'for his country and the cause of civilisation'.[2]

German Alfred Väth was perhaps an extreme example of this sort of attitude, but was by no means unique when he wrote in October 1915:

> The attack was terribly beautiful! The most beautiful and at the same time the most terrible thing I have ever experienced. Our artillery shot magnificently, and after two hours the position was sufficiently prepared for the German infantry. The storm came, as only German infantry can storm! It was magnificent the way our men, especially the youngest, advanced, magnificent! Officers belonging to other regiments, who were

looking on, have since admitted they have never seen anything like it! In the face of appalling machine gun fire they went on with a confidence which nobody can ever attempt to equal. And so the hill, which had been stormed in vain three times, was taken in an hour… But now comes the worst part – to hold the hill! Bad, very bad days are in front of us. One can scarcely hope to get through safe and sound. The French guns are shooting appallingly, and every night there are counter-attacks and bombing raids. Where I am we are only about 20 yards apart.[3]

The problem of the attack was not merely that trenches provided cover, reduced the casualties of the defenders, and tended to bolster the morale of their garrison; it was also one of co-ordination and communication that technology and tactics, as currently pertained, were ill placed to overcome. It is well known that there were many offensives that were more or less bloody failures, but one example will serve to demonstrate that the issue was rather more than a simple equation of trenches acting as a 'force multiplier'. The battle of Aubers Ridge, fought on 9 May 1915, was famously

Previous spread:
German machine gun team in
a log and earth bunker, c.1916.
The MG 08 retains its heavy
'sledge' mount, but rests on a
semi-circular table arrangement
for traversing. It is further
protected by a Mantelpanzer,
an optional 'armoured jacket',
with small crew shield. The
spherical grenades that lie on
the table and hang from the
roof in metal holders are model
1915 Kugelhandgranaten. *This*
cast iron fragmentation bomb
was particularly useful from
cover in defensive situations.
(Author's collection)

described as 'a serious disappointment', and whilst the 10,000 casualties suffered by British and Indian forces were modest compared to some of the engagements that followed, the battle was a significant one. This would be not least in terms of the way it highlighted problems such as ammunition shortages and communication failure, and the subsequent controversies that helped undermine Asquith's government.

On the face of it the plan for a three-division attack was a simple one, formulated at least in part to demonstrate to the French that the British forces were pulling their weight. Field Marshal French deputed the detail of the attack on the 'ridge', in fact a gentle rise of about 27 yards, to General Haig, then commanding First Army. Fourteen of the available battalions would go forward, attempting to break the enemy line, by surprise and in two places, supported by a preliminary bombardment of just 40 minutes' duration. The reserves would mount fresh assaults as required. The attack would cut the road to Lille, forcing an enemy retirement with the ultimate hope of commencing a 'general advance'. Though publicly optimistic Haig was concerned that there were simply not enough human and material resources: his instincts would be proved correct.

The 2nd Welsh were in the forefront of the southern prong of the attack. As Lieutenant B. U. S. Crips recalled:

> We were told that after the bombardment there would not be many people left in the German first and second lines. We were all quite confident and very cheery… My platoon was not to leave the trench for two minutes after the first two platoons had gone. At 5.37am the first two platoons jumped over the parapet ready to charge but they were met with a perfect hail of bullets and many men just fell back into the trench riddled with bullets. A few survivors managed to get back into one of the ditches. My company commander then turned to me before my two minutes were up and said I had better try. So I took my platoon and the other platoon in the company also came and we jumped up over the parapet to charge but we met with the same fate and I with a few men managed to get into the ditch. I was the only officer left in my company, two being killed outright and my company commander and another subaltern serverely wounded. So I had to take command of the company.[4]

On the northern part of the battlefield the position was no better, and arguably worse. The 2nd East Lancashires, for example, faced parts of 6th and 9th companies of the 16th Bavarian Reserve Infantry Regiment; but despite outnumbering their enemy, solidly constructed trenches, and virtually everything else, was against them. One of the worst aspects was the distance that would have to be covered – anything from 150 to 300 yards of open ground – before the enemy position was reached. 'Sally ports' were cut into the British breastworks, but permission to dig further forwards prior to the attack was refused on the grounds that this would ruin the element of surprise. Nevertheless, like the Welsh, the Lancashire men were in high spirits. This hopeful attitude was bolstered by the bombardment, which appeared to be effective. This proved entirely deceptive, for as soon as the first troops left their trenches they were greeted with heavy fire. Indeed many men who had started off from the second-line British trench did not even reach the front line. One platoon was depleted to just one sergeant and a private by the time it reached what was supposed to be the jumping off point.

Later there was even worse to come. In hope of renewing the attack the artillery opened fire again, but the British shells were shared out between the East Lancashires. As one officer recalled:

> Suddenly there broke over us a hail of shrapnel. It seemed to come from everywhere except the enemy, and men were being hit right and left. I realised that our artillery was bombarding the enemy trenches, after which we would assault if there were any of us left. From all around came the cries of wounded men mingled with the splitting crash of shrapnel, and every few minutes one's ears were numbed by bursts of Jack Johnsons behind the forward trench.[5]

German shock troops practise the attack, working from shell hole to shell hole through the remnants of an obstacle zone, 1918. The advance is in no way linear, but by small groups taking advantage of cover and gaps as they present themselves. Smoke and fog were used wherever possible to avoid the fury of defensive fire: by the last months of the war all major armies were using similar ideas on the Western Front. (IWM Q47997)

So enervated was the battalion that it had to be withdrawn, partly down a sap to the main breastwork, then in dribs and drabs under cover of darkness. Ten officers had been killed, and 63 other ranks. The wounded and the missing totalled 376.

This disastrous day was described in the regimental history as the second worst that the unit suffered in the entire war. It was terrible indeed, and made all the more galling by the ingredient of 'friendly fire'. However, it is worth noting that, as was so often the case, the wounded outnumbered the dead by a factor of two or three to one. So often we hear stories that battalions were 'wiped out', or that they 'lost' three quarters of their men – but in fact 'casualties' were not 'fatalities', and slaughter to the last man was vanishingly rare, if not completely unheard of. Often it was the presence of many wounded that made it impossible for the remainder to act – and the realization that this was so gave rise to the now inhuman-sounding orders that so often forbade attacking troops stopping to aid their fallen comrades. What made the war so awful was not so much the presence of the trench, or loss from one attack, but its duration, scale and all-encompassing nature, making the efforts of the individual appear so futile. Cumulatively, therefore, there were some units in which the numbers of the dead did exceed the original strength by the end of the war.

Moreover, to those who were there it could feel as if battalions had been obliterated in a single day. Prisoners would not be seen for years, and even the slightly wounded might be absent for days, and, perhaps unexpectedly, many of the more seriously injured who did make good recoveries were not sent back to their original units, but to wherever they were needed. Under their new cap badge they were much like any other replacement. To their former comrades they were lost in spirit if not in fact. It is also the case that in most major wars the defeated flee the field of death: the victors pursue them as fast as they are able. The battlefield dead are thus quickly out of sight, if not out of mind. In trench warfare both sides must sit and watch the lifeless bodies of friend and foe for days or weeks afterwards, and, like actors in bad feature films with a dearth of extras, the dead of the Western Front got to play multiple roles. For apart from the grief and shock visited upon their immediate comrades, they might be buried, unearthed and reburied more than once. Confined battlefields added to this sense of the charnel house, since the fatalities of every attack and battle that had occurred there were still there, or lay buried not far away, ready to re-enter from the wings.

At Aubers Ridge the attacks went on throughout the afternoon. Amongst the last to go forward were the 2/3 Gurkha Rifles, as Captain W. G. Bagot-Chester recalled:

> We had to advance about 2,000 yards across open country to start with, but we were not fired on until we reached a long communication trench leading up to the front trench line. Of course we advanced in artillery formation [to avoid being caught close together by shells]. Toward the last hundred yards or so German 'Woolly Bears' began to burst overhead, and 'Jack Johnsons' close by, but I had only one man hit at this point.

We then got into a long communication trench leading up from Lansdowne Post to the Gridiron Trenches. Here we were blocked for a long time, shelling increasing every moment, wounded trying to get by us. After a time we got into the Gridiron where it was absolute hell. Hun shells, large and small, bursting everywhere, blowing the parapet here and there, and knocking tree branches off. Here there was fearful confusion. No one knew the way to anywhere. There was such a maze of trenches, and such a crowd of people, many wounded, all wanting to go in different directions, one regiment trying to go back, ours trying to go forward, wounded and stretcher bearers going back, etc. I presently went on to a trench called Pioneer Trench. There I had 26 casualties from shell. Havildar Manbir had his leg blown off, and was in such agony that he asked to be shot. As one got further to the front trench, the place got more of

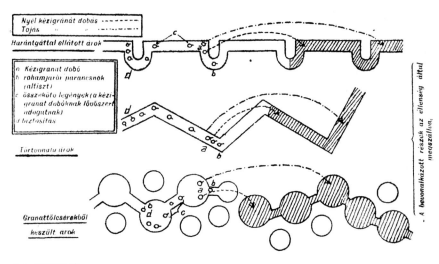

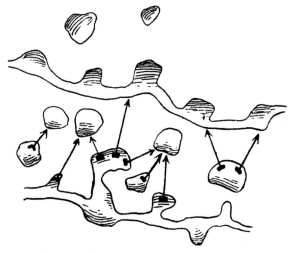

Illustrations showing the German methods of bombing and advancing using trenches and shell holes, 1917. (Author's collection)

a shambles, wounded and dead everywhere. Those who could creep or walk were trying to get back; others simply lying and waiting. The ground in front was littered with Seaforth bodies and 41st Dogras.[6]

Haig wanted to throw in a final bayonet assault as dusk came on at about 8pm, but it was not to be. The congestion that had defeated the earlier wave now prevented new units from gaining their jumping off points. The battle came to an end. Post-war analysis concluded that there had been several causes of failure. The opening bombardment had been the worst of all worlds: enough to thoroughly alert the enemy, but insufficient to prevent him manning his machine guns and trench parapets. Much of the wire was uncut, and could not be cut later by artillery due to British troops in the vicinity. Friendly machine guns played little part in the action, and such reserves as had got through were not directed to where some success had been gained, but into the teeth of failure. Due to primitive communications the commander did not know with any clarity what had happened or why, and simply sent in more men. Counter-battery fire was totally inadequate due to lack of both guns and munitions:

> Our artillery was not able to silence the enemy's machine guns, much of our ammunition was defective, and the guns also suffered by excessive use, and so our troops as they started their attack came under very heavy fire, which was continued as they tried to cross the few hundred yards of open ground in front of the enemy trenches. That a few of our men did actually enter the German front line was marvellous, but it could lead to no definite result, and they could not be supported.

Two months after the attack Captain Owen Buckmaster of the Duke of Cornwall's Light Infantry peered out from the British line at Aubers and could still see British troops from the battle, packs squared, bayonets fixed, 'mummified' on the ground facing an invisible enemy. Rags fluttered in the enemy wire where fragments of uniform had caught upon barbs.

Such is the tragic picture of the infantry attack during World War I. Yet to accept this model as unchanging, and unconsidered, throughout 1914–18 would be entirely wrong. For gradually, if often painfully, the new weapons and techniques were integrated into attacking methods, until an entirely different form of assault had emerged. That this was not immediately reflected in lighter casualties appears to be due to several factors: defenders also learned new techniques and acquired new weapons; communications with attacking formations may have improved but remained problematic; and, last but not least, any attack that involved leaving the relative safety of fieldworks or rear areas was almost bound to involve serious casualties against a determined enemy. Moreover, some of the 'lessons learned' during the first year of war were questionable, and though they might have led to more successful local attacks in the short term, also resulted in even higher casualties.[7]

NORTHERN SECTOR OF THE GERMAN TRENCHES AT AUBERS RIDGE

Taken from a German sketch plan of May 1915 we see the area attacked by Major General F. J. Davies' 8th Division. The British front at the north (top) of the map is shown only as a dotted line, whilst the German front line trench is represented as a schematic series of bays, which are not to scale. The troops occupying the central part of the trench system were of the 16th Bavarian Reserve Infantry Regiment, the various companies being denoted by their number and the abbreviation *Komp*. On either flank the unit was bounded by the positions of the 17th and 21st Reserve Infantry regiments. The opening British attack came from the area directly west of La Cordonnerie Farm and was made by 13th Londons (Kensingtons); 1st Royal Irish Rifles; 2nd Rifle Brigade; and 2nd East Lancashires. The 2nd Northamptonshires attacked further west still, in the vicinity of the point marked 'Tommy Br', which is presumably the bridge across the *Layes Bach*, or *Rivière des Laies*. Note also the words 'Gesprengtes Ms' marked just inside the British position showing blown mines.

The attack on the morning of 9 May at first managed to cross the narrowest part of No Man's Land fairly successfully, entering the 9th Company position: two mines blew craters which the Londons were quick to exploit with a 'magnificent charge'. However, where wider ground was swept by fire, casualties were heavy. As attacks faltered fresh troops from the 2nd Lincolns and 1st Sherwood Foresters were fed in from the rear, Corporal J. Upton of the latter unit being the first of four men to win the Victoria Cross this day. Though the 13th Londons reached the German second line, and two other lodgements were formed by other units, casualties mounted as isolated groups were caught in enfilade fire and confused shelling from both sides. New assaults by other units served only to choke the trenches with dead and wounded. In the mid afternoon and through into the night German counter-attacks gradually forced the British out of the ground they had captured.

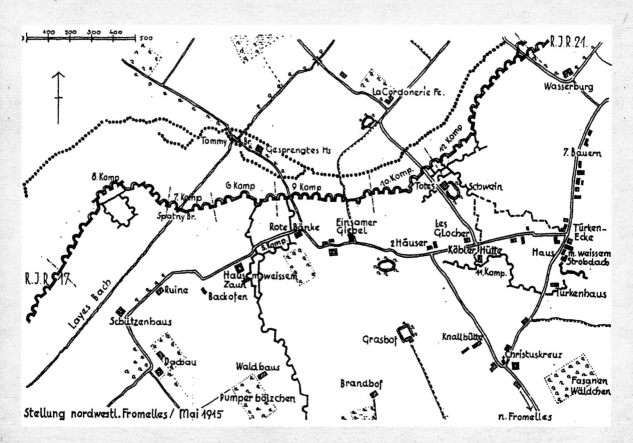

In early 1915, for example, French infantry Captain Andre Laffargue reflected on his experiences at Neuville St Vaast, and in a pamphlet entitled *L'Etude sur L'Attaque*, or 'A Study of the Attack', produced a series of ideas that he believed might lead to better results. His first conclusion was that attacks should not be merely 'progressive' but 'forward bounds' achieving their objectives in a single day. They should be 'unlimited' and aim for breakthrough of the trench lines. Artillery preparation would be as heavy and prolonged as required to destroy barbed wire entanglements; neutralize or destroy the defenders of the trenches; prevent hostile artillery from coming into action; block the passage of enemy reserves; and destroy machine guns as soon as they were located. The infantry attack needed to be big enough, and sustained long enough, to capture the enemy's lines of defence, and by means of reserves pushing through, prevent the enemy from forming other defence lines further back. The advance was to be in lines, preferably with men marching in step to show 'cool resolution', but firing on the move if required. The first attacking wave was to carry on with 'no limit' unless physically prevented; the second wave would set off as soon as the first reached the enemy trench, and be quickly followed by a third. Since it took time for news of progress to filter back attacks were to be pushed on 'in a preconceived and almost unintelligent manner till the moment when the last mesh is broken'.

At the end of 1915 and early in 1916 General Foch offered the opinion that it was artillery which was the prime 'destructive force' and that it should be applied repeatedly, 'increasing all the time'.[8] Artillery preparation indeed became the 'measure of the success' that the infantry could obtain. General Pétain went further still when he stated that artillery conquered the position; infantry occupied it. After the battle of Loos in September and October 1915 British analysts came to the conclusion that lack of any significant success was due to a number of avoidable factors. Important amongst these was the insufficiency of the bombardment, as Field Marshal French had observed:

> They've dug themselves in their entrenchments so deeply and so well that our shrapnel can't get at them, and owing to the bungling and lack of foresight at our fine War Office we have only a very insufficient quantity of high explosive… It's simple murder to send infantry against these powerfully fortified entrenchments until they've been heavily hammered.[9]

Major efforts were put into artillery and shell production so that the scandals of early 1915, when batteries of guns often fell silent through lack of ammunition, should not be repeated. Also deemed of crucial significance was the failure to marshal sufficient reserves at the decisive point – something that French was himself held to task over, and for which he was ultimately sacked. To be successful it was therefore held not only that larger numbers of troops needed to be available close to the centre of the

action, but that they should strive to maintain 'momentum' – not giving the enemy any chance to react or seize the initiative.

The lessons of 1915 therefore seemed to be that attacks should be delivered in a deliberate manner; should be commenced with massive artillery preparation; should be as large as resources allowed; and, crucially, should be pre-arranged so that wave after wave struck the enemy, maintaining 'momentum' without let up. Once started such an attack would not hesitate to take stock of early intelligence that might well be out of date or wrong, but continue until the whole of the enemy battle position had been swallowed. The gaping hole in the front could then be exploited by a handy reserve which would be able to continue quickly to more distant targets or roll up parts of the front from behind. In the British case such notions were codified in various documents, including *The Training of Divisions in Offensive Action* of May 1916. Doubtless it was also the case that Field Marshal Haig sought to demonstrate that he was not about to commit the very error of slowness and hesitancy regarding the commitment of reinforcements over which he had helped to have his predecessor, Field Marshal French, removed. These factors set the scene for the 'Big Push', and specifically for the opening of the battle of the Somme.

Senegalese troops, 20 June 1916. France deployed Tunisian, Algerian and Moroccan troops from North Africa, and Senegalese and others drawn from French West Africa. The Senegalese formed part of the 'Colonial Army' and in 1914 included both volunteers and conscripts. Often village headmen were responsible for providing a quota of troops, initially set at about one, but not more than two, per thousand of the population. Rail transport was quicker than marching, and therefore tended to bestow advantages to defending forces with internal lines of communication. (IWM Q78086)

As the American manual *Notes on the Methods of Attack and Defense* made clear, the British conception of tactics in mid 1916 was by no means unique:

> The general method of attack used almost exclusively at present in Europe is to smother the defense with a torrent of explosive shells, kept up incessantly for from one to three or more days, so shattering the defense that they will be able to offer but slight resistance to the advance of the infantry; then to rush forward with the infantry and seize the enemy's positions while his forces are still demoralized and consolidate them before reinforcements can be brought up through the artillery barrage for counter-attack.

Understandably it is the attacks that lead to heavy casualties which stay longest in the mind – both of those who took part and of those who remember the dead. Nevertheless there were assaults in which few fell, or serious casualties only occurred after an attack had succeeded. At Bernafay Wood on the Somme, for example, the 6th King's Own Scottish Borderers and 12th Royal Scots crossed 500 yards of flat ground and retook the wood at a cost of six casualties. Occupying the wood for six days led to 316 casualties.

British forces had no monopoly on disaster: at various times slaughter fell upon every combatant. At the height of Verdun German infantryman Georg Bucher reviewed the scene across the front line:

> The few hundred yards in front of Douamont was an amazing sight. The dead, mainly Germans, lay in heaps. Then we came to a strip of ground where the French dead lay in rows and groups, the remains of a mass attack which had been repulsed; as they had moved forward, row after row in waves of attack, they must have been mown down by cunningly sited machine gun nests. But where? I could see no sign of such strong points, and I was no longer sure of my direction in the bewildering labyrinth of trenches. Ahead of us more mud-fountains were being thrown up into the air by the heavy shelling.[10]

Ultimately it would be universally recognized that moving as swiftly as possible from one piece of cover to the next was the best way to advance over the moonscapes that many of the battlefields became. The idea of moving portions of units, covered by the fire of the remainder, had in fact existed well before 1914. Shell hole to shell hole movement was used sporadically fairly early in the war, was tried and tested during raids, and did indeed become the norm during the course of the battle for Verdun. Yet getting this generally accepted, and training troops to perform this apparently simple manoeuvre reliably, was no easy, or overnight, task. Crucially, sections and *Gruppe* spread around the empty battlefield in penny packets were extremely difficult to control, and thinly spread there was concern that they would not have sufficient firepower to overcome resistance. There was also worry that untried troops would be more likely to falter without the visible support of their comrades and the overseeing eye of officers. Such issues were very much to mind in mid 1916, when British instructions often stipulated that formations be adhered to, and pace of movement regulated to that of the slowest. The horrific results of the plodding advance of 1 July were due at least in part to such insistence on uniformity. As Field Marshal Haig's notes on a conference with army commanders on 15 June recorded:

> The length of each bound forward by the infantry depends on the area which has been prepared by the artillery. The infantry must for their part, capture and hold the ground which the artillery has prepared with as little delay as possible… The advance of isolated detachments (except for reconnoitring purposes) should be avoided. They lead to loss of the boldest and best without result: enemy can concentrate on these detachments. Advance should be uniform. Discipline and the power of subordinate commanders should be exercised to prevent troops getting out of hand.[11]

Another problem was just what should be carried into the attack. Poor communications and the difficulty of getting supplies across the battlefield suggested that the troops

German Funkstation, *or wireless post. Radios were still heavy pieces of equipment, and whilst they were eventually introduced to the trenches were not easy to move. By 1918 the German establishment included 26 sets per division, though the majority of these were short range only (capable of ranges from 600 to 6,600 yards) – just one set per division was capable of long-range communication. (Author's collection)*

231

should take with them enough food, water and ammunition to last for a couple of days, plus whatever specialist equipment was required to 'turn' trenches, break wire and signal. Conversely the more that was carried the slower and more difficult progress became. French soldier Robert Laloum of the 321st Infantry set out for the recapture of Fort Douamont heavily laden:

> Our equipment is amazing. In addition to the regular infantry equipment and our crammed cartridge pouch, we have two gas masks, a haversack for the biscuits, one for beef and chocolate, a third for grenades, two bottles, one filled with wine and the other with water, a blanket rolled in the tent sheet, a tool, two bags. We were all as large as a casket.[12]

Instructions on equipment given to 1st Irish Rifles on 1 July 1916 were not untypical of the period:

> Rifle, equipment including water-proof sheet (less pack and greatcoat). Haversacks to be carried on the back. Water bottles to be full... Two bandoliers in addition to equipment ammunition (total 220 rounds per man). Bombers and Pioneers will carry equipment ammunition only and Machine Gunners 50 rounds only. Bombers may discard their pouches and carry two bandoliers instead. Iron rations and unexpended portion of day's ration. Not less than two sandbags. Not less than two grenades. Smoke helmets. Every third man a pick or shovel of which 50 per cent will be picks. The following to be carried by selected men. 130 wire cutters with lanyard per battalion. 64 bill hooks per battalion. 100 pairs hedging gloves. 48 bridges for assaulting battalions. 415 flares per battalion for signalling to Aeroplanes. Each bomb squad, of which there will be one to every platoon, will carry not less than 90 grenades.

Albert Andrews of 19th Manchesters also received some additional embellishments to uniform prior to the Somme battle:

> We already had one colour on the back of our tunics, a green and yellow star, which was the battalion colour. We now had to stick a yellow cloth over the flap of our pack – I believe this was for the Artillery Observing Officer to see in the attack how far we had got. On top of this went a tin disc... We had already been wearing short trousers all the summer. These had to be just above the knee and the puttees just below, showing our bare knees, which was all right in the daytime but not at night. Anyway I had a piece of red ribbon which I had to sew round the bottom of the right trouser leg with a bow on the outside. This was to show I was entitled to go down German dugouts after clearing out.[13]

Over his basic uniform went:

Rifle and bayonet with wire cutters attached; a shovel fastened on my back; pack containing two days' rations, oil sheet, cardigan jacket and mess tin; haversack containing one day's iron rations and two Mills bombs; 150 rounds of ammunition; two extra bandoliers containing 50 rounds each, one over each shoulder; a bag of bombs.[14]

How quickly attacking troops could have moved is open to some debate. Early 19th-century experiments suggested that charging at a full run from much more than 100 yards of the enemy, particularly over rough ground or any obstruction, was likely to be prematurely tiring – and the time to move fastest was when closest to danger. In short there was little point in moving very quickly at any distance from an objective if this meant arriving exhausted, and at a snail's pace, to be easily shot down at point blank range by a comparatively fresh, or concealed, enemy. On the other hand some units did run and move more freely, and appeared to have benefited from doing so. Attacking rapidly in short 'bounds' may still have resulted in heavy casualties on many occasions – but there can be little doubting that bursts of swift movement by troops who threw themselves flat in any cover and regained their breath before repeating the process produced less of a target than those who simply walked forwards. On 1 July 1916, 36th Ulster Division are recorded as rushing directly into action without forming up. The relative success of the Ulster attack was no doubt in part due to great courage and *élan*, but was also aided significantly by the fact that it started from trenches at the edge of a battered wood quite close to the enemy. The assault could therefore naturally be launched more rapidly than by those who started from completely open positions further away.

Bringing up Mills bombs near Bernafay Wood during the battle of Bazentin Ridge, Somme, mid July 1916. In addition to the grenades, the men carry rifles, bandoliers and cotton drill bags for gas helmets. The bombs were packed with a dozen, and a tin of detonators, in each rope-handled wooden box. Eight such boxes, or 96 grenades, formed a factory 'lot'. (IWM Q4052)

The Somme was Haig's worst hour, and the British Army's bloodiest. The battle had started as a matter of necessity, due to insistence from above and from the French, that something, indeed anything, that could be done should be done, to relieve the pressure on Verdun. At the same time the French had scaled down their own participation in the offensive. To this extent Haig was a victim of circumstance. Yet the idea that bombardment could simply sweep the enemy away had been tried before – and failed before. Using the New Armies in a largely unimaginative manner, ostensibly because it was believed that they could not handle anything more complicated, was also patronizing at best. It was also an indictment of holding them back for over a year whilst apparently 'training'. By 14 August Haig certainly seems to have realized that the tactics of early July had been a dire mistake – though naturally that of somebody else. According to his own narrative we find him on that day impressing upon General Jacob that the divisions were not 'to employ so many men in the front line' and to use Lewis guns and 'detachments' instead. He also berated him for the slowness of information in reaching HQ – though how Jacob, or anybody else for that matter, could speed this up was unclear. All this was in direct contradiction of his own instructions of a few weeks earlier. Despite the apparent dawning of clarity Haig still spoke in terms of 'maintaining steady pressure', criticized 49th Division for its lack of casualties and failure to salute his car, and greeted his new cavalry general Kavanagh on 9 September with the uplifting news that 'the enemy seemed to have exhausted his reserves'.

Interestingly, German comments of the Somme period confirm some of the stereotypes that have become part of folklore – whilst rejecting other equally cherished notions. In several instances lack of 'tactical sense' was observed, yet increasing skill with small groups and Lewis guns was also seen as a worrying development. The strict discipline in the Kitchener battalions was also remarked upon, which the Germans compared unfavourably with the Territorials. Bavarian reports later noted enemy other ranks as surprisingly physically fit two years into the war, but 'Australian officers are inferior in every respect to the British'. Another report remarked on 3rd and 4th Australian divisions as 'poor'.

A problem that dogged virtually every offensive of the war was lack of adequate communications – and this remained an issue even when an attack succeeded. Field telephone exchanges did excellent work, provided the army stayed still and was not heavily shelled. Radios had existed for some years, but they were large, delicate and impossible for infantry on the move to use, though they were put in some tanks and aircraft. 'Trench sets' were introduced during 1916. Advancing troops therefore quickly outran their communications, and were reduced to the ancient methods of dispatching runners and visual signalling. In the heat of battle such means often went sadly awry: messages sent at different times overtook one another, others arrived very slowly, some not at all.

The usual method to keep communication with the advance was the battalion observation post in the front line equipped with one field telephone, signal flags and runners. Battalions then reported to brigades the progress of the advance by means of telephone or runner. As can be imagined the success of this system rested upon the ability of the observers to see the troops in front of them, or the attacking waves to send back runners. Enemy bombardment might not only hit the attacking infantry but also disable runners and sever telephone wires. Brigades would receive patchy reports, often in the wrong chronological order. Carrier pigeons, signal flares and aircraft could supplement the basic system, but at risk of causing additional confusion. In the event that the attack appeared to be going well battalions would attempt to set up 'forward report centres' – the officer and men responsible for setting this up would follow the last wave of the attack.

The idea of attacking 'waves' remained current for much of the war – yet the emphasis shifted from relatively rigid formations of riflemen, to looser arrangements in which different echelons performed different functions, as, for example, attacking; mopping up; holding and consolidating. This principle had been established by the end of 1915, and by mid 1916 it had become usual to put even smaller groups of specialists out ahead of the already thinned assaulting waves. By the time of the battle of Arras in early 1917 a typical British company attack was formed of waves in which there were

A German 21cm Mörser at the moment of discharge. The shells are delivered in wicker containers, seen to the right of the picture, then carried to the gun for loading using the stretcher device, foreground. The crew have stuffed their ears against potentially deafening noise. (Author's collection)

BANTOUZELLE

From the Bantouzelle sheet 57B S.W. 1, 1:10,000, with German trenches in red corrected to 19 May 1917. Here we see how a classic piece of Hindenburg Line defensive design has been combined with the St Quentin canal to maximum effect. The red hatching along the canal banks denotes flooded areas, crosses indicate obstacle zones. In front of Bantouzelle there are no fewer than three separate belts of wire, and these continue not only into the flooded area but also across the canal itself, the whole space being flanked by trenches and emplacements. A machine gun post is also placed at 90 degrees to the front to rake the streets of Banteux with enfilade fire. The front line is a double trench system, with not only another double obstacle zone between the first and second trenches, but also obstacles running along either side of the communication trenches, making them potential flanking positions – or enemy death traps.

However, the real firepower is to be found in the second line, squares '27' and '33'. Here we see wire – three, four and even five belts deep – shaped into arrow bastions which will have the effect of channelling attackers into narrow zones which are swept by the heaviest fire. Machine guns are positioned not only in the fire trench but also behind yet another obstacle zone another 100–200 yards further back. The eastern half of square 27 alone shows 16 fixed machine gun posts – how many would have been missed by observers and how many weapons could be used in a roving capacity could only be guessed.

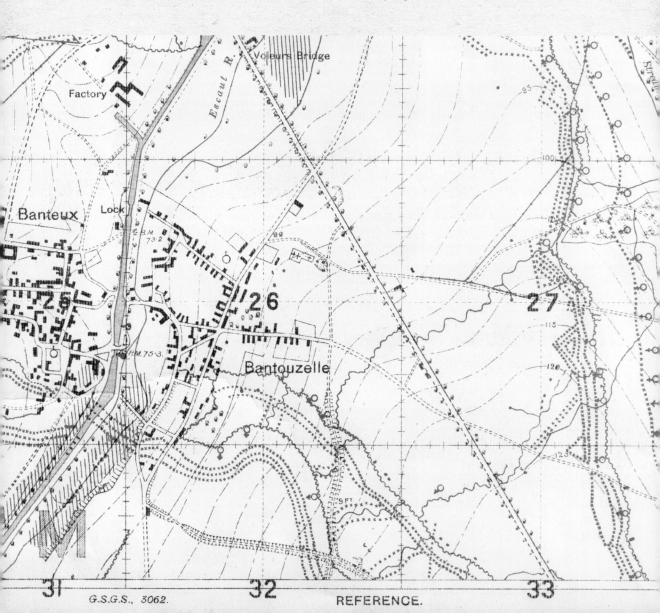

Left:

German field telegraphist of infantry regiment 452. Responsible for setting up field telephone systems the Fernsprecher Trupp usually consisted of an NCO and three men. Equipment of these troops included handsets, cable spools, transmission boxes, pliers, wire cutters, and as seen here on the soldier's back, special poles. These Drahtgabel (literally 'cable forks') could be used to hoist wires into trees or onto telegraph poles. Several poles could be slotted together to obtain greater height. (Author's collection)

Below:

A manual illustration showing a Royal Engineer with the cup discharger used for projecting No 36 Mills bombs in the latter part of the war. Note how the rifle is held upside down, allowing the shock of discharge to be transmitted directly to the ground rather than setting up stress in the butt. (Author's collection)

PLATE 5.

supposed to be about 6 yards between individuals. The first wave consisted of a single platoon, split into four sections – and two sections each comprised a separate line. This first wave was followed by some 'moppers up'. The second wave was again one platoon followed by 'moppers up'; and the third wave a further platoon. The nucleus of the fourth platoon was kept back at transport lines with any remaining men. Part of the logic of keeping back some troops 'out of battle' was that in the event of disaster there would be seasoned troops remaining on which to rebuild the company.

BREAKING THE TRENCHES

It is commonly stated that the 'Stormtroop' tactics that eventually achieved major breakthroughs on the Western Front were introduced only by the Germans, and 'invented' essentially by General von Hutier on the Eastern Front. Though this makes for a dramatic story, and is useful as one more thing with which to castigate supposedly universally unimaginative Allied generals and tacticians, none of these things is actually true. Most, if not all, of the techniques displayed in Operation *Michael* in March 1918 had been used before, and by no means had every one of them been developed by the Germans – and those that were certainly did not appear suddenly, or in isolation. Perhaps the biggest myth of all was the development of the new trench-busting techniques on the Eastern Front. As Ludendorff himself stated:

> On the Eastern Front we had for the most part adhered to the old tactical methods and old training which we had learned in the days of peace. Here [in the West] we met with new conditions and it was my duty to adapt myself to them.[15]

Indeed it may reasonably be argued that the resumption of mobility in the West was a function of a number of different tactical and strategic factors that developed over time. One point easily overlooked is that the latest defensive methods of 1918 no longer regarded continuous linear trench lines as essential to the defence. Though best perfected by the Germans, 'zones' of defence with reliance on machine weapons and artillery had become universally more important than trench 'lines' defended mainly by rifles. Similarly, artillery techniques and hardware, such as new types of shell and fuse, had reached new levels of sophistication – and suitability for use in shorter bombardments. The usefulness of the tank as at least a 'breaking in' weapon – if not a fully developed 'breakthrough' arm – has already been considered.

Finally, the good old-fashioned idea of weight of numbers also had a critical part in the resumption of movement on the Western Front. The revolution of October 1917 and the opening of negotiations at Brest-Litovsk spelled the end of Russia as an Entente partner. This allowed the Germans to achieve at least local and temporary superiorities of numbers in the West, at the very time that British politicians were unwilling to write Haig a blank cheque in terms of replacements after the bloody battles of 1917. During

A gefallener Engländer of the North Staffords. Bodies were often searched – for identification as well as valuables – and boots were removed by the Germans as salvage. (Author's collection)

the spring and early summer of 1918 the wheel of fortune spun again, for whilst the Germans made very significant advances this was at the cost of heavy losses and further stretching of already perilous supply chains. Meanwhile US troop numbers, relatively insignificant the previous year, now built up to a level where American divisions were ready to mount their own offensive battles. French forces, degraded to the point of mutiny in 1917, now also recovered their composure. Taken together these factors helped to give the British in particular the local superiorities required for successful attack.

The artillery techniques of short 'hurricane' bombardments, creeping barrages and fire without registration were not new. German artillery guru Georg Brüchmuller had been using them all for months or years, and creeping barrages in particular had been in use by the British and French, as well as the Germans, since at least 1916. Fire without registration had been a subject of experiment by the Royal Artillery in 1917 and generally dismissed as questionable. Map firing was now the norm, not the exception.

Corporal Amos Wilder of the US 17th Field Artillery described typical long-range artillery techniques of 1918:

> When the camouflaged guns were in firing position in a given sector, orders would come by field telephone or courier from the Colonel at regimental headquarters to our Captain. So many rounds of either explosive or shrapnel shells at such and such times and such frequency. The targets were identified by coordinates on a grid map of the area which showed its features in great detail. Using the map our officers could determine the direction and distance of the target in relation to our position. Allowance had to be made,

however, for such factors as atmospheric conditions as well as distortion in the maps themselves. Trial firings by our guns therefore needed to be observed from a forward position. Our telephone detail would string wires through the woods and fields to such an observation post. Instructing our gunners to fire, the officer would then note how far the shot was 'over' or 'short' right or left, and thus correct the following trial.[16]

The small unit infantry tactics of platoons and sections moving rapidly from cover to cover, working around enemy positions and making copious use of grenades, whilst directly supported by their own light machine guns, evolved – as we have seen – over a period of three years. Small units were deployed experimentally, and in raids, and various sorts of bomb squad and stealthy assault party were in action as early as 1915; the same year in which offensive techniques were developed for light flame-throwers. Light machine gun tactics were more advanced in the British Army than pretty well anywhere, and the French were also well aware of them though sometimes hampered by poor equipment. Aircraft co-operation was at least as advanced in the Allied armies as in the German, and the obvious piece of offensive equipment that the Germans were short of in 1918 was the tank.

In 1916 the reorganization of infantry companies as a combination of specialized groups had already begun. The French were arguably as advanced in this process as any nation. By the end of 1916 the standard French infantry company of four platoons contained as its fighting complement:

12 NCOs armed as automatic riflemen or bombers
12 Rifle armed NCOs
24 Automatic riflemen
68 Riflemen
28 Bombers
16 Rifle grenade men
8   Grenade carriers

Each of the four platoons was made up of two full and two half sections. The half sections comprised one with a corporal and seven bombers, the other, two Chauchat teams of three led by a corporal. The full sections were eight or nine riflemen each, backed by two rifle grenadiers and a grenade carrier – these full sections being led by sergeants. As far as possible individuals were taught more than one specialism, and all were trained to use the rifle and hand grenade.

Within the French battalion there was also a machine gun company, armed with not only eight medium machine guns but a 37mm gun for light close support. As an American commentary in the publication *Notes on the Methods of Attack and Defense* observed, 'The battalion has thus come to be a very strong unit, capable of progressing by its own means, and of breaking most resistance it encounters.' The organization within the French companies allowed the 'introduction of new arms into the infantry without upsetting the organic channels of command as they are now established'. Whilst the specialists could remain within their sections it was also possible for the company or battalion commander to concentrate them for a particular tactical requirement.

For the British the introduction of Lewis gun teams with the infantry battalions in 1915, and the use of 'Grenadier Parties', had marked the beginning of a shift from lines to more flexible attacking tactics; but the idea that the platoon was the 'unit of attack' was not general until after the battle of the Somme. In February 1917 the important manual *Instructions for the Training of Platoons for Offensive Action* laid down a scheme for platoon organization somewhat similar to the French model. The British platoon was now to number from 28 to 44 with an 'average strength' of 36 in four sections. These sections were designated bombers, Lewis gunners, riflemen and rifle bombers, and each section was led by an NCO. Men with particular aptitude for shooting, throwing or scouting were to be allotted accordingly. The platoon 'HQ' was an additional four men led by an officer. Each of the weapons had something different to contribute. The rifle and bayonet – with which all troops were to be proficient – were defined as 'the most efficient offensive weapons of the soldier' and intended primarily for assault, repelling of attack, and 'obtaining superiority of fire'. The grenade was the 'secondary weapon' of all, being ideal for 'dislodging the enemy from behind cover or killing him below ground'. The rifle bomb was the infantry 'howitzer', attacking the enemy from behind cover and perhaps driving him underground. The Lewis gun, as 'weapon of opportunity', could kill the enemy above ground or drive him below. The fact that it was mobile and presented a small target made it useful to work round a flank or protect a flank.

Whilst *Instructions for the Training of Platoons* still assumed that major assaults would be launched in a series of rough 'waves' (not parade ground lines), there were many instances in which the platoon would be expected to operate as sections. In a 'trench to trench' attack, for example, the rifle section was expected to 'gain a position on a flank', attacking with both 'fire and the bayonet'. The bombers with hand grenades would similarly and 'without halting' gain a position on a flank from which to attack. Meanwhile, the rifle bombing section was to lend support, gaining the nearest cover possible, and from here 'open a hurricane bombardment'. The Lewis gunners were to take cover and open a 'traversing fire' upon the point of resistance, being later available to work round a flank. Though by no means general for all purposes, section-strong 'blob' and 'worm' formations were also in use by this time. For attacking in woods a 'line of skirmishers' was recommended, followed by small section columns. Under threat of artillery fire the platoon would also move as sections, in 'fours, file, or single file, according to the ground and other factors of the case'.

Just a month later, in March 1917, Canadian 4th Division issued a memorandum instructing that it was 'the mobility of the platoon' and nothing else which could deal with the sudden and unexpected discovery of a machine gun. General Arthur Currie investigated French methods, as had been applied at Verdun, and concluded that capturing useful topography was a better aim than simply attacking trench lines. Moreover, careful training, particularly of companies and platoons, paid better dividends than the painstaking organization of 'jumping off' trenches and other somewhat predictable forms of preparation.

That the art of attack had moved on significantly was underlined by the instruction *Assault Training*, issued in September 1917:

> Fire and movement are inseparable in the attack. Ground is gained by a body of troops advancing while supported by the fire of another body of troops. The principle of fire and movement should be known to all ranks, and the one object of every advance, namely to close with the enemy, should be emphasised on all occasions.

Assault training was now to be divided into three stages: training the individual in the 'combination of rifle fire and bayonet work'; training in bullet, bayonet and bomb and the use of 'the weapon appropriate to the situation'; and collective training in 'all infantry weapons by means of a tactical exercise'. Departure from the start line was still 'at a steady pace' – but might include 'firing from the hip', and was to lead to a charge close to the enemy position. Some of the most advanced methods were borrowed from those of the scout, as is illustrated by an exercise given in *Scouting and Patrolling* of December 1917:

> A group of men, covering each other's advance, rush from cover to cover, a distance of 200 to 300 yards, to shell holes within 50 yards of the butts. Targets, stationary, representing Machine Guns or loopholes at longer ranges, moving figures at closer ranges. Dummy figures just in front of the butts. Scouts in the butts watch the advancing men with periscopes, noting the mistakes and learning how difficult a mark the good scout presents.

Opposite:
The damp subterranean central passageway of Fort Douamont. Outdated, but still a substantial obstacle, Douamont was arguably the most formidable of Verdun's 19 major forts. Occupied by only a skeleton garrison it was seized by the Germans in an unexpected, and possibly accidental, coup on 25 February 1916. Repeated and bloody attempts to take it back followed. On 8 May several hundred German soldiers were killed in an accidental explosion and fire, stoked by hand grenades, a munitions dump and flame-thrower fuel. Following massive bombardment the French re-entered Douamont in October 1916. (Author's collection)

By May 1918 *Hints on Training*, published under the auspices of Lieutenant General Ivor Maxse, gave further indication of just how far things had changed. General principles of training were now to be 'on simple lines' and to cover the essentials. These were discipline, the importance of keeping direction, the 'value of the bullet', the use of ground, immediate counter-attack – and, perhaps critically, 'fire and movement'. All tactical training at platoon level was to include the use of a Lewis gun, and training was to be designed 'to interest, not bore'. Sections were now to comprise six men and an NCO, and all sections were to be trained first and foremost as 'rifle sections'. Any section that fell below three was to be disbanded and reintegrated with others to provide viable units. Sergeants and corporals were to be trained to fulfil the roles of platoon commander in case of lack of replacement officers: 'A battalion must be organized into 16 platoons and 64 sections. This is the basis of all training.'

Though bomb, rifle grenade and bayonet training were still part of the curriculum, the maxim now was that 'the bullet beats the bomb and bayonet'. Rifle training was to concentrate on rapid loading, aiming and firing, with an expectation of 15 accurate rounds per minute. Where possible rapid loading could be used as subject for a competition, perhaps with one man attempting to load faster than another could empty a rifle. Practice for the attack was now to focus on objectives, covering fire by Lewis guns and machine guns, fire and movement, and liaison with units to the flank. The mantra for the attack was now, 'When in doubt go ahead. When uncertain do that which will kill most Germans. Don't fear an exposed flank. Teach the exposed flank to hang on, or to push out and protect itself.' Somme veteran D. V. Kelly was just one of many convinced that the British methods had made 'enormous advances' between the opening of the Somme and 1918.[17] 'Tremendous' artillery bombardments – poorly synchronized, but lasting days – gave way to shorter but cleverly planned efforts which did not disclose the objectives in advance. Advances in plodding waves by daylight were often replaced by movement or attack under darkness. Large daylight operations were commonly fronted by tanks.

As we have seen, changes to German infantry tactics commenced very early with the use of small grenade-armed *Stoss* and *Handgranaten* troops for specific actions,

such as attacks on strong points or raids. Experimental units, or *Versuchstruppen*, for testing trench mortars, small 'assault cannon' and flame-throwers were started in March 1915. The unit that tested the *Sturmkanonen* under Major Kalsow and later Hauptmann Wilhelm Rohr subsequently became recognized as the forerunner of all 'Stormtroops'. Following the barrage as closely as possible, and movement from shell hole to shell hole, were established techniques by the time of Verdun, as the account of a lieutenant of the 115th Hessian Leibgarde Infantry Regiment made clear:

> I had already established with my people that 'with the barrage we were out'. Everything then hung between life and death. The advance began immediately, creeping and jumping from crater to crater. A shell which struck on the edge of our crater showered my brave lad Franz at my side with stones and earth, but the effect was trivial. Forwards, only forwards, called my inner voice. My undaunted colleague Martin S. quickly found another hole and raised his rifle: we were beside him in an instant. Often we held craters only a few metres from each other, but without being aware of it in the crazy noise – bullets whistling over us, and amongst the roar of the arrival of shells.[18]

New manuals for the weapons of close combat, *Nahkampfmittel*, issued in August 1916 and again in January 1917, stressed the role of grenades, pistols and close range work from one shell hole to another. There was also a widespread willingness on the part of commanders, generally unmatched in Allied armies, to allow latitude to juniors – to lead by 'directive', and target driven means, rather than prescription. Crucially, however, producing the new equipment required to re-equip the entire infantry arm, and to retrain it in new methods, would take a long time. Integrating small unit tactics with the bigger picture could also be problematic. Moreover, as Clausewitz had once remarked, 'War consists of a continuous interaction of opposites' – and many methods would evolve to perfection only through a process of trial and error, and of learning by observing enemy successes and failures. Some new techniques were also honed by the mountain troops of the *Alpenkorps*, where, by necessity, small gun batteries and machine gun units were attached at a low organizational level to the rifle-armed troops, and terrain offered opportunities for small unit actions on non-continuous fronts. So it was that for quite some time 'shock units' were just a small part of the army, drawn out from existing battalions and regiments to spearhead an attack or perform a specific role. This process was regularized in May 1916 when the High Command ordered that all armies on the Western Front should send cadres of officers and men to the new *Sturmbataillon* to learn techniques, and then return to their units to teach the latest ideas. By November most divisions, and many regiments, could boast at least one *Sturmabteilung*, or 'assault detachment', of company strength.

Arguably the full development of self-supporting platoons and squads was held back by heavy losses, the need to maintain a very long perimeter on two fronts, and a failure to fully realize Germany's industrial potential until 1916. Nevertheless *Stoss* troops had been employed at Verdun, and the use of small detachments and infiltration techniques was well advanced by 1917. In August 1917, for example, German 451st Regiment launched an operation on the ridge of Hill 124 based almost entirely on the deployment of *Stoss* troops and 'Storm companies'. The attackers were both special companies drawn from ordinary units, and detachments from a *Sturmbataillon*. Part of the force moved out of the German front line under cover of darkness, taking position from 80 to 220 yards from the French, and a second wave then occupied the jumping off trenches. The assault was supported by brief mortar and artillery fire, aimed mainly at the neutralization of French batteries, and the sealing off of the target area. The *Stoss* troops were under orders to seize the objectives, but to retire back on the German lines when other troops arrived to relieve them.

In September 1917 1st Bavarian Division prepared plans for a limited attack, or giant raid, in the Champagne – 'Operation *Sommerernte*' (Summer Harvest) – which was to integrate gas with no fewer than 12 'shock troops' drawn from the division, three from the 2nd *Sturmbataillon*, and some specially formed 'destruction' and 'salvage'

US official photograph showing Lieutenant V. A. Browning firing the machine gun invented by his father at Thillombois, 5 October 1918. The 1917 model .30 Browning was manufactured by Colt, Westinghouse and Remington, with 68,000 produced by the end of the war. (IWM Q70559)

A gunner major at the awesome breech of a 12-inch howitzer of 444 Battery, Royal Garrison Artillery, near Arras, 19 July 1918. The weapon weighed well over 20,000lb, and 20 tons of soil were loaded into its 'earth box' to counteract the massive recoil. The officer's rank is denoted by the crown and three lines of lace on his cuff: a gold 'wound stripe' worn above his rank insignia shows that he has been wounded once. (IWM Q6873)

squads. Further shock troops from neighbouring divisions would also attack, leaving the enemy in doubt of the extent of the operation and reducing the possibility of enemy interference from a flank. There would be no drawn out advanced bombardment, but artillery and trench mortars would fire to 'neutralize' enemy artillery with shells and gas. As a document later translated by the Americans explained:

> The role of the shock troops will be to open a passage through the enemy's positions for the salvage and destruction squads, to break down the remaining resistance, to attain the objectives assigned to them, and to protect the salvage and destruction squads during their operations.

The individual shock troop units were of about 50 men each, led by an officer, and mixed together infantry and pioneers to match the tasks to hand. The basis of each troop was a light machine gun squad, bombing squad and attached specialists and riflemen. The majority were organized as follows:

From the infantry

1 Officer

3 NCOs

16 Men

5 Man light machine gun squad

2 Signallers

From the pioneers

1 NCO

4 Pioneers

3 Gas specialists

From the *Sturmbataillon*

2 NCOs

3 Pioneers

6 Grenadiers

2 Stretcher bearers

Towards the end of 1917, during the battle of Cambrai, British commentators noted German use of what were virtually fully developed 'Stormtroop tactics'. As the *Official History* recorded:

> Preceded by patrols the Germans had advanced at 7am in small columns bearing many light machine guns, and in some cases flame-throwers. From overhead low flying airplanes, in greater numbers than had hitherto been seen, bombed and machine gunned the British defenders, causing further casualties and, especially, distraction at the critical moment. Nevertheless few posts appear to have been attacked from the front, the assault sweeping in between them to envelop them from flanks and rear.

By the end of 1917 Allied intelligence therefore had quite a good idea of the latest German techniques. In the US this knowledge was summarized as 'Tactics of the German Assault Detachments' as part of the manual *German Notes on Minor Tactics*. The key factors identified were good advanced preparation; a brief but 'very violent' application of artillery and mortars which 'caged' the area under attack; and finally the actual attack of the *Stosstrupp* units. Their method was to advance 'by groups, using the shell holes' with the wings of attack having 'reinforced groups' for flank protection. Study of a specific action at Sechamp Woods suggested a model of a *Stosstrupp* that numbered 106 men, carrying with them two light machine guns and an automatic rifle. Probably in addition to some long arms, individuals were equipped with 'a Mauser pistol, a trench knife, a bayonet, and in a sandbag 16 stick grenades and 8 egg shaped grenades'.

What was different about the German Spring Offensive of 1918 therefore was not the application of any individual technique, but its scale, reinforced by troops drawn

The 'New Armies' – a soldier of the Durham Light Infantry in full marching order including the 'large pack', which was normally deposited before entering the trenches. Note the fearsome model 1907 'sword bayonet' with its 17 inch blade, much of the time it was more of a weapon of morale than practical impact on the modern 'empty battlefield'. The 1914 type leather equipment with its distinctive large pouches was a stop gap but never as popular as the 1908 webbing with its ten small ammunition pouches. (Author's collection)

from the East, the general equipment of the assaulting divisions to the latest standard with items such as new mortars and light machine guns, and the willingness of Ludendorff to take this all or nothing gamble to finish the war with a 'Peace Offensive'. Also of significance was the existence of an overarching doctrine in the form of the new manual *Der Angriff im Stellungskrieg* – 'The Attack in Position Warfare'. This document, published on 1 January 1918 under the authorship of Hauptmann Hermann Geyer, served to pull together all previous experience from all fronts into a general blueprint for the attack – not only limited attacks, significantly, but full-scale offensive battles leading from 'position warfare to the breakthrough'.

Preparation for the assault was to be thorough but subtle, so as not to give away time or place. The bombardment likewise would be intensive and include gas, with a view towards 'neutralization', but would not be so prolonged as to give the enemy the chance to react. Where the shells were aimed at trenches a density of one German howitzer battery was deemed desirable for every hundred yards of trench line. The assault would be an attack 'in depth', with each division so deployed that it had a frontage of 2,000–3,000 yards. Reserves were to be pushed in where there was success, not failure, and the keeping back of a portion of fresh artillery was seen as even more important than fresh infantry. Some of the lighter units, such as light trench mortars, would be designated as 'accompanying artillery', moving up with the infantry to fire at close range over open sights on arrival.

The infantry were to advance so hard on the bombardment that it was deemed preferable that they take casualties from their own guns, rather than appear after the enemy had any chance to recover. Assault detachments would as a matter of course lead the attack, but whether the main effort was 'waves of skirmishers' or waves of assault detachments was left up to circumstance. The battle was to be seen not so much as a matter of numbers as of comparative 'fighting power', that is, training and equipment, preparation and skill, 'combined with rapid and determined action'. As far as possible the distance from the attackers to their objective would be minimized, the forces being gathered as far forward as practical in trenches, shell holes and dugouts. The effect of the enemy artillery response would be further reduced through surprise, and the fact that the first wave would be across the barrage zone before it could be badly hit. Subsequent reinforcing waves would be less dense and therefore suffer fewer casualties accordingly.

As *Der Angriff* observed:

Besides making full use of the weapons at their disposal and exploiting the enemy's known weaknesses, the troops must have dash if the assault is to be successful. Success is gained by determined and reckless drive and initiative on the part of every individual man. A check in the attack in one place must not spread to the whole line; infantry which pushes well forward will envelop the parties of the enemy that are standing fast.

CONCLUSION

On the basis of many accounts we might be forgiven for thinking that the trench war of 1914–18 was the war in which nothing of significance, bar death and destruction, ever happened – as the original German title of *All Quiet on the Western Front* put it, *Nothing New in the West*. Bloody as the Western Front was, however, this is but the most superficial of interpretations. For in the first place trenches were dug specifically as refuges against the worst that modern war could deliver, and as a way to economize on troops, some of whom could now be freed to be used elsewhere. Given the population growth of the 19th century, and the fact that the trench lines soon reached from Switzerland to the sea, there was, unfortunately, in the West at least, no 'elsewhere'.

Nevertheless this was very far from the whole story, for as Lieutenant Charles Carrington of the Royal Warwickshires observed, the lines were only 'rigid' during 1915 and 1916: 'during 1917 bomb fighting in the trenches gave way to shell hole warfare, and in 1918 to open fighting'[1] – in which tanks and cavalry played a part. It was also the case that technological and tactical virtuosity led, fairly quickly, to a wide range of new weapons and techniques that eventually culminated not only in breakthroughs but in a revolution in the way that war was fought. The revival of the grenade, the transformation of the artillery, the inventions of new shells and fuses, the rapid development and use of observation, fighting and bombing aircraft, the first use of the flame-thrower and the start of modern chemical warfare were just the most obvious manifestations of this revolution. For there were many other, more subtle, developments, which were also crucial. One of these was the transformation of the trench itself.

The first trenches of August 1914 were usually just that – one long ditch, with only minor embellishments, in which a unit stood, more or less as it might have done on the open battlefield. By early 1915 trenches had become 'systems', with reserve lines, bunkers, posts for specialists and a growing culture of a sort of existence alien not only to the civilian but also to the pre-war soldier. Men now rotated in and out of the various lines in a long and exhausting ballet of movements, enjoying the

dubious experience of the front line trench for only a small minority of the time they spent at or near the Western Front.

By the end of that year it was usual for there to be two or more systems forming the defence, and there was an awareness that as far as possible trench garrisons should be kept small. By 1916 it was clear that machine weapons were key to holding the trench with economy and that concrete and individual posts within zones was the way forward. So it was that by 1917 linear defence was gradually on the wane.

The Ossuary, Verdun. Built between 1922 and 1932 the basement of the building contains the skeletal remains of 130,000 dead – some of which may still be viewed through ground-level portholes. Another 15,000 identified bodies are in the adjoining cemetery. The building also contains 18 chapels for different parts of France, and other areas for Allied nations. Its solid eclectic design is part fort, part cathedral. (Author's collection)

Human organization also changed. Where once battalions and companies had been the clear units of attack, and the rifle, used mainly by men in lines, had been backed only by a couple of fairly static and heavy machine guns, the tactical focus was pulled ever tighter. The infantry battalion soon included grenades of many types, new machine guns and snipers, catapults and light mortars. The Engineers adopted gas, flame and other examples of frightfulness. By 1917 the platoon was considered vital. Eventually the squad and the individual were accounted worthwhile – the tank crew, the machine gun team, and other groups which were small enough either to be placed in one vehicle, or to hide together in a shell hole or bunker on the 'empty battlefield'. For some this was the start of a new age, when, as Ernst Jünger put it, 'the spirit of the machine took possession' of the battlefield, and new types of leader were born.[2]

All wars end; even this war will some day end, and the ruins will be rebuilt and the field full of death will grow food, and all this frontier of trouble will be forgotten. When the trenches are filled in, and the plough has gone over them, the ground will not long keep the look of war. One summer with its flowers will cover most of the ruin that man can make, and then these places, from which the driving back of the enemy began, will be hard to trace, even with maps.

John Masefield, 1917[3]

NOTES

INTRODUCTION

1   Edmund Dane, *Trench Warfare*, London, 1915, p.3

THE ARMIES OF 1914 AND THE PROBLEM OF ATTACK

1   Captain E. G. Hopkinson, *Spectamur Agendo*, Cambridge, 1926, p.73

2   Corporal Amos Wilder, *Armageddon Revisited*, Yale, 1994, p.67

3   Frederic Manning, *The Middle Parts of Fortune*, 1929, London, 1986 (new edition), pp.10–11

4   Gustav Ebelshauser, *The Passage*, Huntingdon, 1984, p.101

5   N. Fraser-Tytler, *Field Guns in France*, London, 1922, pp.102–103

6   Unteroffizier Hundt, 'Reserve Infantry Regiment 17', in J. Sheldon, *The German Army on the Somme*, Barnsley, 2005, p.235

7   Private C. E. D. Dunn quoted in I. Uys, *Delville Wood*, Rensburg, 1983, p.76

8   Report of the War Office Committee, 1922, pp.9, 44, 58–58, 62, 81, 138

9   Captain Henry Dundas, *A Memoir* (reprinted letters), Edinburgh, 1921, p.103

10 Corporal W. F. Lowe, eyewitness account in L. MacDonald, *1915: The Death of Innocence*, London, 1993, pp.425–427

11 Herbert W. McBride, *A Rifleman Went to War*, Ottawa, 1935, p.160

12 Marc Bloch, *Memoirs of War* (English edition), Cambridge, 1988, p.140

13 Private R. G. Bultitude quoted in B. Purdom (ed.) *Everyman at War*, London, 1930, p.219

14 Lieutenant D. W. J. Cuddeford, *And All For What? Some War Time Experiences*, reprinted in T. Donovan (ed.), *The Hazy Red Hell*, Spellmount, 1999, pp.108–115

15 Jean Norton Cru, *Témoins Essai d'analyse*, Paris, 1929; Ian Ousby, *The Road to Verdun*, London, 2003, pp.70, 270

16 George Coppard, *With a Machine Gun to Cambrai*, London, 1980, pp.37–38; C. E. Crutchley (ed.), *Machine Gunner*, Northampton, 1973

17 Marshal Ferdinand Foch, *Memoirs*, London, 1931, p.43. See also G. Blond, *The Marne*, London, 2002 and E. D. Bose, *The Kaiser's Army*, Oxford, 2001

THE BEGINNING OF THE TRENCHES

1   Edmund Dane, *Trench Warfare*, London, 1915, pp.33, 58–63

2   Erich von Falkenhayn, *General Headquarters, 1914–1916 and its Critical Decisions*, Berlin and London, 1919, p.40

3 Lieutenant F. P. Roe, *Accidental Soldiers*, London, 1981, p.42

4 R.E. Harris, *Billie: The Nevill Letters*, London, 1991, pp.61–78

5 Guy Chapman, *A Passionate Prodigality*, London, 1985 (third edition), pp.39–40

6 Private Edward Roe quoted in P. Downham (ed.), *Diary of an Old Contemptible*, Barnsley, 2004, p.54

7 Marc Bloch, *Memoirs of War*, (English edition), Cambridge, 1988, p.130

8 P. Witkop (ed.), *German Students' War Letters*, London, 1929, p.3

9 Sidney Rogerson, *Twelve Days on the Somme*, London, 2006, p.65

10 Anon., *A Month at the Front: The Diary of an Unknown Soldier*, Bodleian Library, Oxford, 2006, p.37

11 Lieutenant John Reith, *Wearing Spurs*, London, 1966, pp.64–65

12 Private Edward Loxdale, *A Souvnir of a Soldier*, London, 1916, p.2

13 Dane, *Trench Warfare*, pp.47–48

14 German 3rd Army Headquarters, *Experiences Gained in the Winter Battle in Champagne, 14th April, 1915*, translated as 'CDS 303', p.2

15 John Masefield, *The Old Front Line*, Bourne End, 1972 (reprint), p.89

16 Harris, *Billie: The Nevill Letters*, p.63

17 Lieutenant N. F. Percival, manuscript journal, Duke of Lancaster's Own Yeomanry Museum, Preston

18 Ibid.

19 Rudyard Kipling, *The Irish Guards in the Great War: Second Battalion*, Staplehurst, 1997 (new edition), p.37; Ernst Jünger, *Storm of Steel*, London, 1994 (reprint), pp.92–110

20 Edmund Blunden, *Undertones of War*, London, 1982 (reprint), pp.105–106

21 C.T. Atkinson, *History of the South Wales Borderers 1914–1918*, London, 1931, pp.215–216, 349

'TRENCHTOWN'

1 Sidney Rogerson, *Twelve Days on the Somme*, London, 2006, p.35

2 List of stores taken by 'C' Company, 5th S. Lancs, August 1916. Queen's Lancashire Regiment collection, Fulwood

3 Albert W. Andrews quoted in S. Richardson (ed.), *Orders are Orders*, Manchester, 1987, pp.28–31

4 J. W. Taylor, *The 1st Royal Irish Rifles in the Great War*, Dublin, 2002, pp.189–201; D. Winter, *Death's Men*, London, 1985 (second edition), pp.42–44; E. C. Vaughan, *Some Desperate Glory*, London, 1981, pp.67–68; J. Peaty in B. Bond (ed.), *Look to Your Front: Studies in the First World War*, Spellmount, 1999, pp.89–104

5 G. D. Sheffield and G. I. S. Inglish (eds.), *From Vimy Ridge to the Rhine: The Great War Letters of Christopher Stone*, Marlborough, 1989, pp.63–37

The grave of Private G. E. Ellison, 5th Lancers, St Symphorien Cemetery, Mons. Ellison is acknowledged as the last British soldier to be killed in World War I, though many actually succumbed to wounds after 11 November 1918. By a quirk of fate Ellison is buried within feet of Private J. Parr of the Middlesex Regiment, who is believed to be the first British soldier killed. (Author's collection)

6 Claude Prieur, *De Dixmude A Nieuport: Journal de Campagne d'un Officier de Fusiliers Marins*, Paris, 1916, p.105

7 A. Williamson, *Henry Williamson and the First World War*, Stroud, 2004 (second edition) pp.42, 58

8 M. Glover (ed.), *The Fateful Battle Line: The Great War Journals and Sketches of Captain Henry Ogle*, London, 1993, pp.13, 82, 136

9 Anon., *The War History of the 1st/4th Battalion The Loyal North Lancashire Regiment*, Preston, 1921, p.46

10 Sheffield and Inglish (eds.), *From Vimy Ridge to the Rhine*, p.100

11 George Coppard, *With a Machine Gun to Cambrai*, London, 1980, pp.262–263

12 Lieutenant N. F. Percival, manuscript journal, Duke of Lancaster's Own Yeomanry Museum, Preston; J. Ellis, *Eye Deep in Hell*, London, 1976, pp.54–55; M. Brown, *Tommy Goes to War*, London, 1978, pp.88–90

13 Williamson, *Henry Williamson and the First World War*, pp.120, 122, 124–127

14 Rogerson, *Twelve Days on the Somme*, pp.57, 75–76

15 Glover (ed.), *The Fateful Battle Line*, p.136; D. Jones, *In Parenthesis*, New York, 1961, p.205

16 Private Edward Roe quoted in P. Downham (ed.), *Diary of an Old Contemptible*, Barnsley, 2004, p.78; S. Bull, *An Officer's Manual of the Western Front*, London, 2008, pp.63–64, 83

17 The trench life of the Royal Welch Fusiliers is especially well recorded by not only Robert Graves, Frank Richards, and Siegfried Sassoon, but medical officer J. C. Dunn, author of the excellant *The War the Infantry Knew*, London, 1987

18 Private A. Stuart Dolden, *Cannon Fodder*, London, 1980, p.104

19 Eric Hiscock, *The Bells of Hell go Ting-Aling-Aling*, London, 1976, pp.37, 42; Richardson (ed.), *Orders are Orders*, pp.28–29

20 Ernest Parker, *Into Battle*, London, 1994 (second edition), preface and pp.10, 40, 42; S. Chapman, *Home in Time for Breakfast*, London, 2007, pp.16–17, 19, 42

21 Vaughan, *Some Desperate Glory*, pp.106, 169, 184–185; Williamson, *Henry Williamson and the First World War*, pp.41–42, 50, 105, 109–110

22 P. Witkop (ed.), *German Students' War Letters*, London, 1929, pp.210–220; A. P. Linder, *Princes of the Trenches*, Drawer, 1996, pp.61–63

23 Sheffield and Inglish (eds.), *From Vimy Ridge to the Rhine*, pp.72, 86; P. T. Scott, *Home For Christmas: Cards, Messages and Letters of the Great War*, London, 1993

24 Downham (ed.), *Diary of an Old Contemptible*, pp.45, 46, 61, 67, 73, 77, 80, 83, 124, 173, 291

25 Anon., *The War History of the 1st/4th Battalion The Loyal North Lancashire Regiment*, pp.5–21

26 Ibid., p.11

27 US Intelligence, General Staff, *Histories of the Two Hundred and Fifty One Divisions of the German Army*, Chaumont, 1919; H. H. Herwig, *The First World War: Germany and Austria Hungary*, London, 1997, pp.246–249, 421–422

NEW WEAPONS AND TACTICS

1 Frank Richards, *Old Soldiers Never Die*, London, 1993 (second edition), pp.92–93; *History of the Ministry of Munitions*, London, 1921, vol XI 'Supply of Munitions'

2 Letter reproduced in T. Donovan (ed.), *The Hazy Red Hell*, Spellmount, 1999, pp.157–158

3 George Coppard, *With a Machine Gun to Cambrai*, London, 1980, pp.39–41

4 P. Witkop (ed.), *German Students' War Letters*, London, 1929, pp.39–43; A. Saunders, *Weapons of the Trench War*, Stroud, 1999, pp.28–51

5 L. Wyn Griffith, *Up the Line to Mametz*, London, 1931, p.45

6 C. J. Arthur quoted in B. Purdom (ed.), *Everyman at War*, London, 1930, pp.179–180

7 Guy Chapman, *A Passionate Prodigality*, London, 1985 (third edition), p.190

8 'Man pack' means flame throwers that were carried rather than mounted on the ground, see E. Koch, *Flamethrowers of the German Army*, (English translation) Atglen, 1997, pp.4–12

9 Captain P. Christison, memoir. Imperial War Museum, Documents, pp.66–67

10 Georg Bucher, *In the Line*, (English translation) Uckfield, 2005, p.157

GAS

1 Lance Corporal J. D. Keddie quoted in L. MacDonald, *1915: The Death of Innocence*, London, 1993, p.194

2 See D. Richter, *Chemical Soldiers*, University of Kansas, 1992, pp.6–86

3 W. A. Quinton memoir, quoted in B. MacArthur (ed.), *For King and Country*, London, 2008, pp.97–101

4 Private A. Stuart Dolden, *Cannon Fodder*, London, 1980, p.160; another mustard gas victim was Henry Lawson, see *Vignettes of the Western Front*, Oxford, 1979, pp.53–56

5 Captain F. C. Hitchcock, *Stand To: A Diary of the Trenches*, London, 1937, pp.53–54

6 See C. H. Foulkes, *Gas! The Story of the Special Brigade*, Edinburgh, 1934

7 Captain P. Christison, memoir. Imperial War Museum, Documents, p.63. Also on this subject see A. Palazzo, *Seeking Victory on the Western Front: The British Army and Chemical Warfare*, University of Nebraska, 2000, passim, and G. Hartcup, *The War of Invention*, London, 1988, pp.94–117

8 Edmund Blunden, *Undertones of War*, Penguin Classics (new edition) pp.26–27

Signpost to Fricourt German Cemetery, Somme. Fricourt was a strong point assaulted on 1 July 1916, but did not fall until the following day. The cemetery was temporarily the resting place of Manfred von Richthofen, shot down in 1918. Somewhat bizarrely the 'Red Baron' was first interred by the Australians at Bertangles, but moved to Fricourt after the war. The remains – or at least some of them – were exhumed and transferred to Berlin in 1925. In 1975 they were moved yet again to the family vault at Wiesbaden. (Author's collection)

RAIDING AND SNIPING

1   Corporal Sidney Amatt, Imperial War Museum sound archives, transcribed in M. Arthur, *Forgotten Voices*, London 2002, pp.201–202

2   One of many first hand accounts collected in *The War the Infantry Knew* (London, 1987). Instructions of enemy items to look out for were contained in *Collection of Information Regarding the Enemy*, 1915

3   Captain F. C. Hitchcock, *Stand To: A Diary of the Trenches*, London, 1937, pp.188–189

4   Rudyard Kipling, *The Irish Guards in the Great War: Second Battalion*, Staplehurst, 1997 (new edition), pp.84–88

5   L. Nicholson and H. T. MacMullen, *History of the East Lanacshire Regiment in the Great War*, Liverpool, 1936, pp.145–146

6   Ibid., pp.209–291

7   General Staff (UK), *Scouting and Patrolling*, 'SS 195', 1917, p.20

8   Lieutenant Colonel J. S. Y. Rogers to the 'Shell Shock' enquiry, *Report of the War Office Committee*, p.62

9   Major H. Hesketh-Pritchard, *Sniping in France*, London, 1994 (new edition) p.16

10 Major F. M. Crum, *With Riflemen, Scouts and Snipers*, Oxford, 1921, p.52: Crum was the author of the unofficial 1916 manual, *Scouts and Sniping in Trench Warfare*

11 See *Scouting and Patrolling*, pp.14–18 and T. F. Fremantle, *Notes of Lectures and Practices of Sniping*, Leicester, 1916

12 Hesketh-Pritchard, *Sniping in France*, p.83; see also E. Parker, *A Memoir*, London 1924

The French memorial at Ayette, about 16km south of Arras and scene of fierce fighting in 1918. The colouring of the figure is not usual – even for French memorials – but does hark back to similar ideas from ancient Rome and the medieval period. The meaning of 'horizon blue' suddenly becomes apparent, though the uniform colour was more 'grey blue' than that seen here. (Author's collection)

MINING

1   Lieutenant Geoffrey Malins, *How I Filmed the War*, London, 1920, pp.162–163

2   This and other accounts appear in W. G. Grieve and B. Newman, *Tunnellers*, London, 1936. See also A. Barrie, *War Underground*, London, 1961

3. See G. H. Addison, *The Work of the Royal Engineers in the European War: Military Mining*, Uckfield, 2004 (reprint); and P. Barton (et al) *Beneath Flanders Fields: The Tunneller's War*, Staplehurst, 2004

CONCRETE AND *STELLUNGSBAU*

1   P. von Hindenburg, *Out of My Life*, (English translation) London, 1919, p.261

2   General Gough on the experiences of V Army, see also P. Oldham, *Pillboxes on the Western Front*, London, 1995

3   For electrics see G. H. Addison, *The Work of the Royal Engineers in the European War*, Chatham, 1926, pp.271–294

4   Major E. Pickard quoted in H. C. Wylly, *The Green Howards in the Great War*, Regimental Publication, 1926

5   Signaller Stanley Bradbury, Imperial War Museum documents, typescript memoir, p.29

THE TANK

1 Many first hand accounts were published in the *Tank Corps Journal* between 1920 and 1924. A convenient selection is D. Fletcher (ed.), *Tanks and Trenches*, for Lieutenant B. L. Q. Henriques see pp.12–14

2 Ibid., pp.14–17. See also C. Duffy, *Through German Eyes: The British and the Somme*, London, 2006, pp.297–304

3 G. Sheffield and J. Bourne (eds.), *Douglas Haig: War Diaries and Letters*, London, 2005, pp.195–261

4 Major W. H. L. Watson, *A Company of Tanks* (Imperial War Museum with N&M Press reprint, undated), p.69

5 Fletcher, *Tanks and Trenches*, pp.53–55

6 Ibid., pp.70–94. See also D. Crow (ed.), *Armoured Fighting Vehicles of the World: World War I*, Retford, 1988, and D. Fletcher, *Landships*, London, 1984

7 Document translated in Y. Buffetaut, *The 1917 Spring Offensives*, Paris, 1997, p.151

8 Frank Mitchell, *Tank Warfare*, London, 1933, pp.189–192

'OVER THE TOP'

1 Harold MacMillan, in a letter to his mother Nellie, dated 13 May 1916

2 The Liddell Hart Archive at King's College, London, remains a significant source for military history. For context of the 'nobler end' letter see A. Danchev, *Alchemist of War*, London, 1998, pp.42–68

3 P. Witkop (ed.), *German Students' War Letters*, London, 1929, pp.164–175

4 Letter reprinted in A. Bristow, *A Serious Disappointment: The Battle of Aubers Ridge*, London, 1995, p.75

5 L. Nicholson and H. T. MacMullen, *History of the East Lancashire Regiment in the Great War*, pp.129–133

Above left: The German Cemetery, Fricourt. The plain and sober, even sombre, appearance is typical of German burial grounds, as is the presence of a mass grave with a list of known occupants. Whilst France and Belgium were happy to give plots for the bodies of their Allies, 'German' space was constrained to an absolute minimum. Even where individual crosses appear, these usually commemorate two, or four, of the fallen. (Author's collection)

Above right: The grave of Congressional Medal of Honor winner Lieutenant William Bradford Turner, 105th Infantry, Somme American Cemetery. On 27 September 1918 Turner led an attack near Le Catelet in which he rushed two machine gun posts and led his men over three trench lines and on to a fourth, personally shooting or bayoneting several of the enemy. Already wounded three times he was finally killed, and was posthumously awarded the highest US decoration. Interestingly whilst British families were discouraged from taking home their dead from the theatre of war, many bodies of US servicemen were returned to the United States. (Author's collection)

6 Bristow, *A Serious Disappointment*, p.130

7 The simplistic picture presented by Alan Clark in *The Donkeys* (London, 1961) has been widely challenged, initially, and probably too dogmatically, in a series of books by John Terraine. More telling has been the detailed work of Paddy Griffith, whilst Gordon Corrigan's *Mud, Blood and Poppycock* (London, 2003) has brought revisionist lines of thought to a wide contemporary audience.

8 Marshal Ferdinand Foch, *Memoirs*, London, 1931, pp.168, 202, 217, 240–244. On shells shortages see R. J. Q. Adams, *Arms and the Wizard: Lloyd George and the Ministry of Munitions*, Texas A&M University, 1978

9 Field Marshal French in a letter to Winifred Bennett earlier in 1915, cited in R. Holmes, *The Little Field Marshall: A Life of Sir John French*, London, 2004 (second edition) p.286

10 Georg Bucher, *In the Line*, (English translation) Uckfield, 2005, p.43. See also J. H. Lefebvre, Die Hölle von Verdun, Fleury, 1997 (new edition), passim

11 G. Sheffield and J. Bourne (eds.), *Douglas Haig: War Diaries and Letters*, London, 2005, pp.190–191. A first hand record of training in the lead up to July 1916 is contained in M. A. Argyle (ed.), *Fallen on the Somme: The War Diary of Harold Harding Linzell, 7th Border Regt*, Barnstaple, 1981, pp.11–44

12 For accounts of Verdun in English see Ousby Op Cit; M. Brown, *Verdun: 1916*, Stroud, 1999, and A. Horne, *The Prince of Glory*, London, 1962

13 Albert Andrews quoted in S. Richardson (ed.), *Orders are Orders*, Manchester, 1987, p.44

14 Ibid., p.48. For first hand accounts of 36th Ulster Division see P. Orr, *The Road to the Somme*, Belfast, 1987

15 E. Ludendorff, *Meine Kriegserinnerungen*, Berlin, 1919, translated as *My War Memories*, p.342

16 Corporal Amos Wilder, *Armageddon Revisited*, pp.67–67. For an upbeat assessment of Brüchmuller see D. T. Zabecki, *Steel Wind*, Westport, 1994

17 There have been a number of interpretations of pre and post Somme tactics. For example see P. Griffith, *Battle Tactics of the Western Front*, New Haven, 1994, pp.65–82; S. Bidwell and D. Graham, *Firepower*, London, 1982, pp.66–93; M. Middlebrook, *The First Day on the Somme*, London, 1971, pp.244–316; G. Sheffield, *The Somme*, London, 2003

18 W. Foerster, *Wir Kämpfer im Weltkrieg*, Reichsarchiv, 1929, pp.255–258

CONCLUSION

1 Lieutenant Charles E. Carrington, *A Subaltern's War*, London, 1984 (new edition), pp.150–155

2 Ernst Jünger, *Das Wälchen 125*, translated as *Copse 125*, 1985 (new edition) p.3. See also S. Bull, *Stosstrupptaktik*, Stroud, 2007, passim

3 John Masefield, *The Old Front Line*, Bourne End, 1972 (reprint), p.75; see also J. Giles, *The Somme Then and Now*, Folkstone, 1977, and *The Ypres Salient*, London, 1970

SELECT BIBLIOGRAPHY

MEMOIRS AND OTHER FIRST HAND ACCOUNTS

Bauer, Max, *Der Grosse Krieg in Feld und Heimat*, Tübingen, 1921

Bloch, Marc, *Memoirs of War* (English edition), Cambridge, 1988

Coppard, George, *With a Machine Gun to Cambrai*, London, 1980

Dundas, Captain Henry, *A Memoir* (reprinted letters), Edinburgh, 1921

Dunn, J. C., *The War the Infantry Knew*, reprinted London, 1987

Ebelshauser, Gustav, *The Passage*, Huntingdon, 1984

Foch, Marshal Ferdinand, *Memoirs*, London, 1931

Foch, Marshal Ferdinand (et al.), *The Two Battles of the Marne*, London, 1927

Foerster, Wolfgang, *Wir Kämpfer im Weltkrieg*, Reichsarchiv, Berlin, 1929

Fraser-Tytler, N., *Field Guns in France*, London, 1922

Hiscock, Eric, *The Bells of Hell Go Ting-a-ling-a-ling*, London, 1976

Hitchcock, Francis C., *'Stand To': A Diary of the Trenches, 1915–1918*, London, 1937

Hopkinson, Captain E. G., *Spectamur Agendo*, Cambridge, 1926

'In Flanders Fields' Museum, *Eye-Witness Accounts of the Great War*, Ypres, undated

Jünger, Ernst, *Storm of Steel*, London, 1929

Lefebvre, Jacques-Henri, *Die Hölle von Verdun: Nach Den Berichten von Frontkämpfern*, Verdun, 1997

McBride, Herbert W., *A Rifleman Went to War*, Ottawa, 1935, reprinted Mt. Ida, 1987

Ogle, Henry, *The Fateful Battle Line*, London, 1993

Roe, Lieutenant F. P., *Accidental Soldiers*, London, 1981

Sassoon, Siegfried, *Memoirs of an Infantry Officer*, London, 1930

MANUALS

Beher, Francis J. (trans.), *Drill Regulations for the Infantry, German Army*, Washington, 1907

Bull, S. (ed.), *An Officer's Manual of the Western Front, 1914–1918* (compendium of British Manuals), London, 2008

Crum, F. M., *Scouts and Sniping in Trench Warfare*, Cambridge, 1916

Dane, Edmund, *Trench Warfare*, London, 1915

Fitschen, Heinrich, *Der Spatenkrieg*, Berlin, 1915

French Official, *Manual of the Chief of Platoon of Infantry* (English translation), 1918

General Staff (German), *Feld-Pionierdienst Aller Waffen*, Berlin, 1911

Monument on the Voie Sacrée, *Verdun. Now an insignificant secondary road, the route from Bar-le-Duc was the vital artery keeping Verdun supplied – hence the nose to tail lorries depicted here. The popular name, meaning literally 'Sacred Way', was coined by journalist-politician Maurice Barrès during a visit in April 1916. (Author's collection)*

General Staff (German), *Stellungsbau*, Berlin, 1916

General Staff (German), *Nahkampfmittel*, Berlin, 1916 (2nd ed. 1917)

General Staff (German), *Der Angriff im Stellungskrieg*, Berlin, 1918

General Staff (UK), *Manual of Field Engineering*, 1911

General Staff (UK), *Handbook of the French Army*, 1914

General Staff (UK), *Notes From the Front*, Parts I–IV, 1914–15

General Staff (UK), *German Instructions Regarding Gas Warfare*, 1916

General Staff (UK), *Instructional Handbook for the 2in Trench Howitzer*, 1916

General Staff (UK), *Scouting and Patrolling*, 1918

General Staff (UK), *Field Works for Pioneer Battalions*, 1918

General Staff (UK), *The Principles and Practice of Camouflage*, 1918

Laffargue, Andre, *L'Etude Sur L'Attaque*: translated as *A Study of the Attack in the Present Phase of War*, 1915

Law, R., *Grenades and Their Uses*, Melbourne, 1916

Maxse, Ivor, *Hints on Training: Issued by XVIII Corps*, 1918

North, E. B., *Trench Standing Orders: 124th Infantry Brigade*, London, undated

Northern Command School, *Notes of Lectures and Practices of Sniping*, Leicester, 1916

Solano, E. John, *Field Entrenchments: Spadework for Riflemen*, London, 1914

War Department (US), *Notes on the Construction and Equipment of Trenches*, Washington, 1917

GENERAL

Addison, G. H., *The Work of the Royal Engineers in the European War 1914–1918* (8 vols), Chatham, 1920–27

Barton, Peter (et al.), *Beneath Flanders Fields*, Staplehurst, 2004

Blond, G., *The Marne*, London, 2002

Brown, Malcolm, *Verdun, 1916*, Stroud, 1999

Bose, E. D., *The Kaiser's Army*, Oxford, 2001

Buchner, Adolf, *Der Minenkrieg auf Vauquois*, Karsfeld, 1982

Buffetant, Yves, *The Battle of Verdun*, Louviers, 2005

Bull, Stephen, *Trench Warfare* (2 vols), Oxford, 2002

Bull, Stephen, *Battle Tactics: Trench Warfare*, London, 2003

Chasseaud, Peter, *Topography of Armageddon*, Lewes, 1991

Coombs, Rose E. B., *Before Endeavours Fade: A Guide to the Battlefields of the First World War*, London, 4th ed. 1983

Crutchley, C. E. (ed.), *Machine Gunner*, Northampton, 1973

Dean, Bashford, *Helmets and Body Armor in Modern Warfare*, New Haven, 1930

Desfosses, Yves (et al.), *L' Archéologie de la Grande Guerre*, Rennes, 2008

Donovan, T. (ed.), *The Hazy Red Hell*, Spellmount, 1999

Edmonds, James E. (ed., et al.), *History of the Great War Based on Official Documents* (in 27 vols and appendices), London 1922–49

Van Emden, R., *The Trench*, London, 2003

Von Falkenhayn, Erich, *General Headquarters, 1914–1916 and its Critical Decisions*, Berlin and London, 1919

Griffith, Paddy, *Battle Tactics of the Western Front*, New Haven, 1994

MacDonald, L., *1915: The Death of Innocence*, London, 1993

Manning, Frederic, *The Middle Parts of Fortune*, 1929, new edition London, 1986

Marshall, George C. (et al.), *Infantry in Battle*, Infantry Journal, Washington, 1939

de Meyer, Mathieu (et al.), *The A19 Project: Archaeological Research at Cross Roads*, Zarren, 2004

Oldham, Peter, *Pill Boxes on the Western Front*, London, 1995

Ousby, Ian, *The Road to Verdun*, London, 2002

Purdom, B. (ed.) *Everyman at War*, London, 1930

Samuels, Martin, *Command or Control? Command Training and Tactics in the British and German Armies, 1888–1918*, London, 1995

Samuels, Martin, *Doctrine and Dogma: British and German Infantry Tactics in the First World War*, New York, 1992

Saunders, Nicholas J., *Killing Time: Archaeology and the First World War*, Stroud, 2007

Sheffield, Gary (ed.), *War on the Western Front: In the Trenches of World War I*, Oxford, 2007

Sheldon, Jack, *The German Army on the Somme*, Barnsley, 2005

Strachan, Hew, *The First World War*, Vol 1, Oxford, 2001

Uys, I., *Delville Wood*, Rensburg, 1983,

Winter, Denis, *Death's Men*, London, 1978

Wilder, Corporal Amos, *Armageddon Revisited*, Yale, 1994

INDEX

Note: numbers in **bold** refer to
illustrations, maps and diagrams